SNOW ANGELS ™

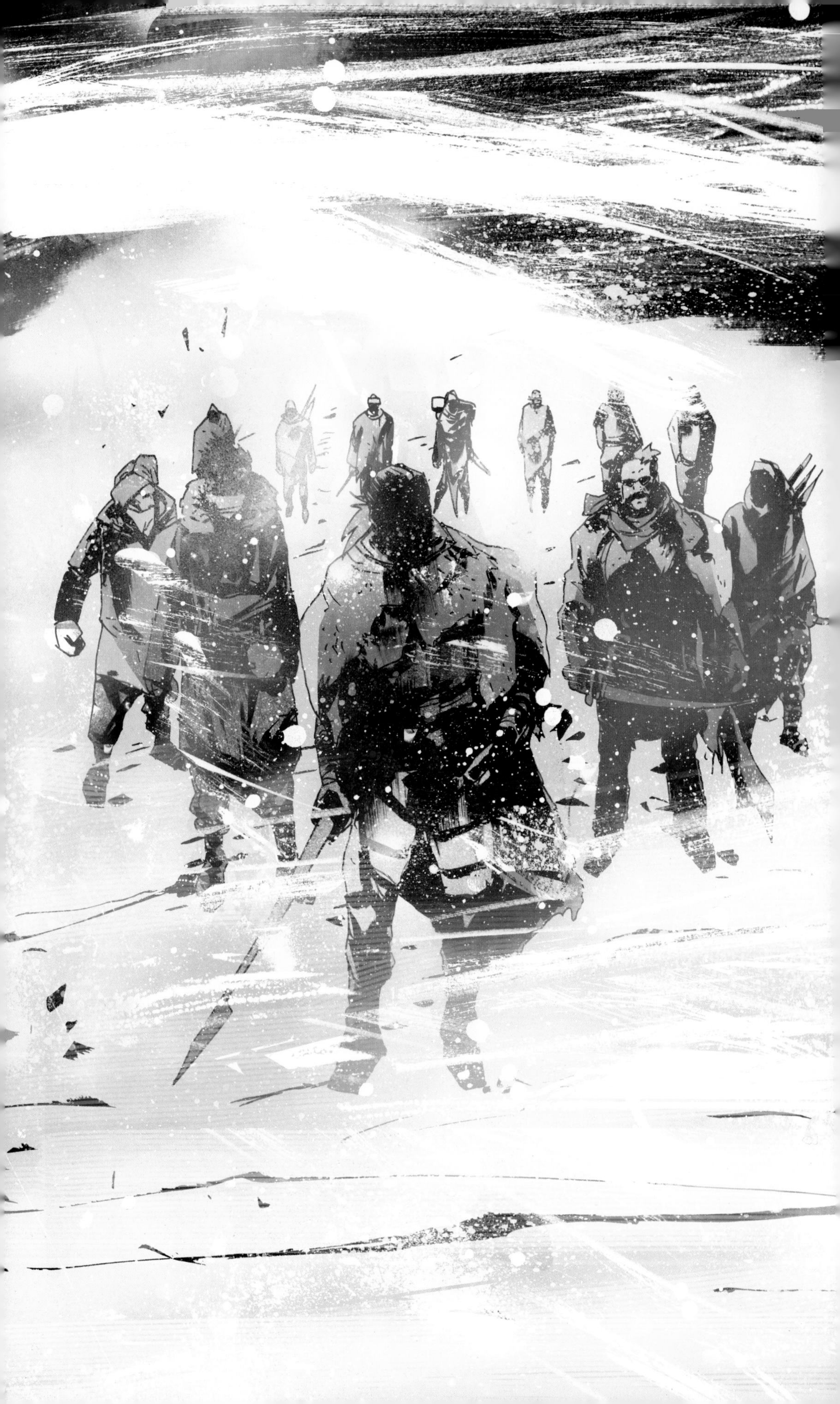

SNOW ANGELS ™

VOLUME 2

- **SCRIPT**
  JEFF LEMIRE

- **ART AND COVER**
  JOCK

- **LETTERING**
  STEVE WANDS

SNOW ANGELS CREATED BY JEFF LEMIRE AND JOCK

_____

EDITOR
WILL DENNIS

ASSISTANT EDITOR
TYLER JENNES

DARK HORSE BOOKS

DARK HORSE TEAM

PRESIDENT & PUBLISHER
MIKE RICHARDSON

EDITOR
DANIEL CHABON

ASSISTANT EDITORS
CHUCK HOWITT & MISHA GEHR

DESIGNER
MAY HIJIKURO

DIGITAL ART TECHNICIAN
JASON RICKERD

SPECIAL THANKS

DAVID STEINBERGER

CHIP MOSHER

BRYCE GOLD

NEIL HANKERSON Executive Vice President TOM WEDDLE Chief Financial Officer DALE LAFOUNTAIN
Chief Information Officer TIM WIESCH Vice President of Licensing MATT PARKINSON Vice
President of Marketing VANESSA TODD-HOLMES Vice President of Production and Scheduling
MARK BERNARDI Vice President of Book Trade and Digital Sales RANDY LAHRMAN Vice President
of Product Development KEN LIZZI General Counsel DAVE MARSHALL Editor in Chief DAVEY
ESTRADA Editorial Director CHRIS WARNER Senior Books Editor CARY GRAZZINI Director of
Specialty Projects LIA RIBACCHI Art Director MATT DRYER Director of Digital Art and Prepress
MICHAEL GOMBOS Senior Director of Licensed Publications KARI YADRO Director of Custom
Programs KARI TORSON Director of International Licensing

PUBLISHED BY DARK HORSE BOOKS
A DIVISION OF DARK HORSE COMICS LLC
10956 SE MAIN STREET, MILWAUKIE, OR 97222

FIRST EDITION: JUNE 2022
TRADE PAPERBACK ISBN: 978-1-50672-649-6

10 9 8 7 6 5 4 3 2 1
PRINTED IN CHINA

COMIC SHOP LOCATOR SERVICE: COMICSHOPLOCATOR.COM

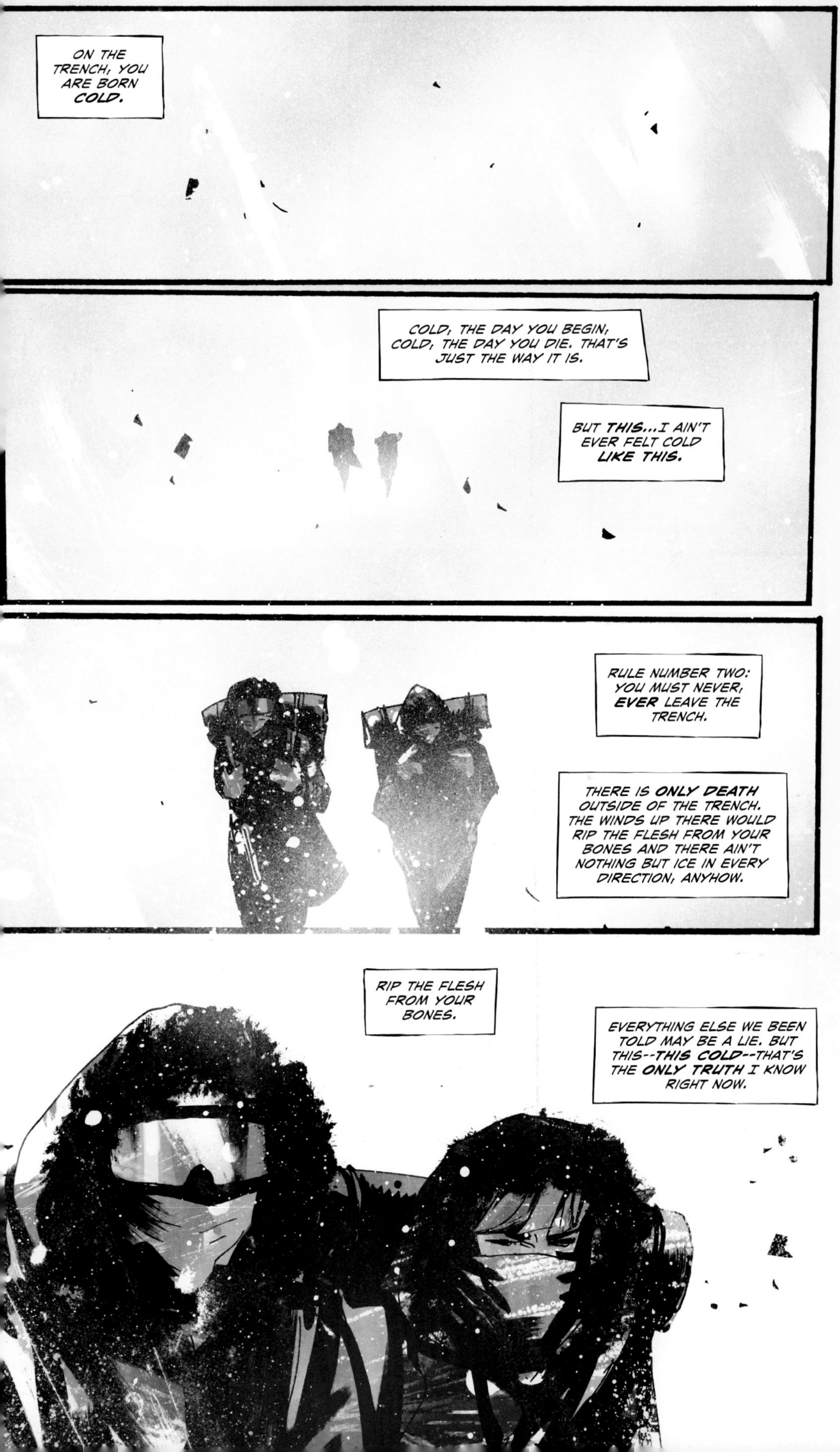
ON THE TRENCH, YOU ARE BORN COLD.
COLD, THE DAY YOU BEGIN, COLD, THE DAY YOU DIE. THAT'S JUST THE WAY IT IS.
BUT THIS...I AIN'T EVER FELT COLD LIKE THIS.
RULE NUMBER TWO: YOU MUST NEVER, EVER LEAVE THE TRENCH.
THERE IS ONLY DEATH OUTSIDE OF THE TRENCH. THE WINDS UP THERE WOULD RIP THE FLESH FROM YOUR BONES AND THERE AIN'T NOTHING BUT ICE IN EVERY DIRECTION, ANYHOW.
RIP THE FLESH FROM YOUR BONES.
EVERYTHING ELSE WE BEEN TOLD MAY BE A LIE. BUT THIS--THIS COLD--THAT'S THE ONLY TRUTH I KNOW RIGHT NOW.

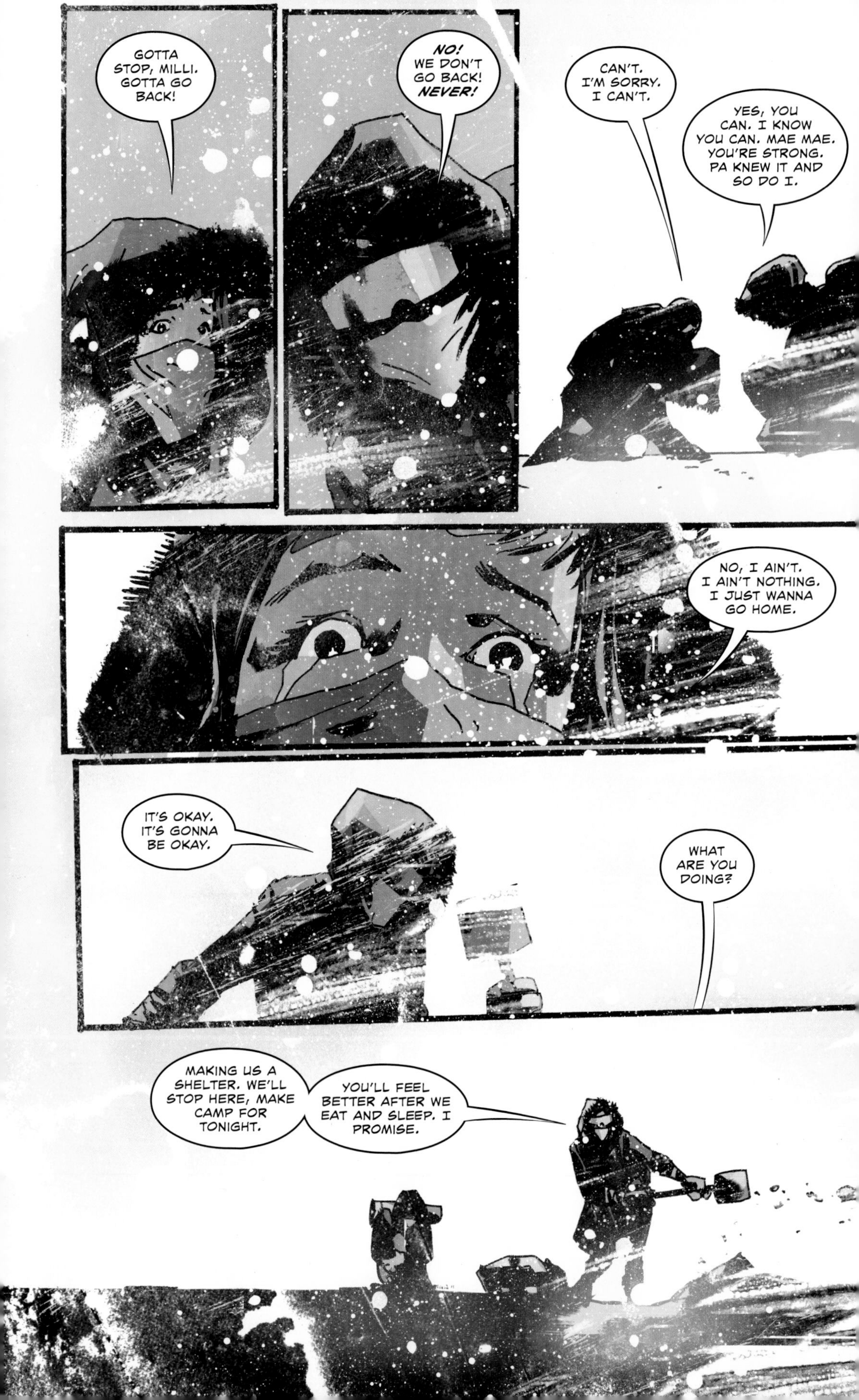

GOTTA STOP, MILLI. GOTTA GO BACK!
NO! WE DON'T GO BACK! NEVER!
CAN'T. I'M SORRY. I CAN'T.
YES, YOU CAN. I KNOW YOU CAN. MAE MAE. YOU'RE STRONG. PA KNEW IT AND SO DO I.
NO, I AIN'T. I AIN'T NOTHING. I JUST WANNA GO HOME.
IT'S OKAY. IT'S GONNA BE OKAY.
WHAT ARE YOU DOING?
MAKING US A SHELTER. WE'LL STOP HERE, MAKE CAMP FOR TONIGHT.
YOU'LL FEEL BETTER AFTER WE EAT AND SLEEP. I PROMISE.

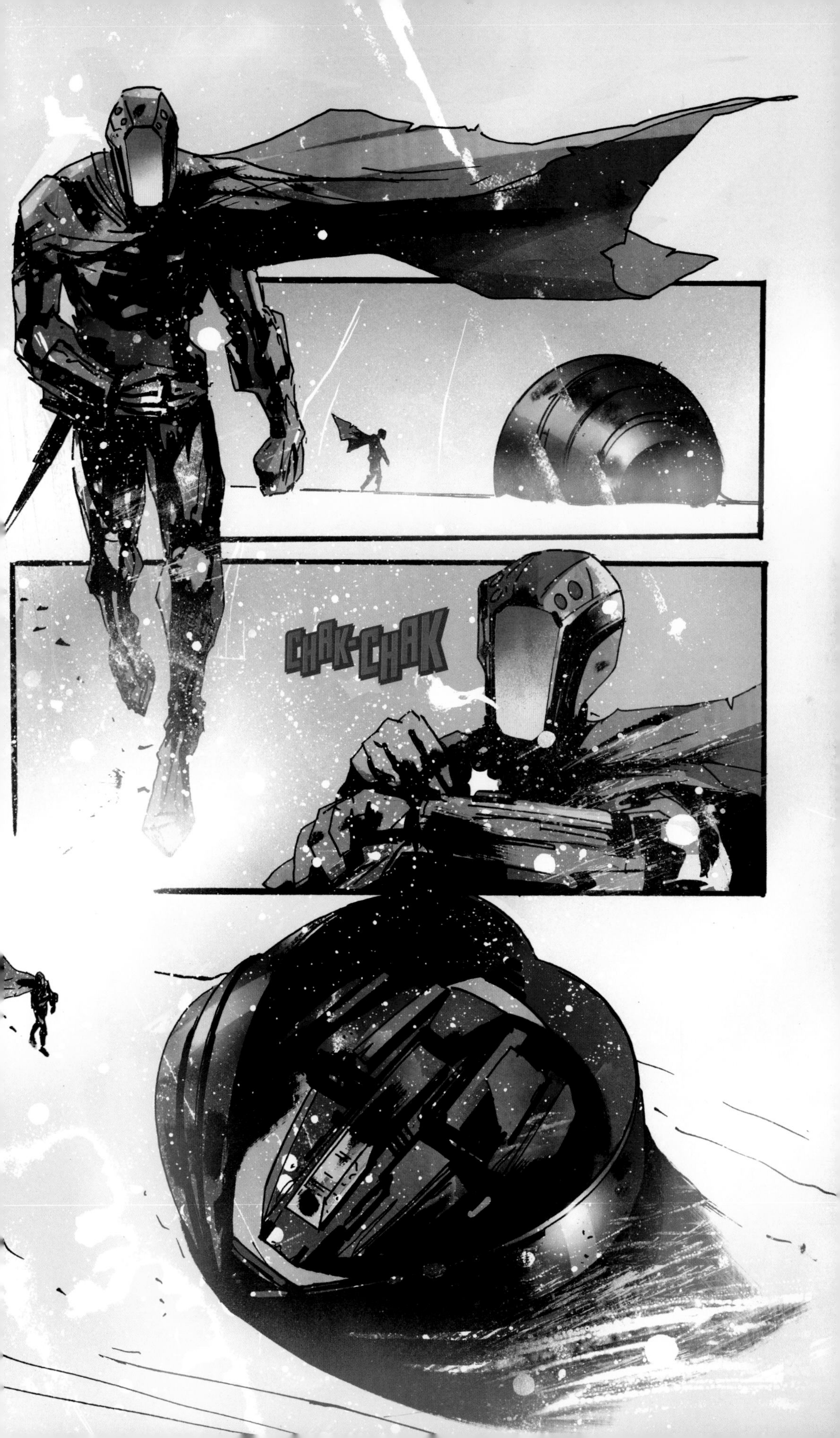
CHAK-CHAK

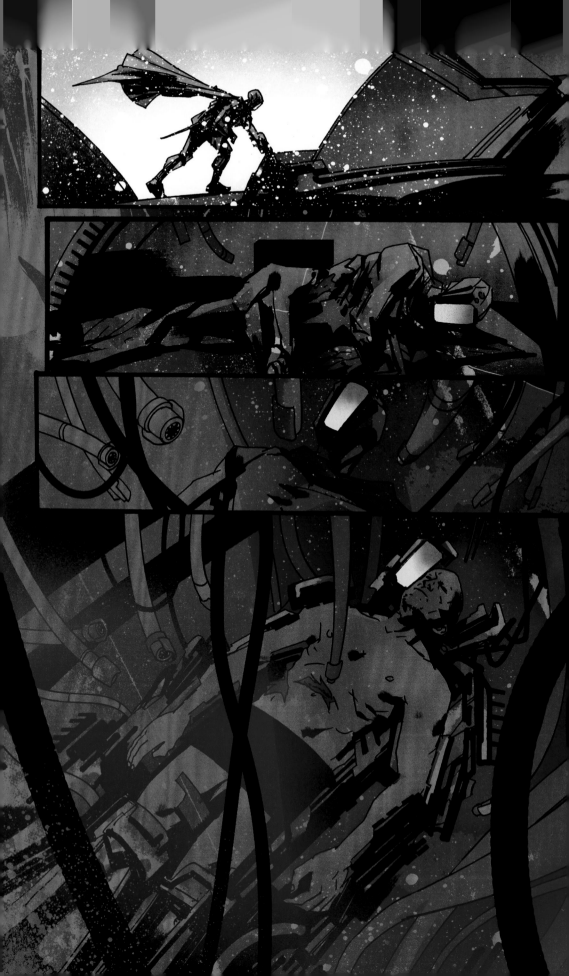

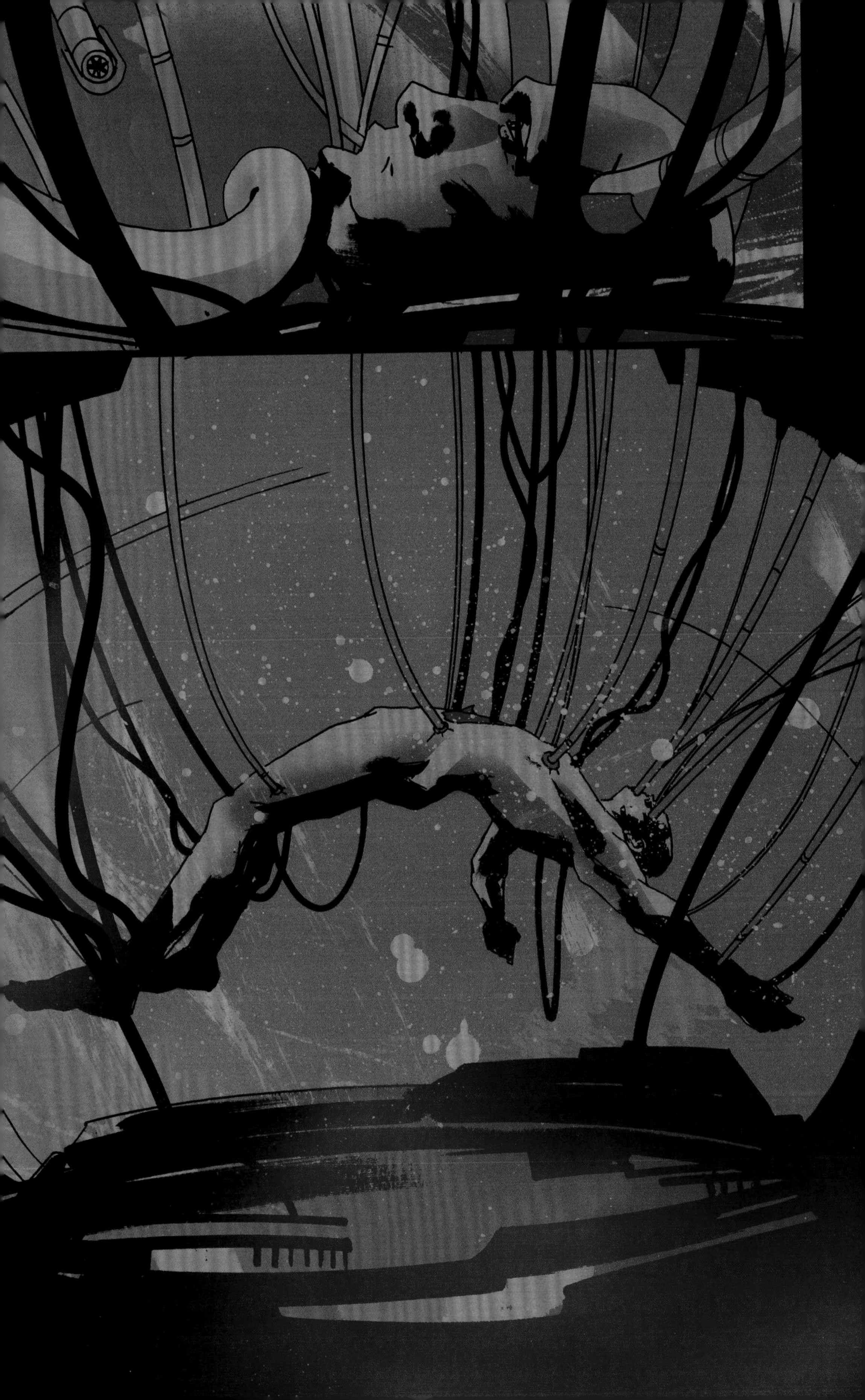

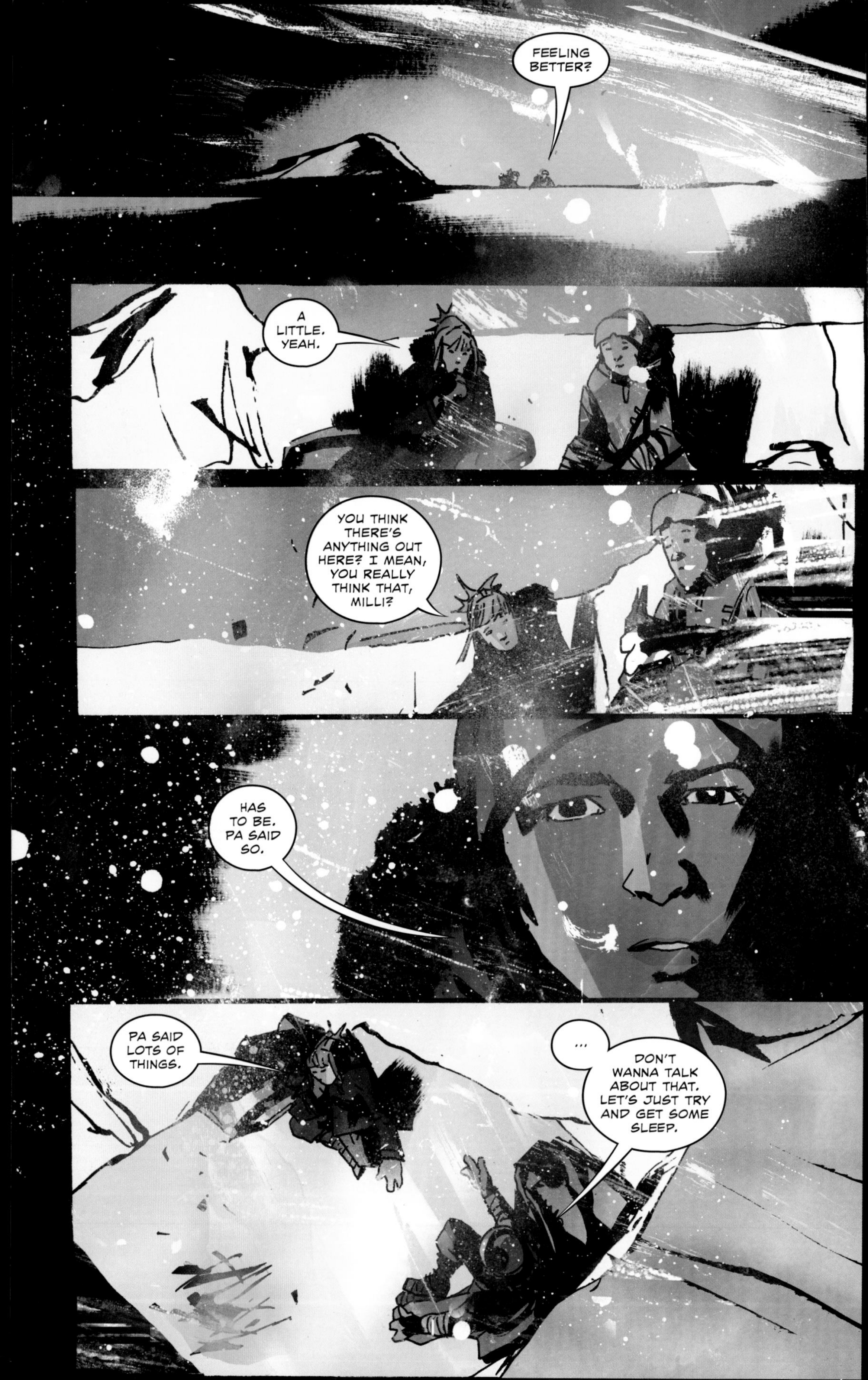
FEELING BETTER?
A LITTLE. YEAH.
YOU THINK THERE'S ANYTHING OUT HERE? I MEAN, YOU REALLY THINK THAT, MILLI?
HAS TO BE. PA SAID SO.
PA SAID LOTS OF THINGS.
...
DON'T WANNA TALK ABOUT THAT. LET'S JUST TRY AND GET SOME SLEEP.

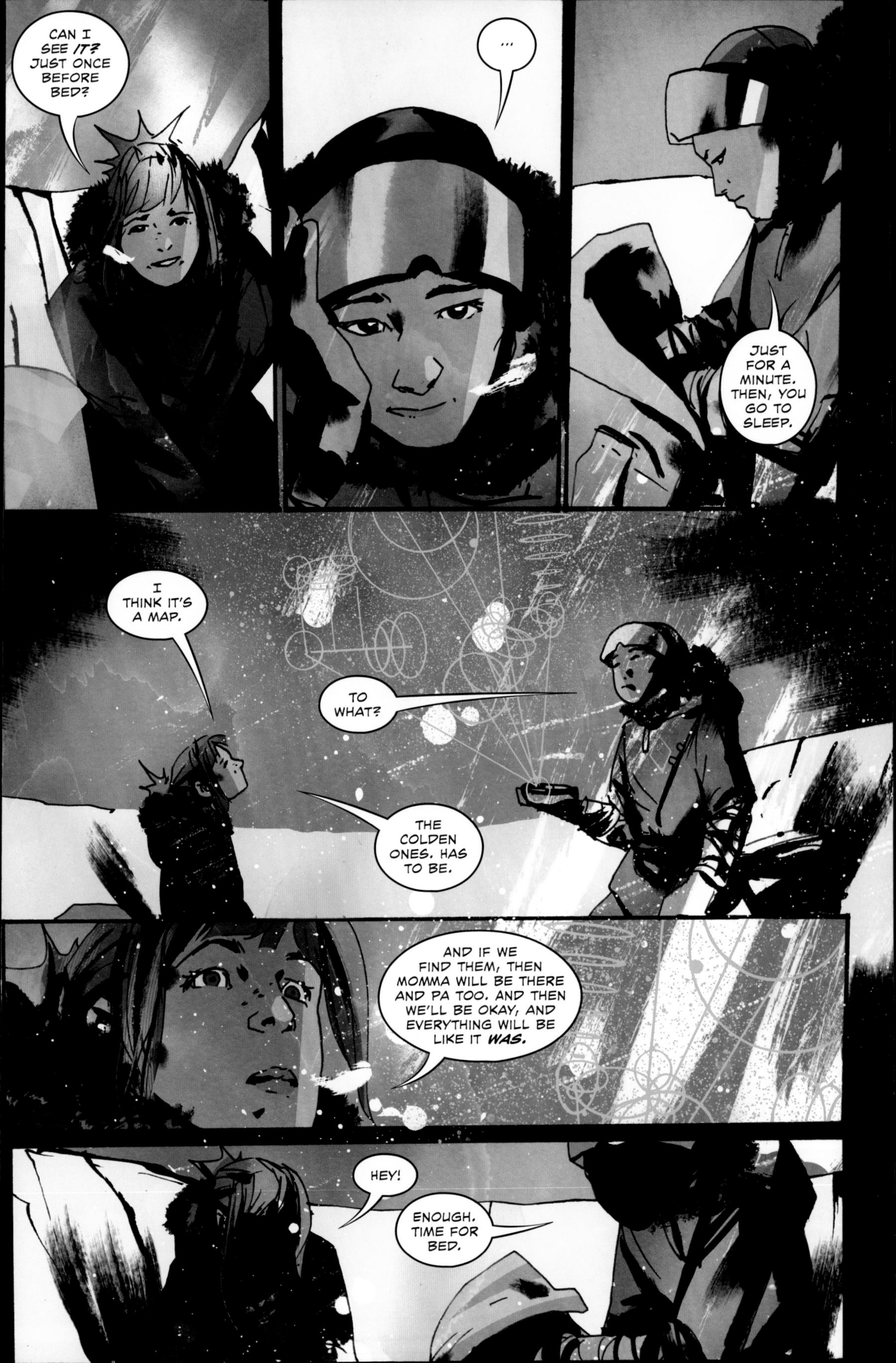
CAN I SEE *IT?* JUST ONCE BEFORE BED?
...
JUST FOR A MINUTE. THEN, YOU GO TO SLEEP.
I THINK IT'S A MAP.
TO WHAT?
THE COLDEN ONES. HAS TO BE.
AND IF WE FIND THEM, THEN MOMMA WILL BE THERE AND PA TOO. AND THEN WE'LL BE OKAY, AND EVERYTHING WILL BE LIKE IT ***WAS.***
HEY!
ENOUGH. TIME FOR BED.

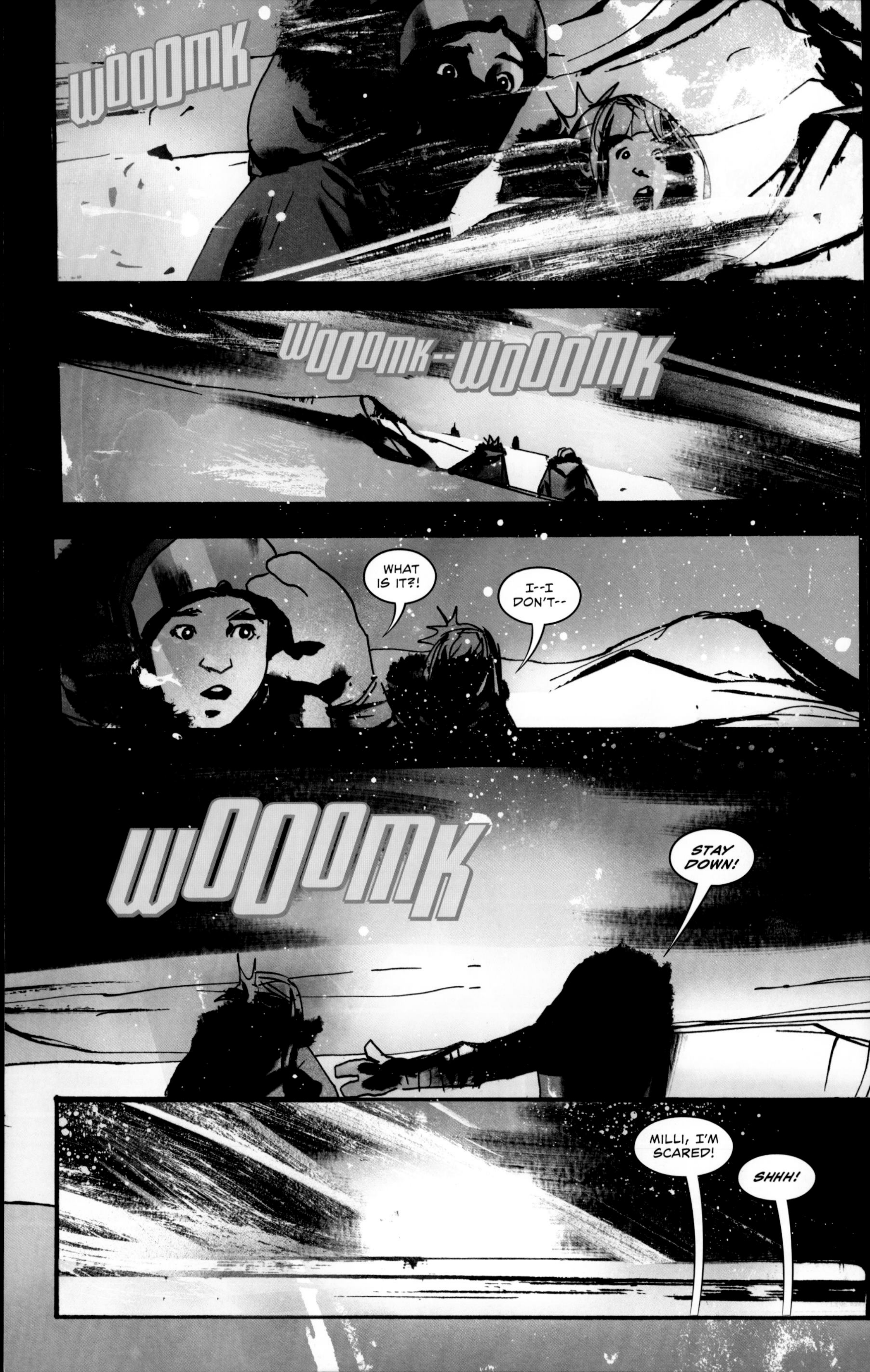
WOOOMK
WOOOMK--WOOOMK
WHAT IS IT?!
I--I DON'T--
WOOOMK
STAY DOWN!
MILLI, I'M SCARED!
SHHH!

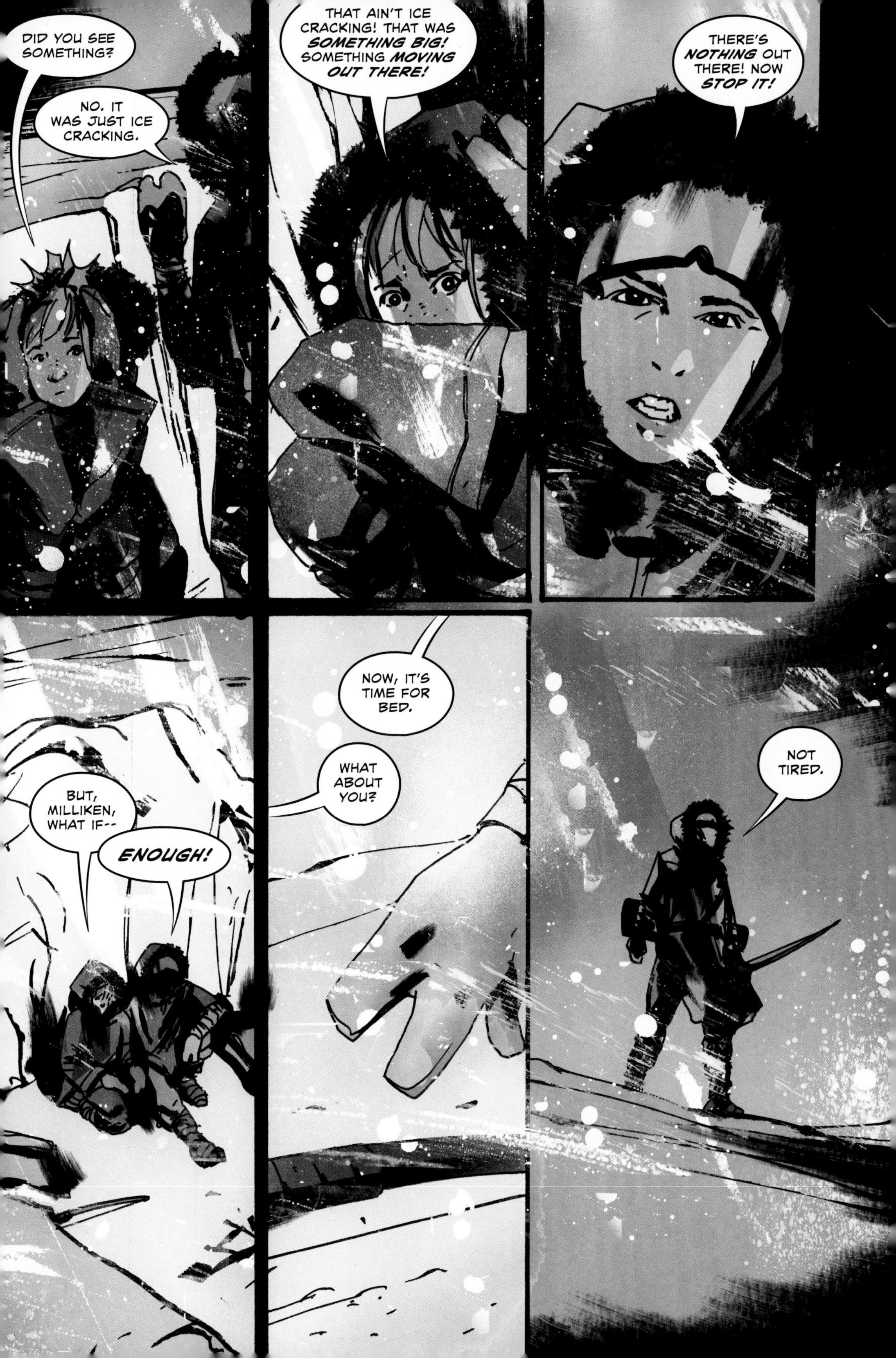

DID YOU SEE SOMETHING?
NO. IT WAS JUST ICE CRACKING.
THAT AIN'T ICE CRACKING! THAT WAS SOMETHING BIG! SOMETHING MOVING OUT THERE!
THERE'S NOTHING OUT THERE! NOW STOP IT!
BUT, MILLIKEN, WHAT IF--
ENOUGH!
NOW, IT'S TIME FOR BED.
WHAT ABOUT YOU?
NOT TIRED.

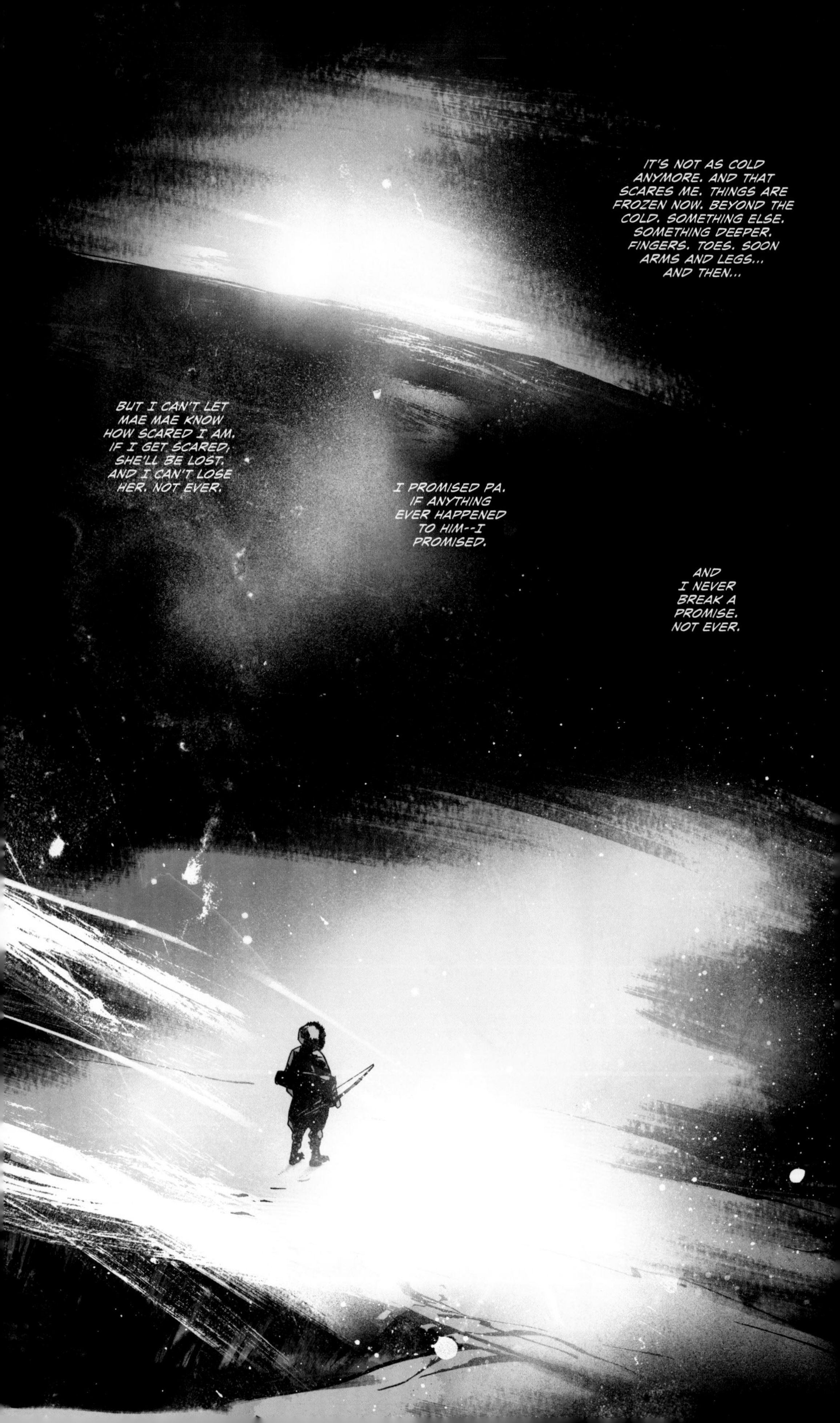
IT'S NOT AS COLD ANYMORE. AND THAT SCARES ME. THINGS ARE FROZEN NOW. BEYOND THE COLD. SOMETHING ELSE. SOMETHING DEEPER. FINGERS. TOES. SOON ARMS AND LEGS... AND THEN...
BUT I CAN'T LET MAE MAE KNOW HOW SCARED I AM. IF I GET SCARED, SHE'LL BE LOST. AND I CAN'T LOSE HER. NOT EVER.
I PROMISED PA. IF ANYTHING EVER HAPPENED TO HIM--I PROMISED.
AND I NEVER BREAK A PROMISE. NOT EVER.

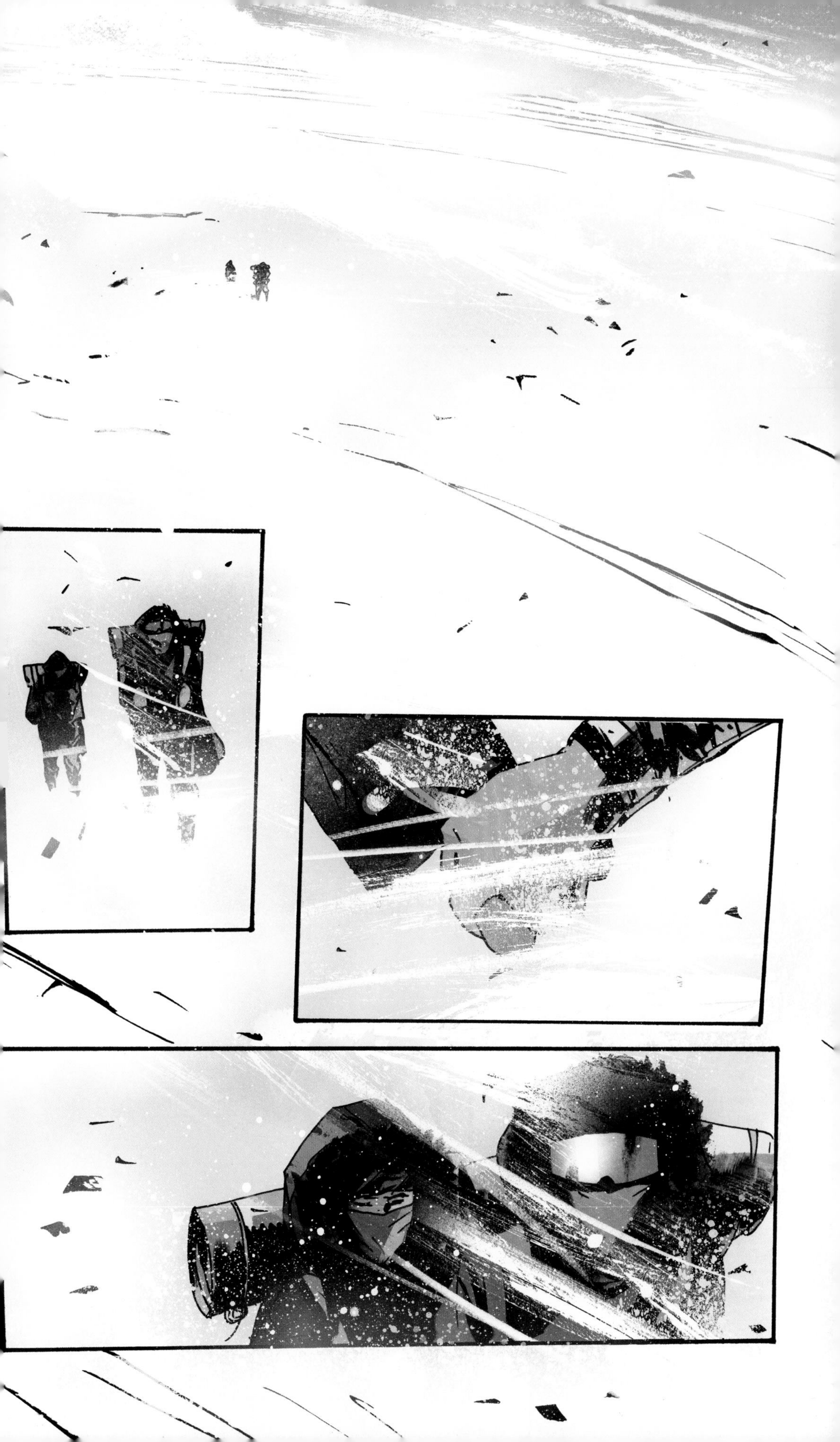

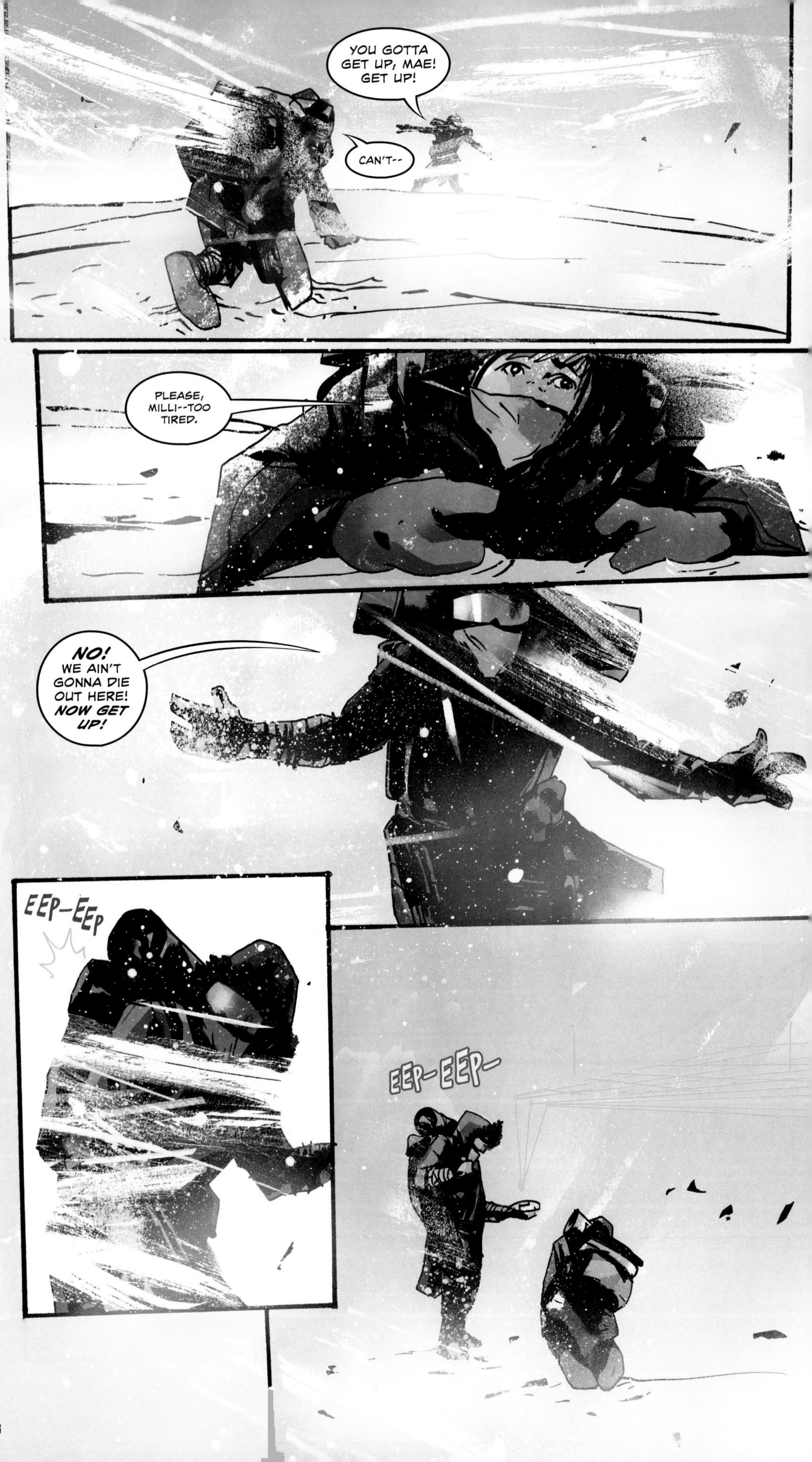
YOU GOTTA GET UP, MAE! GET UP!
CAN'T--
PLEASE, MILLI--TOO TIRED.
NO! WE AIN'T GONNA DIE OUT HERE! NOW GET UP!
EEP-EEP
EEP-EEP-

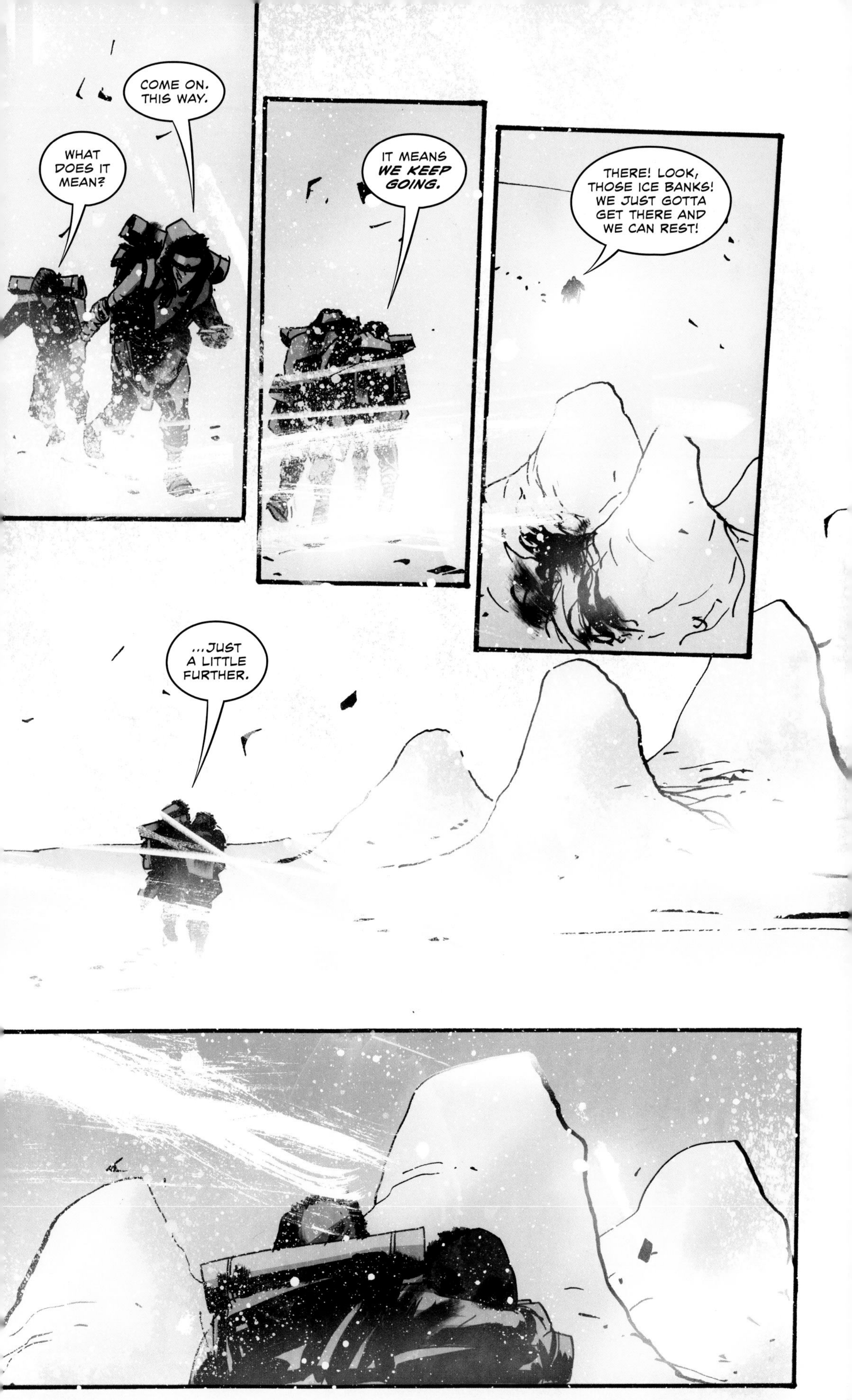
COME ON. THIS WAY.
WHAT DOES IT MEAN?
IT MEANS *WE KEEP GOING.*
THERE! LOOK, THOSE ICE BANKS! WE JUST GOTTA GET THERE AND WE CAN REST!
...JUST A LITTLE FURTHER.

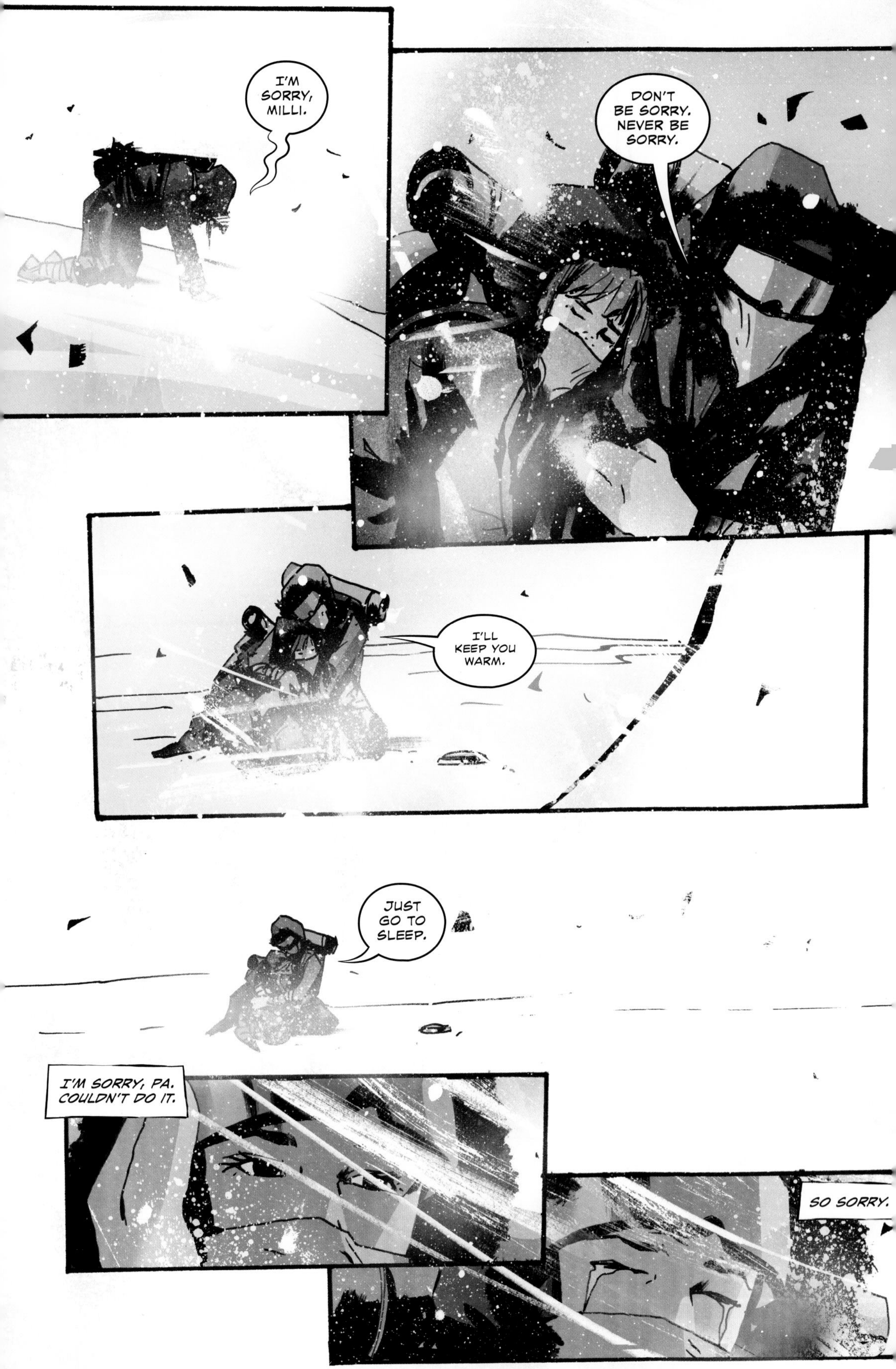
I'M SORRY, MILLI.
DON'T BE SORRY. NEVER BE SORRY.
I'LL KEEP YOU WARM.
JUST GO TO SLEEP.
I'M SORRY, PA. COULDN'T DO IT.
SO SORRY.

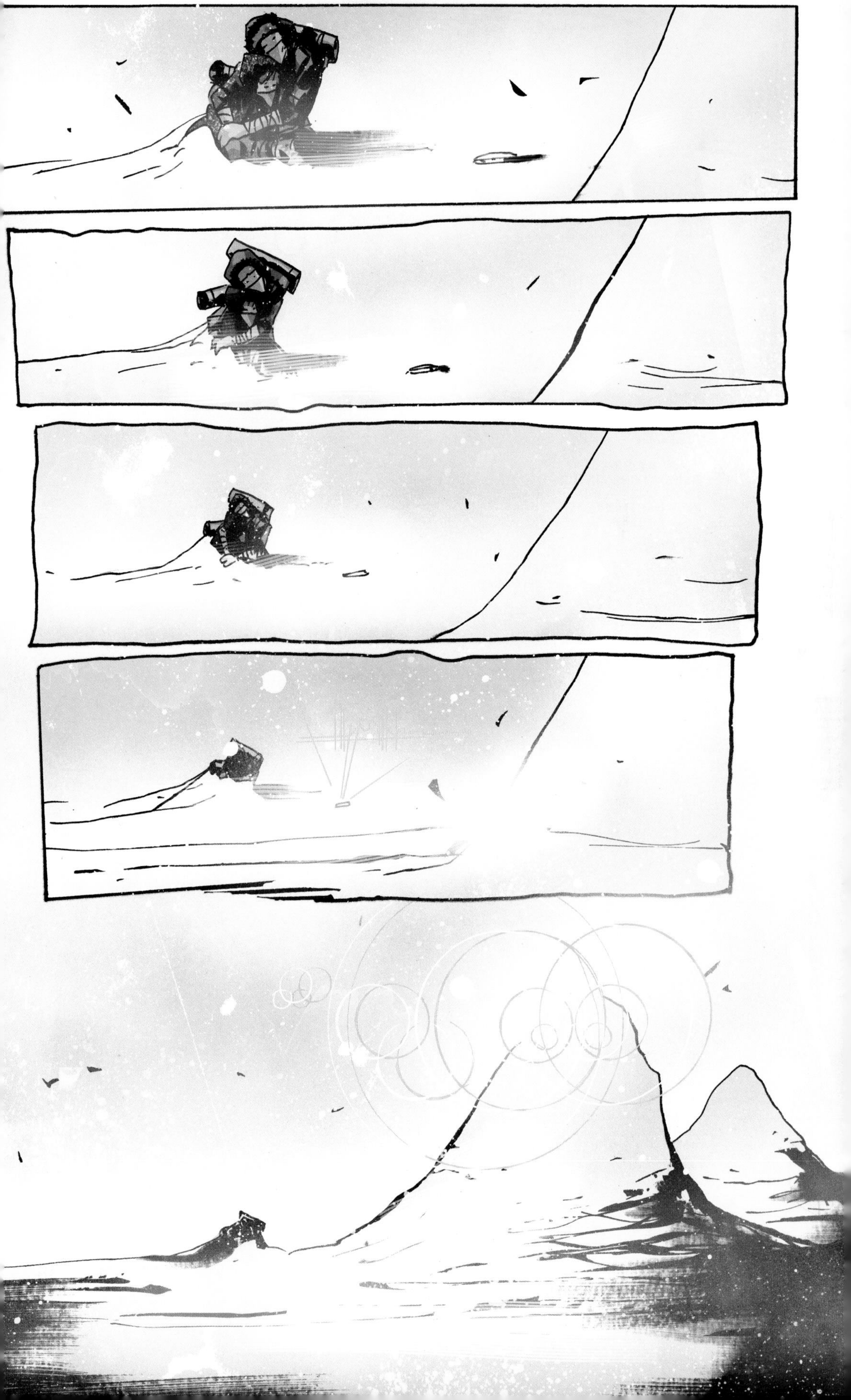

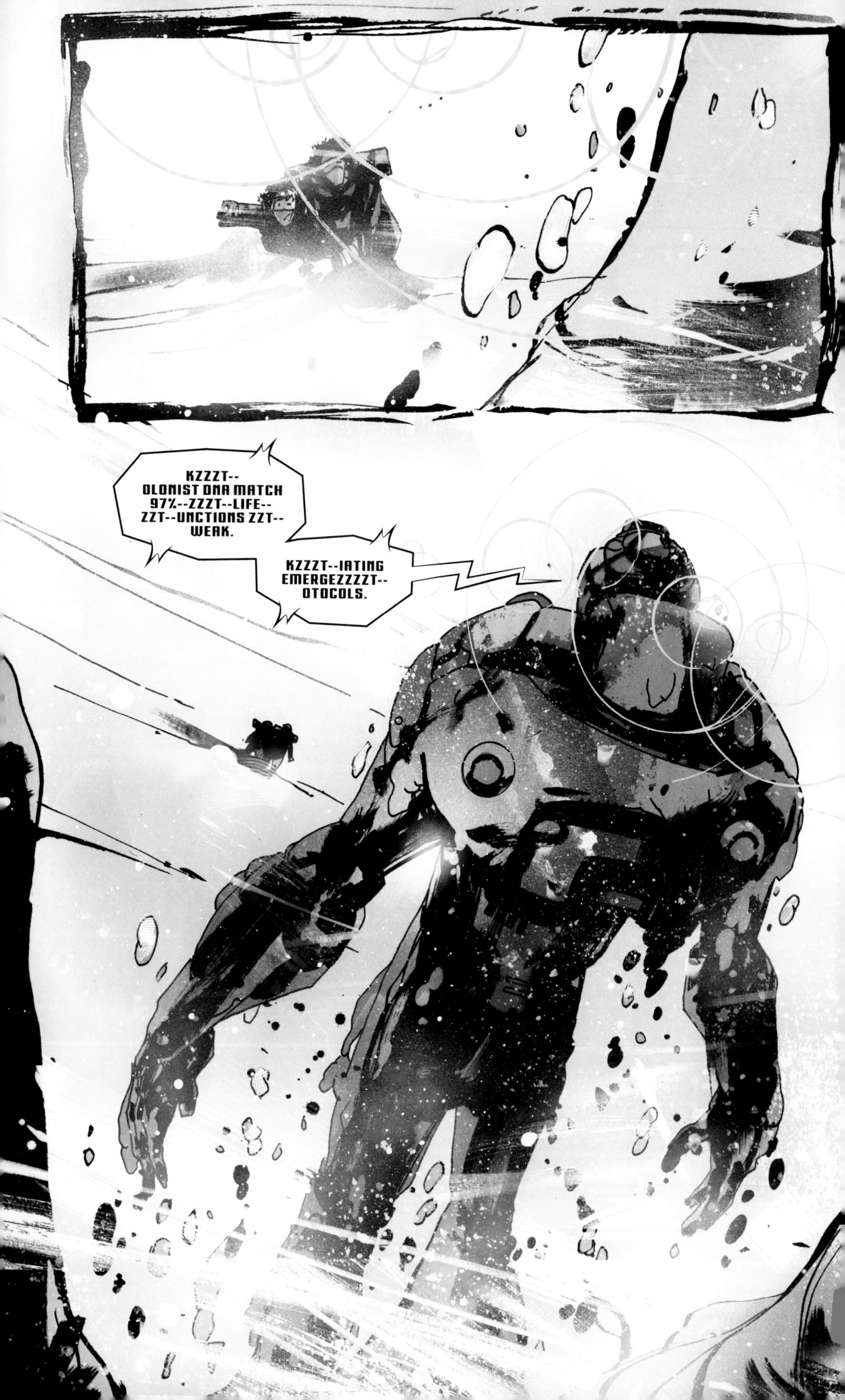
KZZZT-- OLONIST DNA MATCH 97%--ZZZT--LIFE-- ZZT--UNCTIONS ZZT-- WEAK.
KZZZT--IATING EMERGEZZZZT-- OTOCOLS.

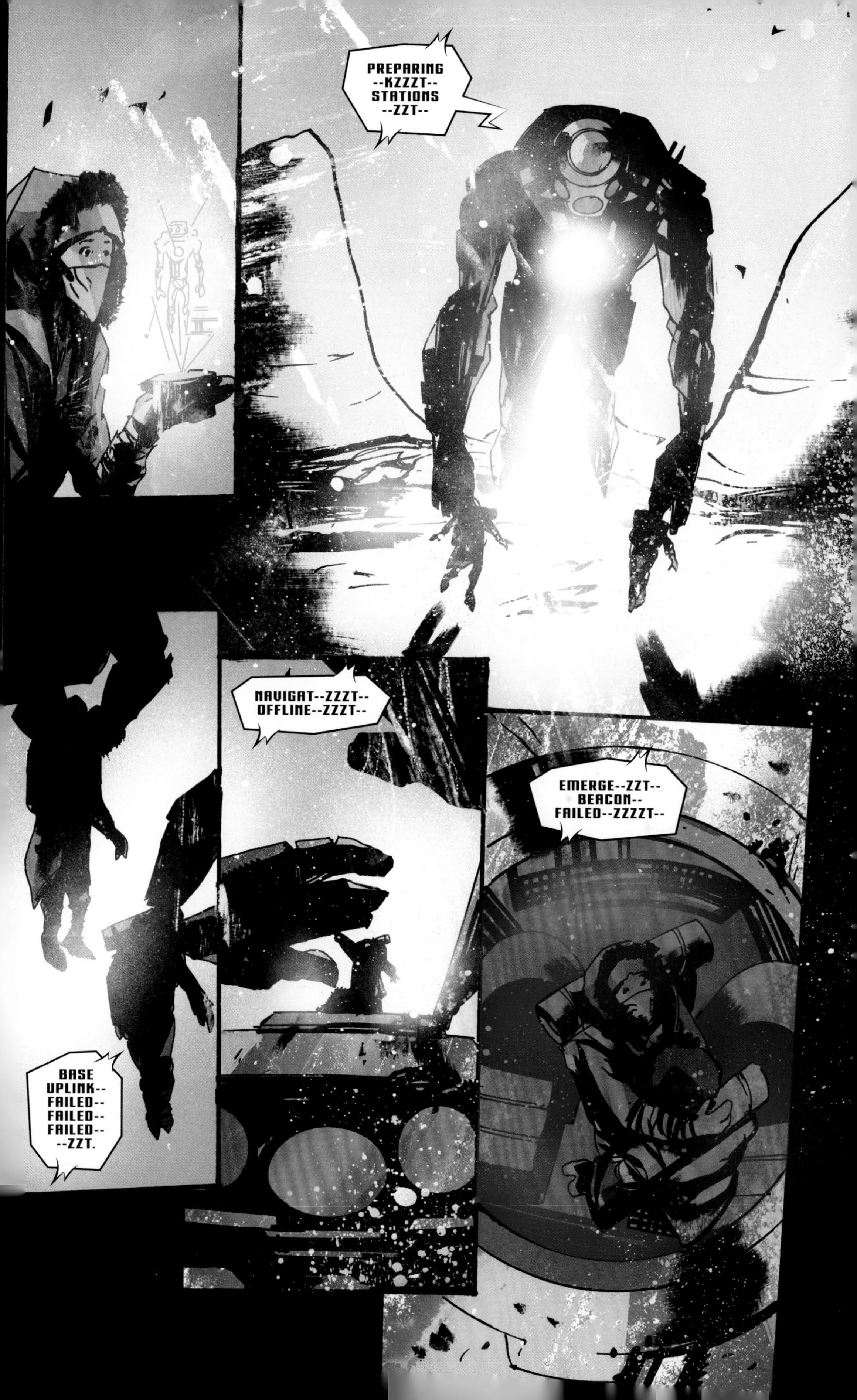
PREPARING --KZZZT-- STATIONS --ZZT--
BASE UPLINK-- FAILED-- FAILED-- FAILED-- --ZZT.
NAVIGAT--ZZZT-- OFFLINE--ZZZT--
EMERGE--ZZT-- BEACON-- FAILED--ZZZZT--

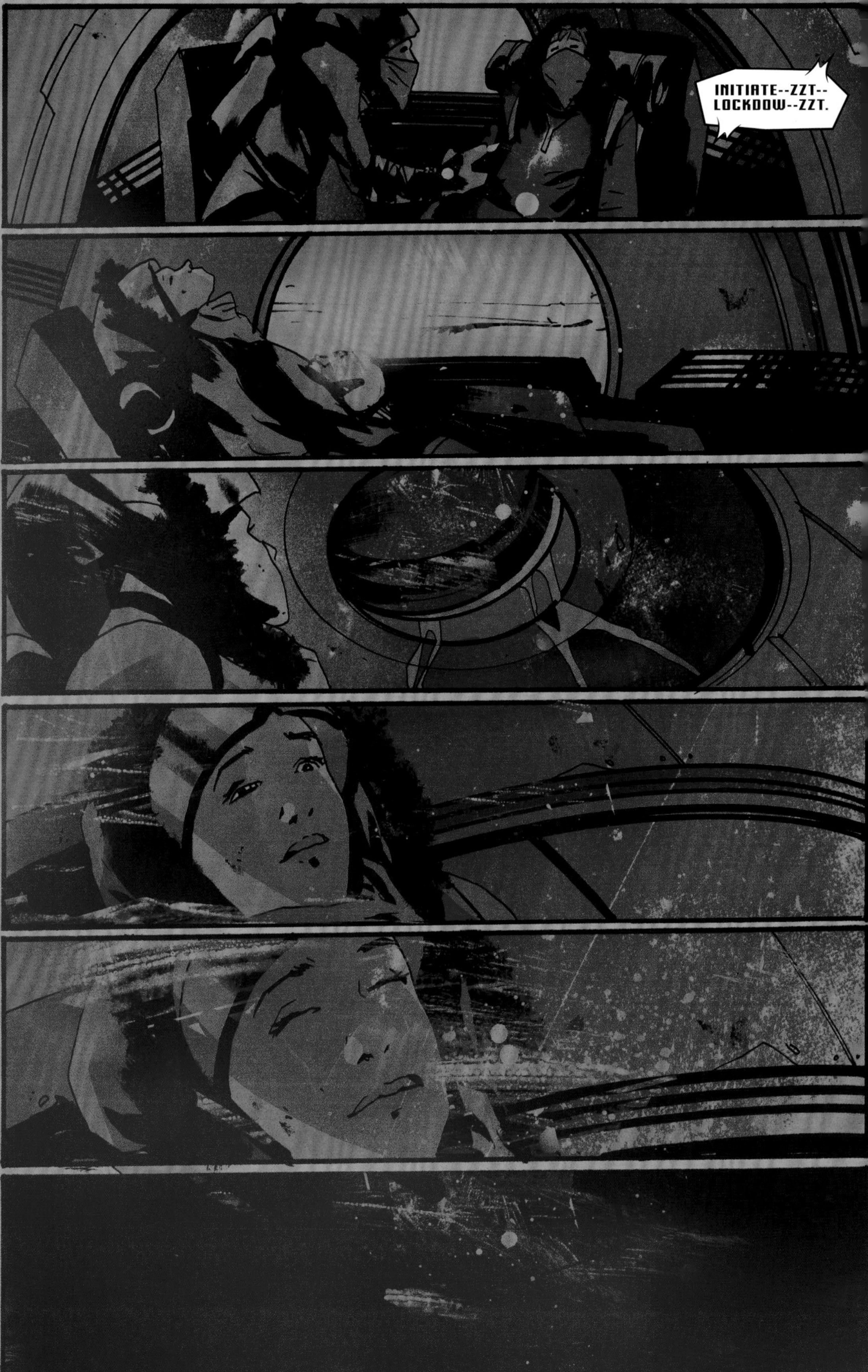
INITIATE--ZZT--
LOCKDOW--ZZT.

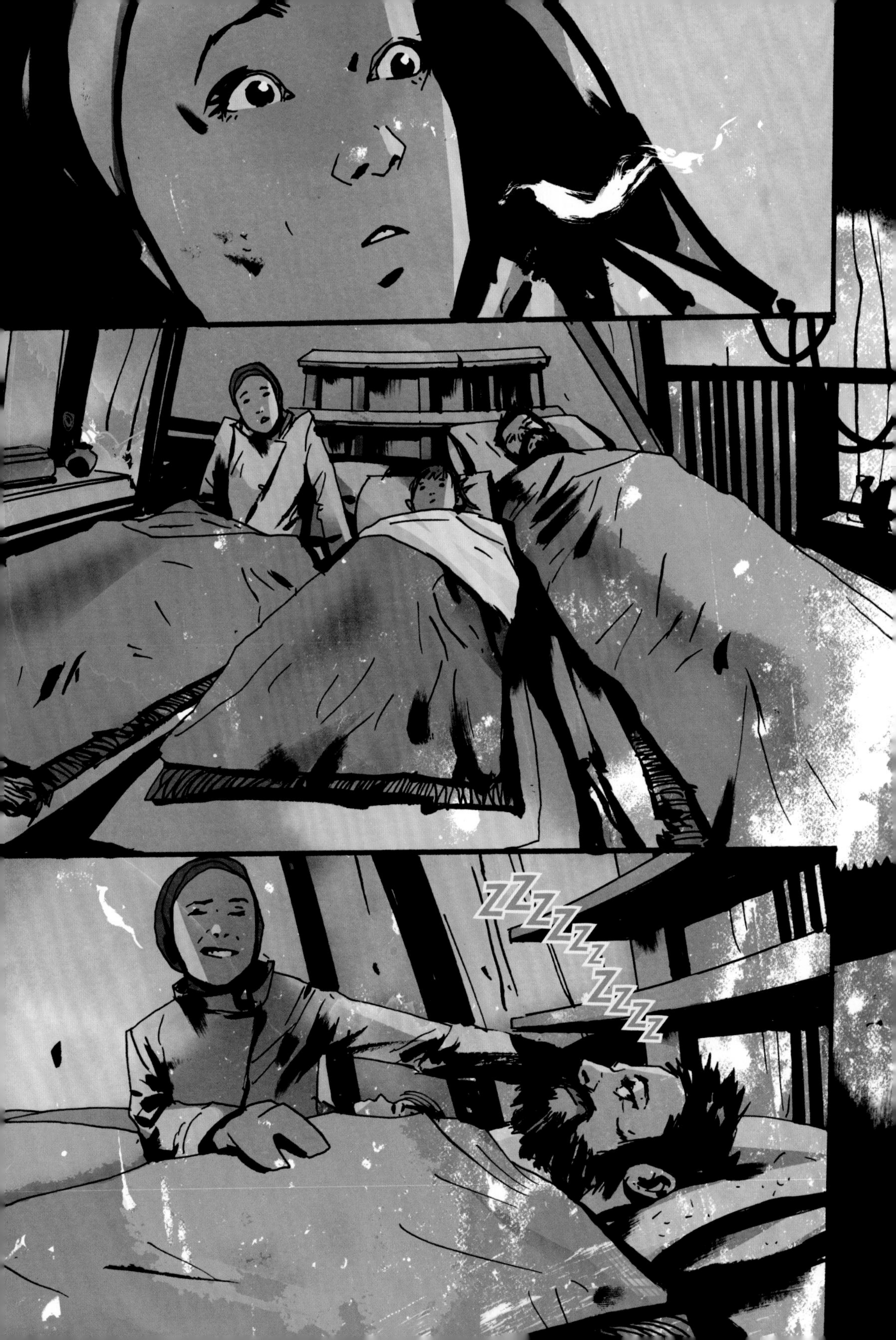
ZZZZZZZ

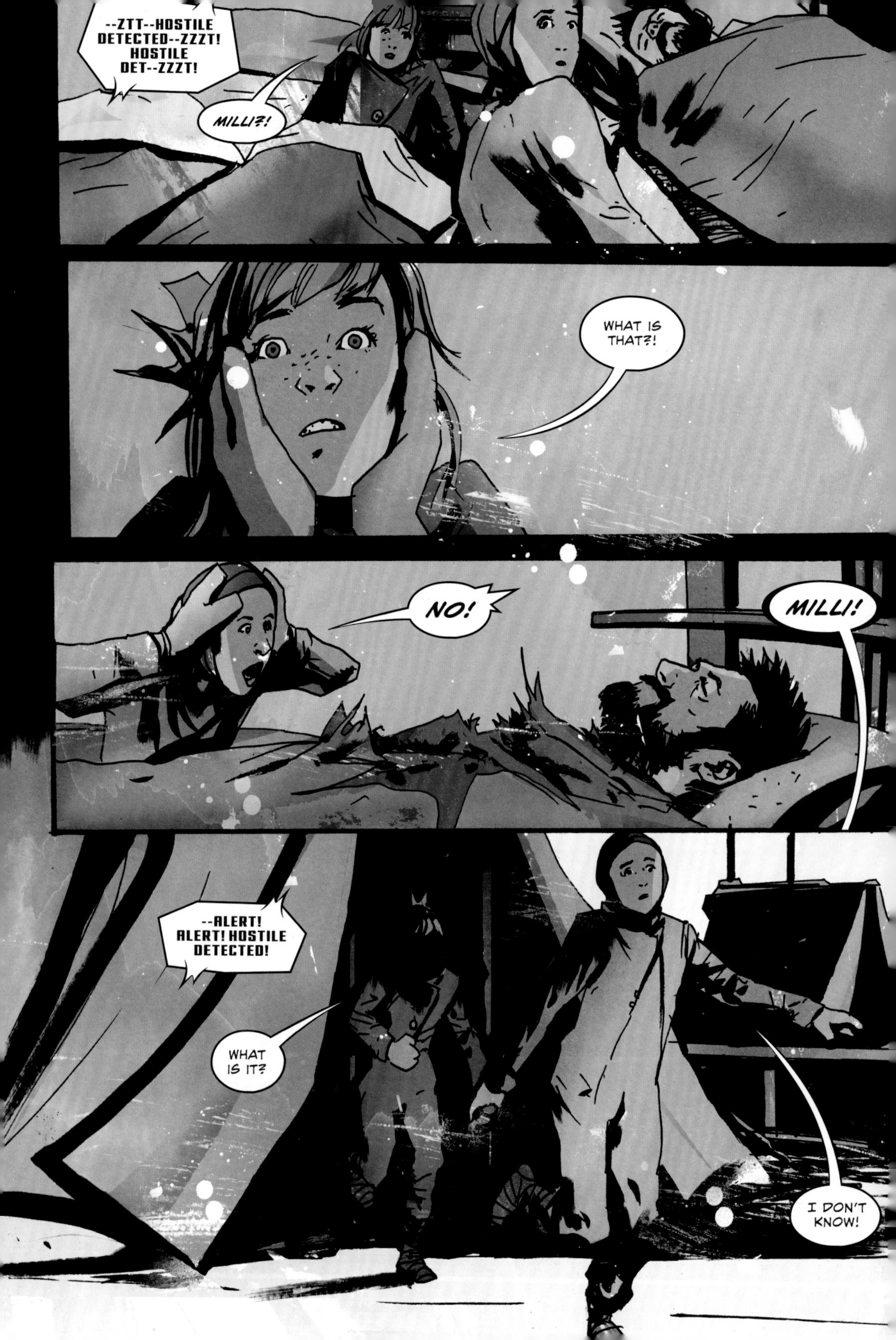
--ZTT--HOSTILE DETECTED--ZZZT! HOSTILE DET--ZZZT!
MILLI?!
WHAT IS THAT?!
NO!
MILLI!
--ALERT! ALERT! HOSTILE DETECTED!
WHAT IS IT?
I DON'T KNOW!

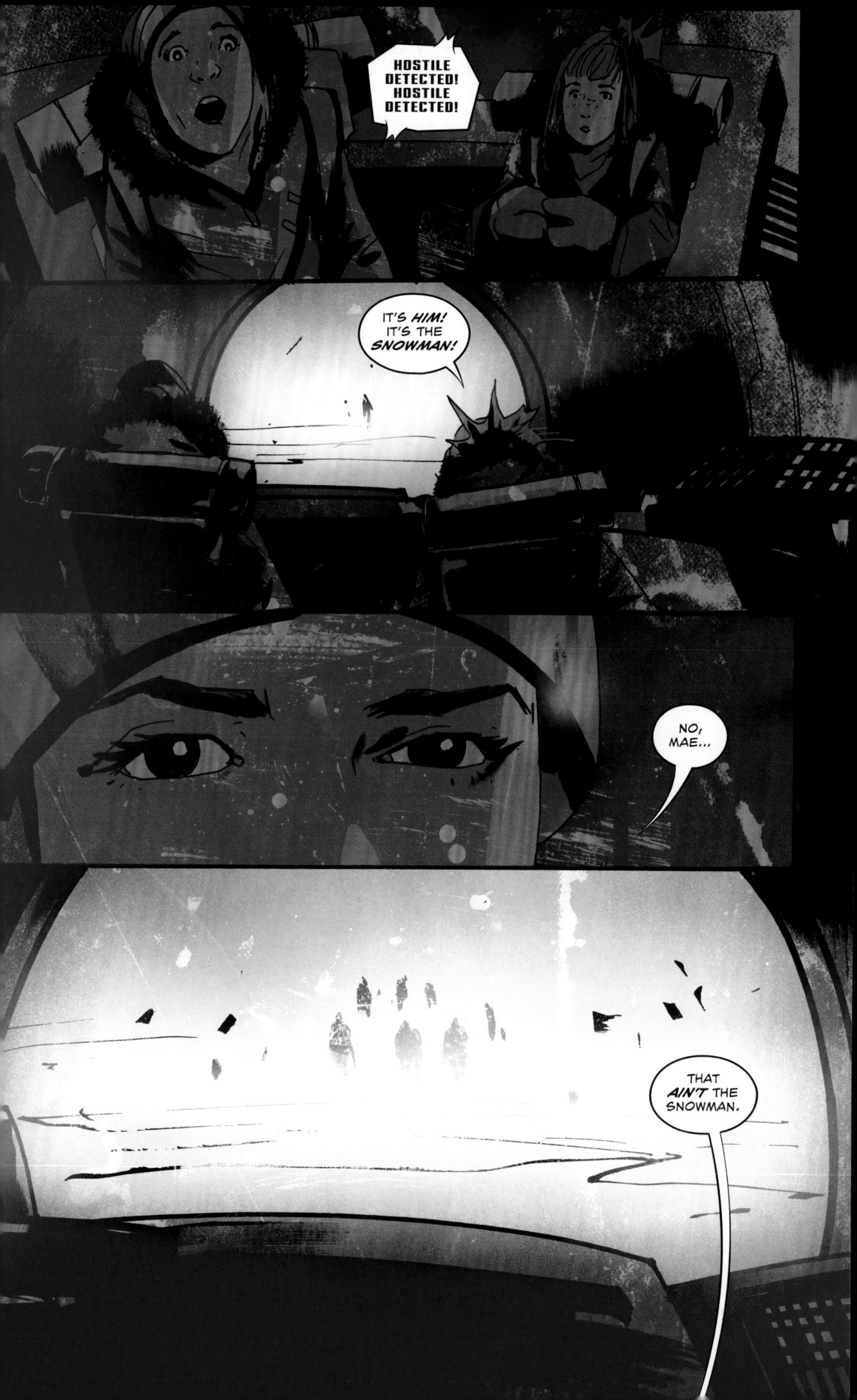
HOSTILE DETECTED! HOSTILE DETECTED!
IT'S HIM! IT'S THE SNOWMAN!
NO, MAE...
THAT AIN'T THE SNOWMAN.

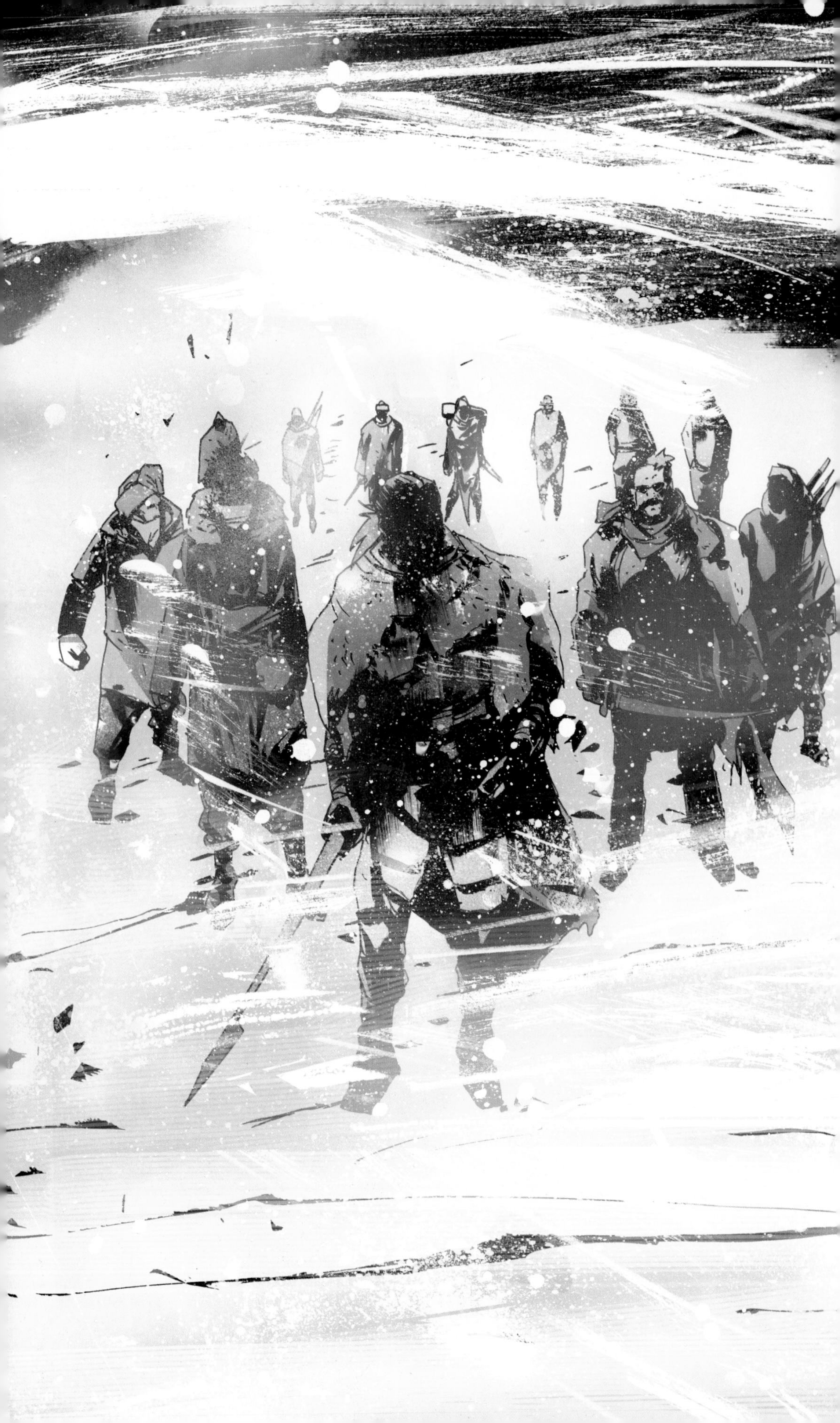

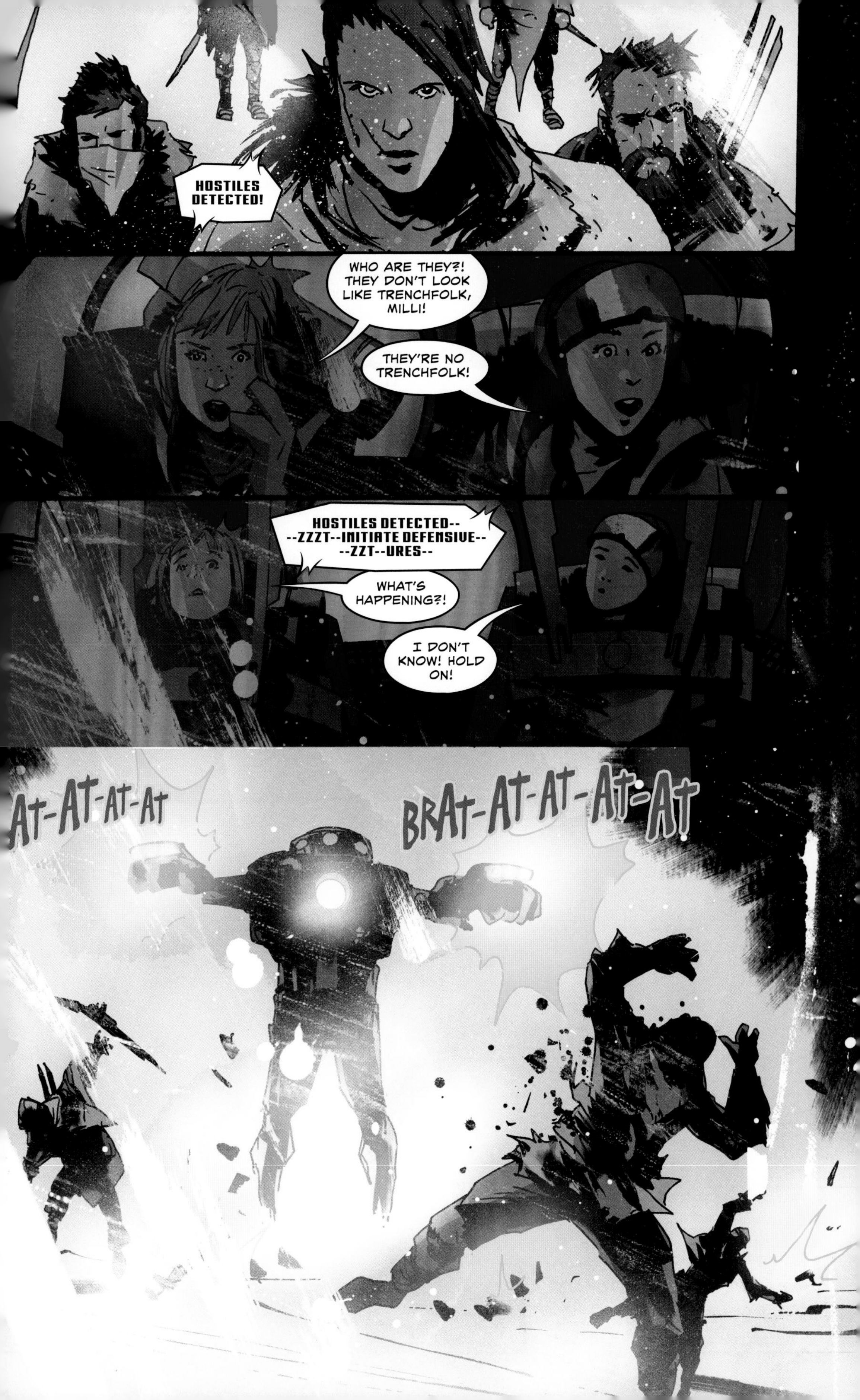
HOSTILES DETECTED!
WHO ARE THEY?! THEY DON'T LOOK LIKE TRENCHFOLK, MILLI!
THEY'RE NO TRENCHFOLK!
HOSTILES DETECTED-- --ZZZT--INITIATE DEFENSIVE-- --ZZT--URES--
WHAT'S HAPPENING?!
I DON'T KNOW! HOLD ON!
AT-AT-AT-AT
BRAT-AT-AT-AT-AT

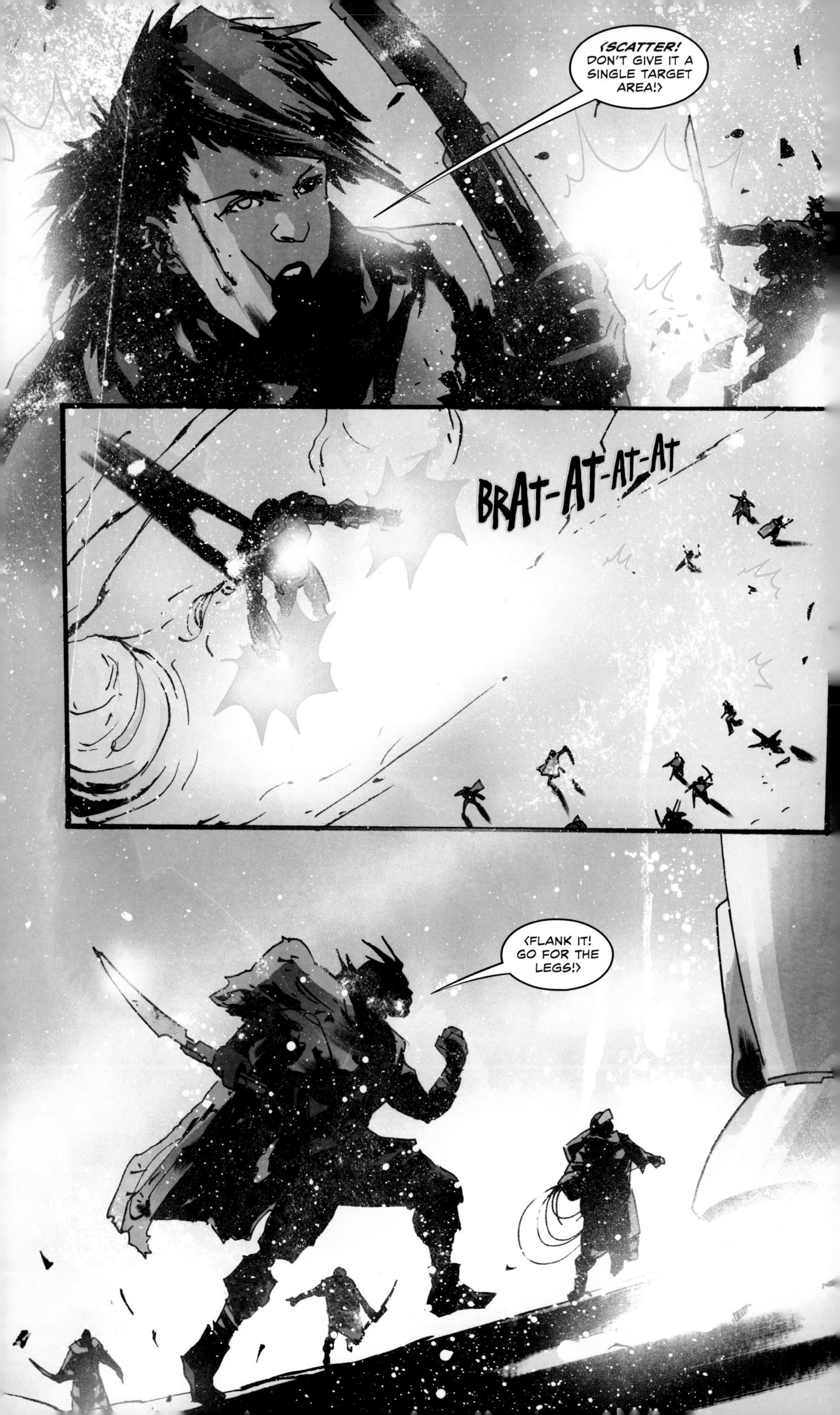
‹SCATTER! DON'T GIVE IT A SINGLE TARGET AREA!›
BRAT-AT-AT-AT
‹FLANK IT! GO FOR THE LEGS!›

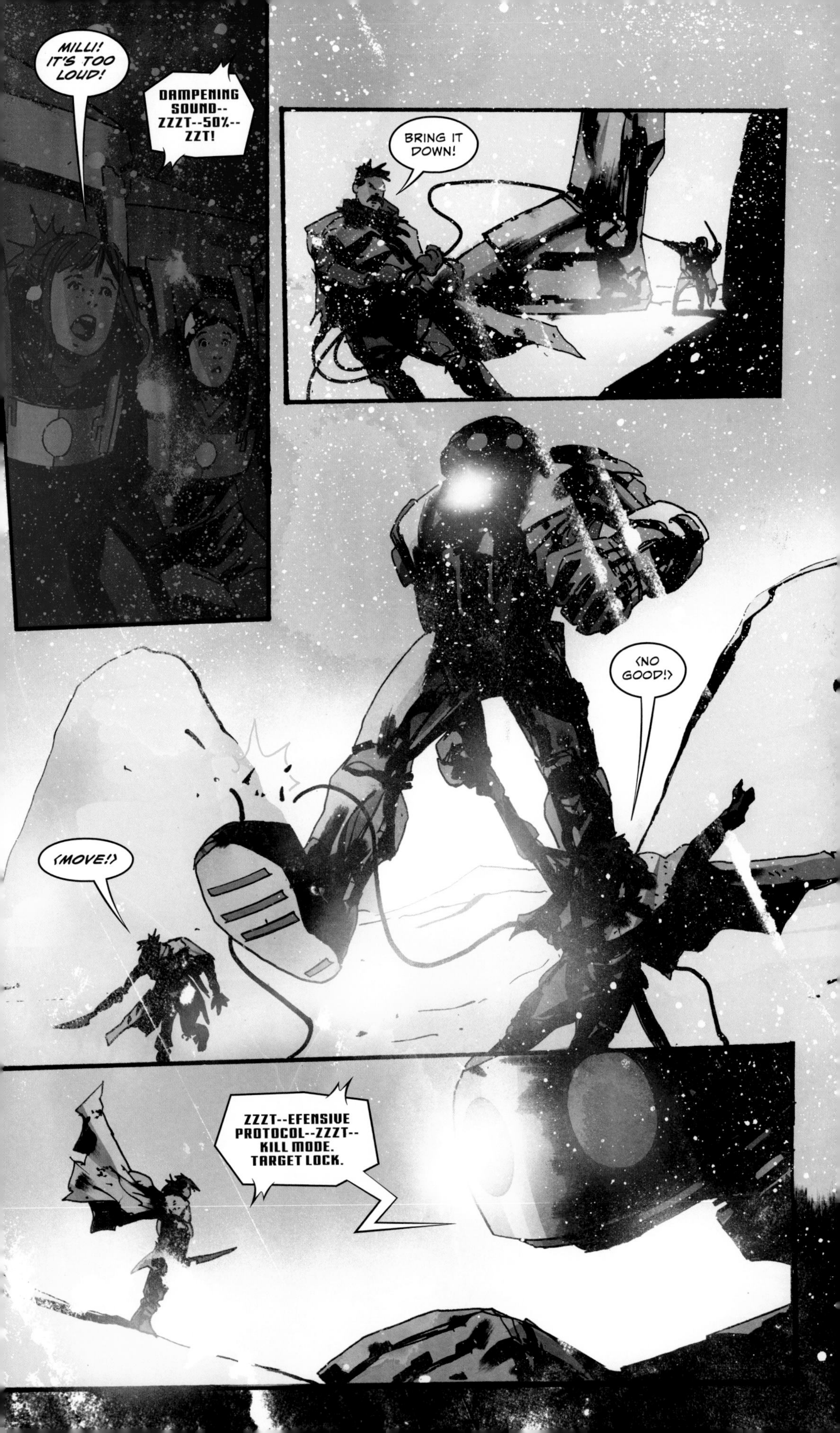
MILLI! IT'S TOO LOUD!
DAMPENING SOUND--ZZZT--50%--ZZT!
BRING IT DOWN!
‹NO GOOD!›
‹MOVE!›
ZZZT--EFENSIVE PROTOCOL--ZZZT--KILL MODE. TARGET LOCK.

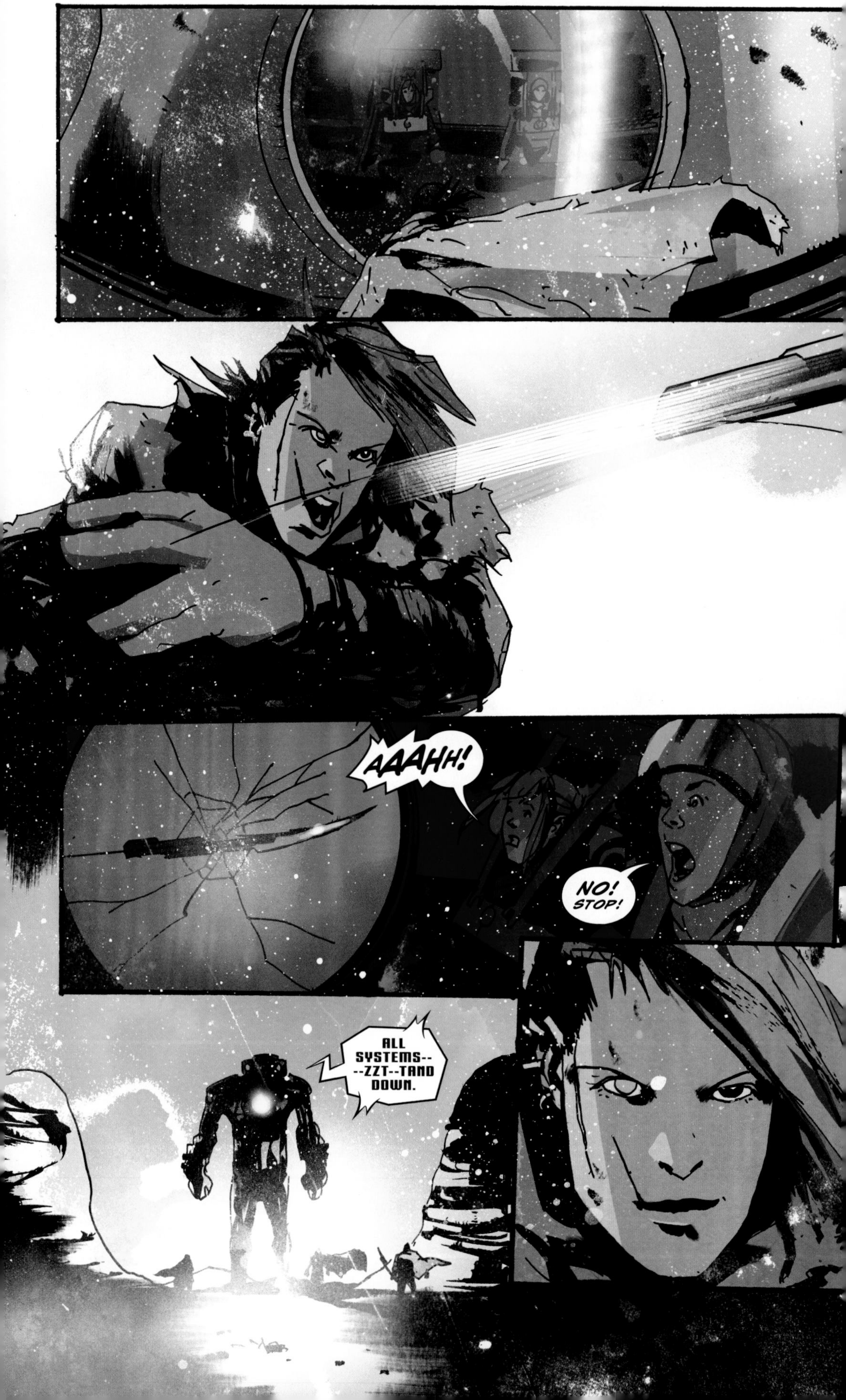
AAAHH!
NO! STOP!
ALL SYSTEMS-- --ZZT--TAND DOWN.

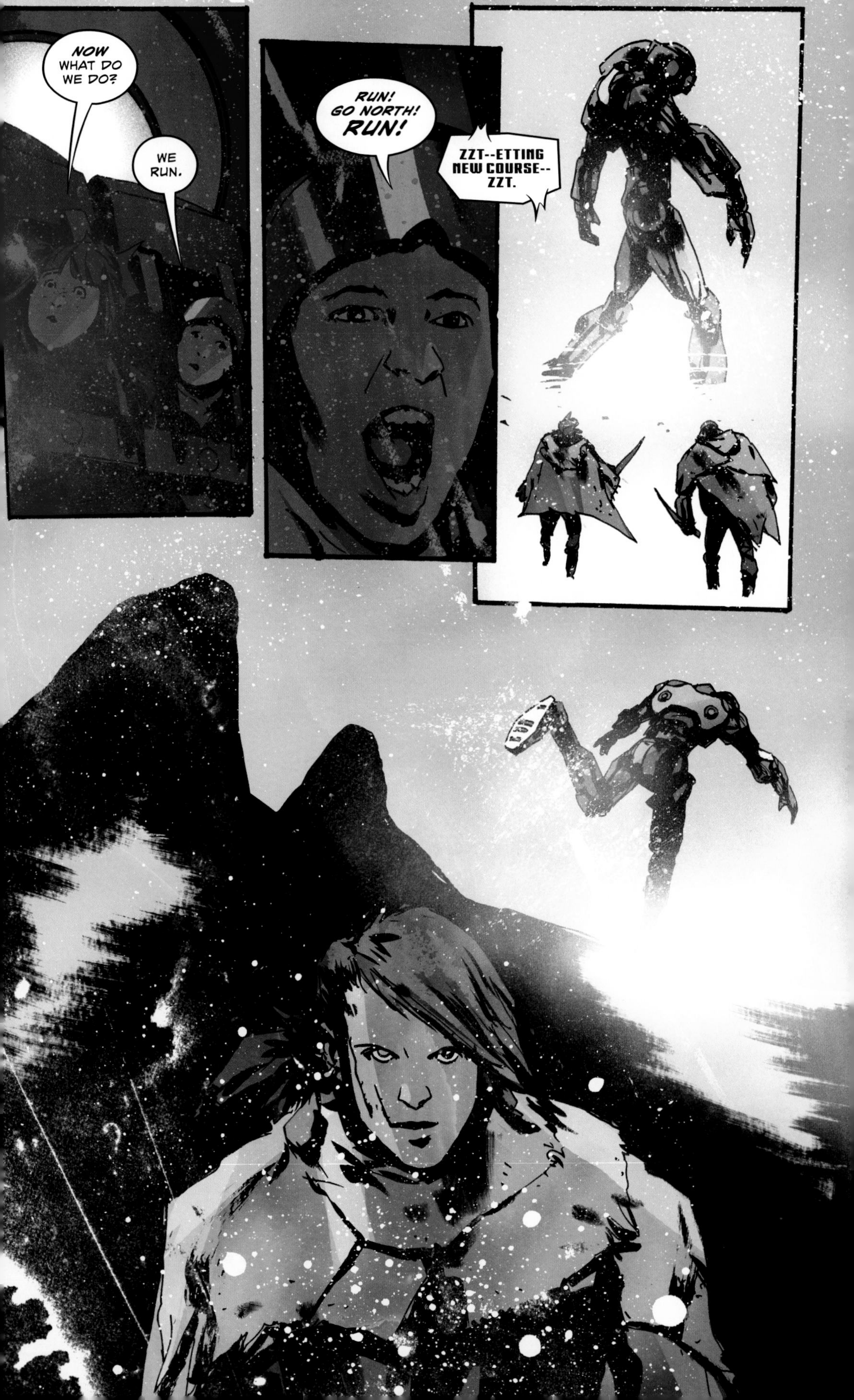
NOW WHAT DO WE DO?
WE RUN.
RUN! GO NORTH! RUN!
ZZT--ETTING NEW COURSE-- ZZT.

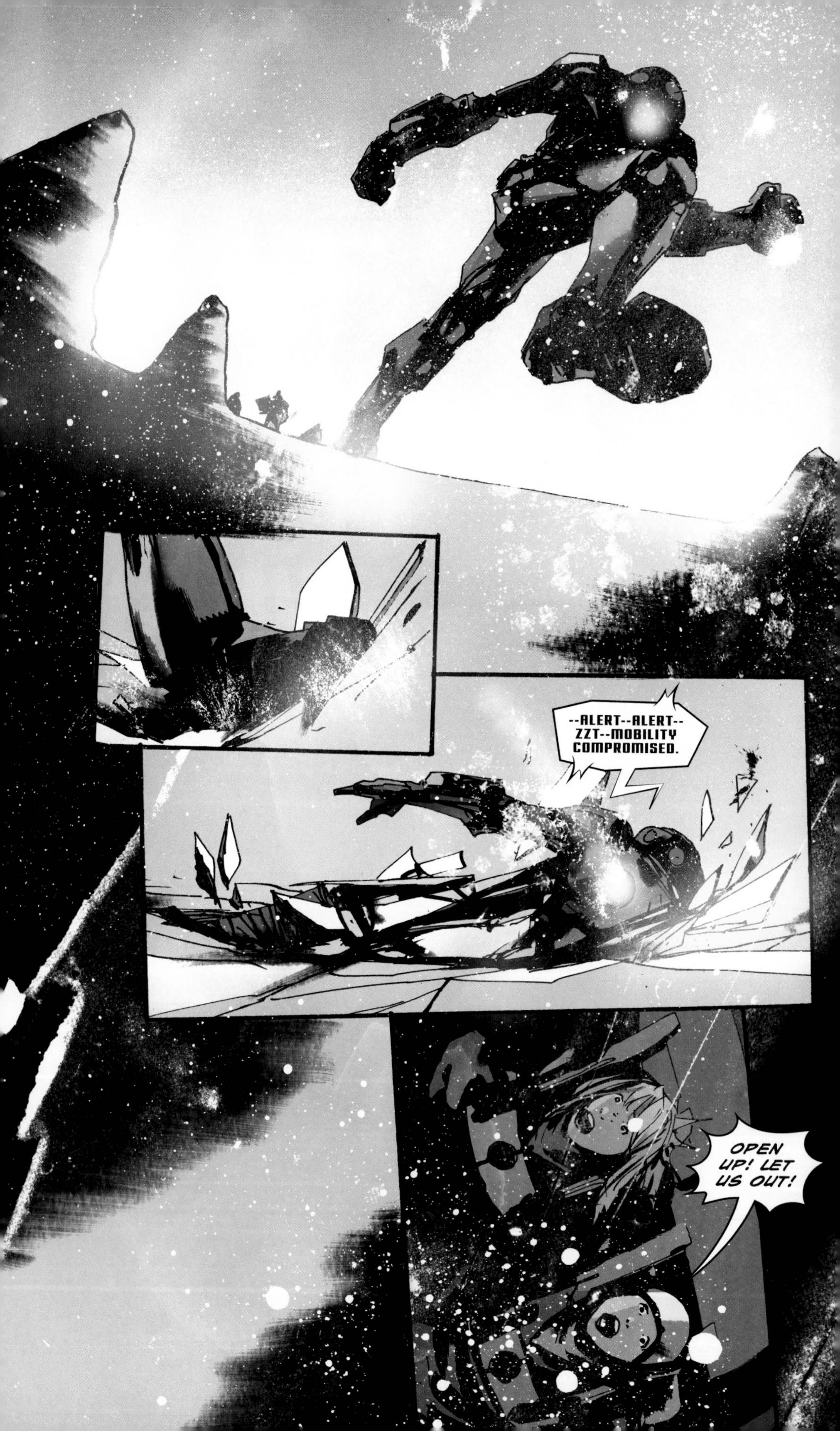
--ALERT--ALERT--
ZZT--MOBILITY
COMPROMISED.
OPEN UP! LET US OUT!

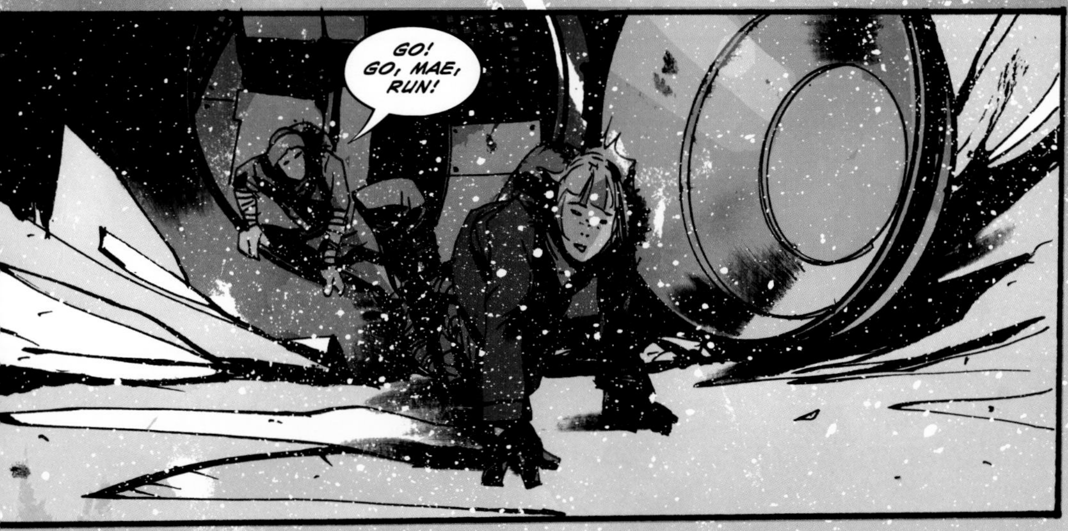
GO! GO, MAE, RUN!

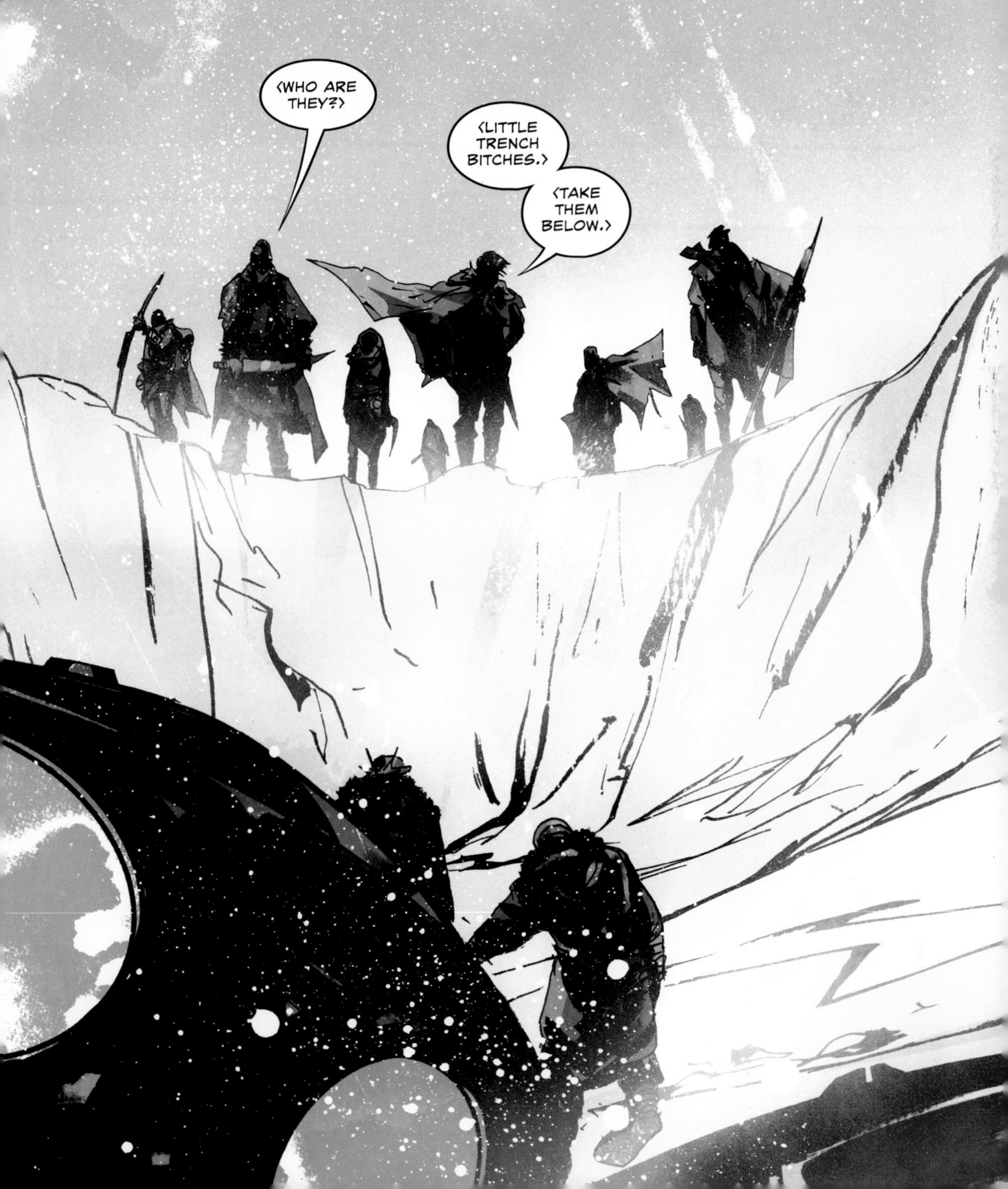
<WHO ARE THEY?>
<LITTLE TRENCH BITCHES.>
<TAKE THEM BELOW.>

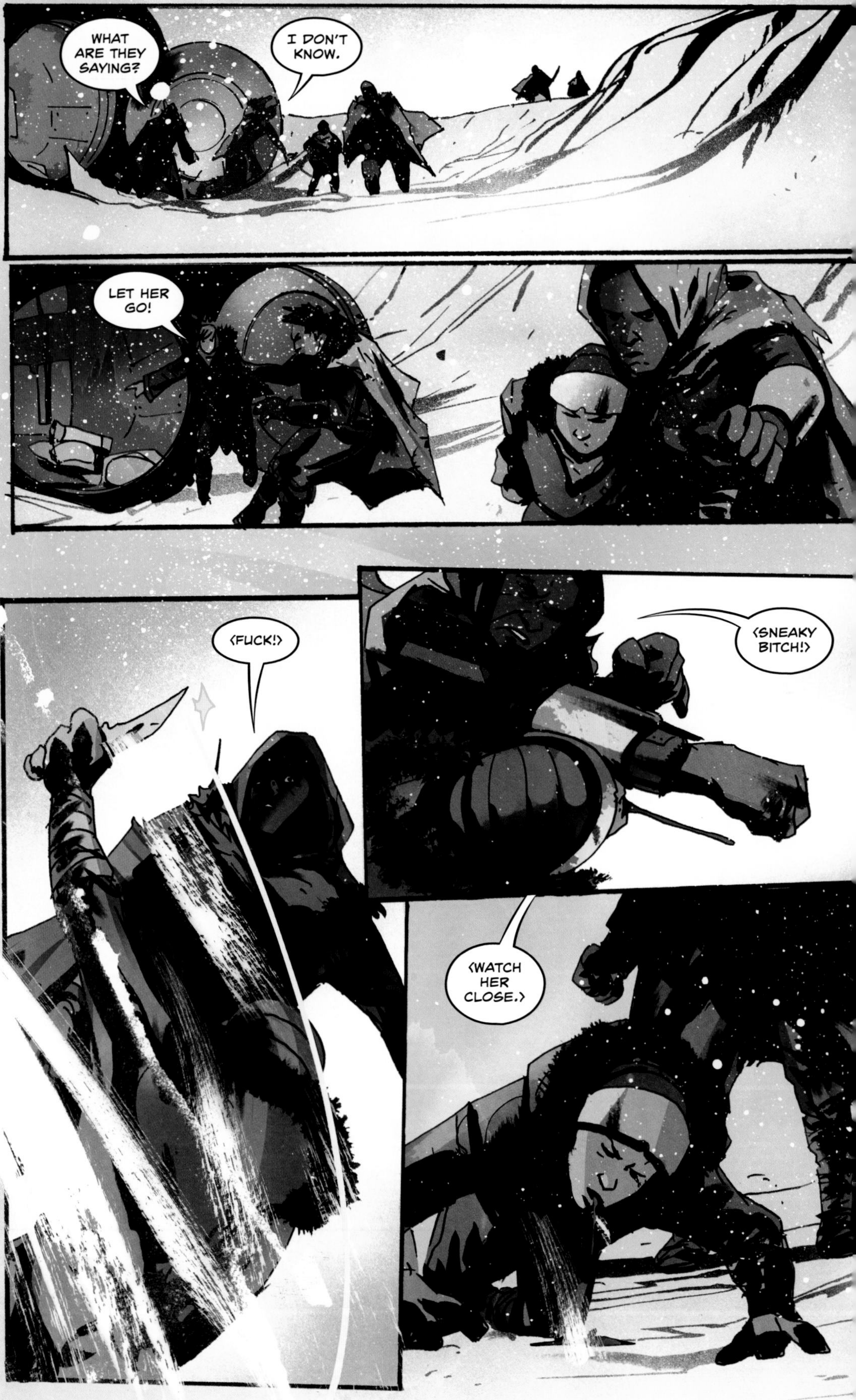
WHAT ARE THEY SAYING?
I DON'T KNOW.
LET HER GO!
‹FUCK!›
‹SNEAKY BITCH!›
‹WATCH HER CLOSE.›

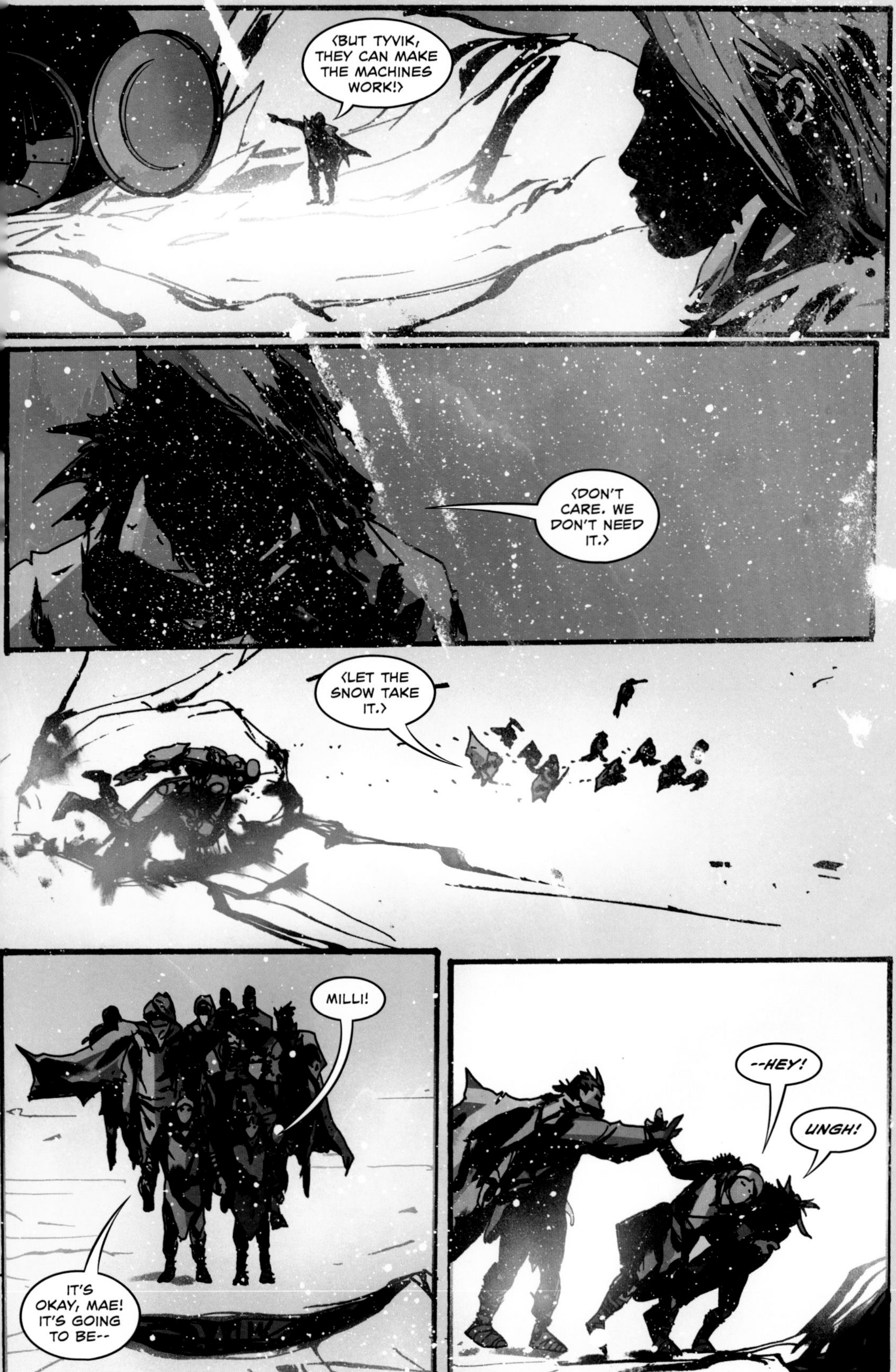

<BUT TYVIK, THEY CAN MAKE THE MACHINES WORK!>
<DON'T CARE. WE DON'T NEED IT.>
<LET THE SNOW TAKE IT.>
MILLI!
IT'S OKAY, MAE! IT'S GOING TO BE--
--HEY!
UNGH!

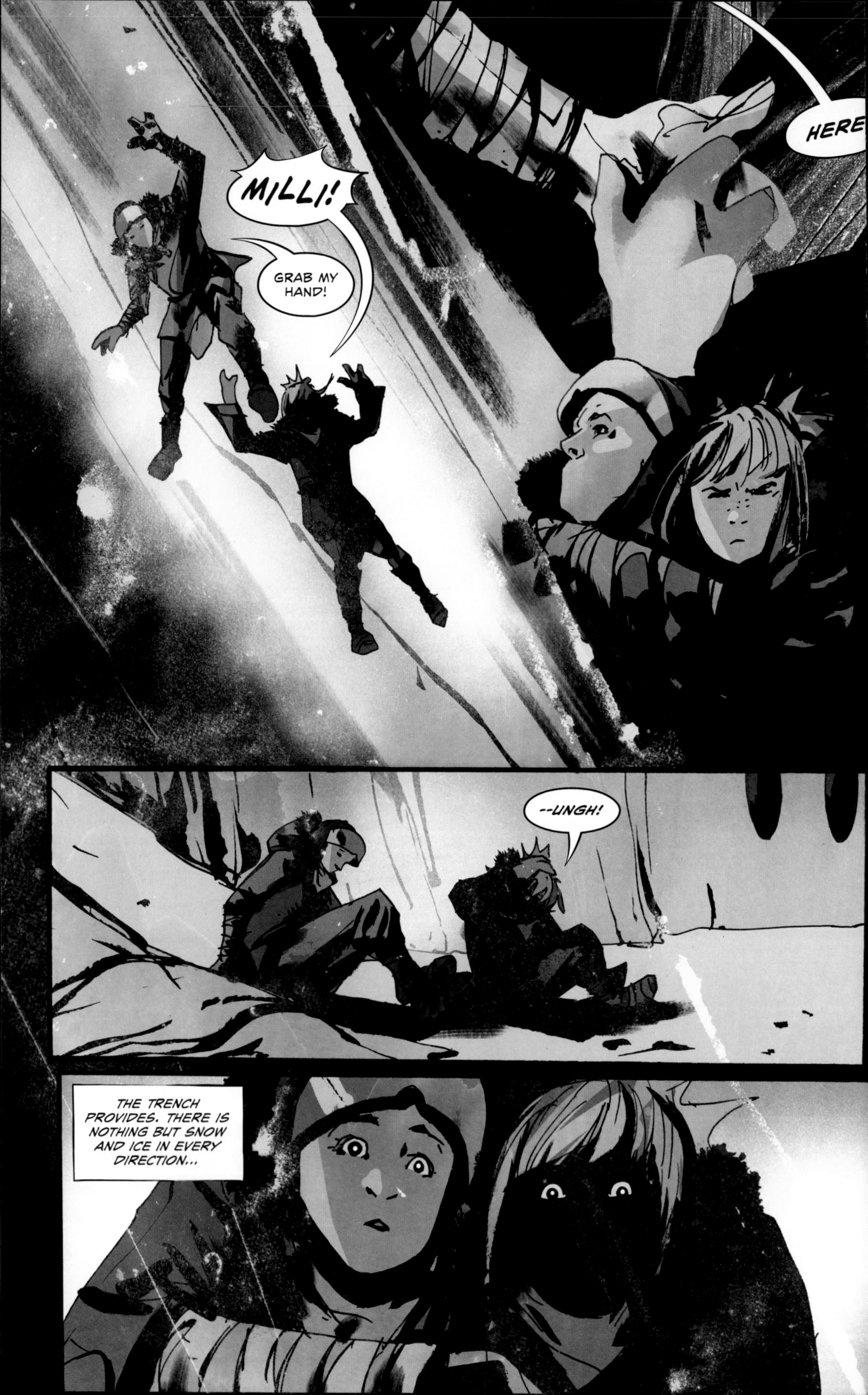
HERE
MILLI!
GRAB MY HAND!
--UNGH!
THE TRENCH PROVIDES. THERE IS NOTHING BUT SNOW AND ICE IN EVERY DIRECTION...

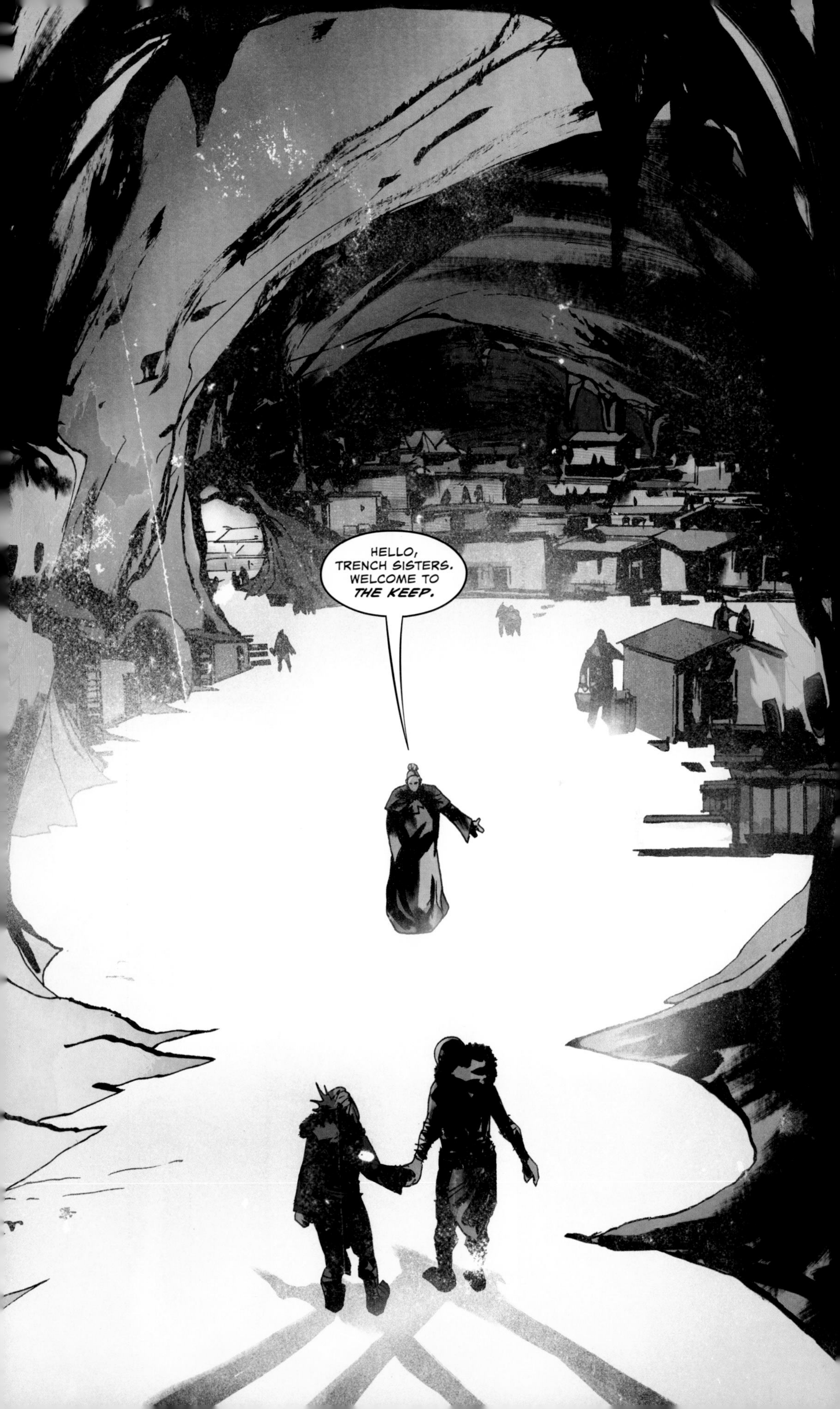
HELLO, TRENCH SISTERS. WELCOME TO *THE KEEP.*

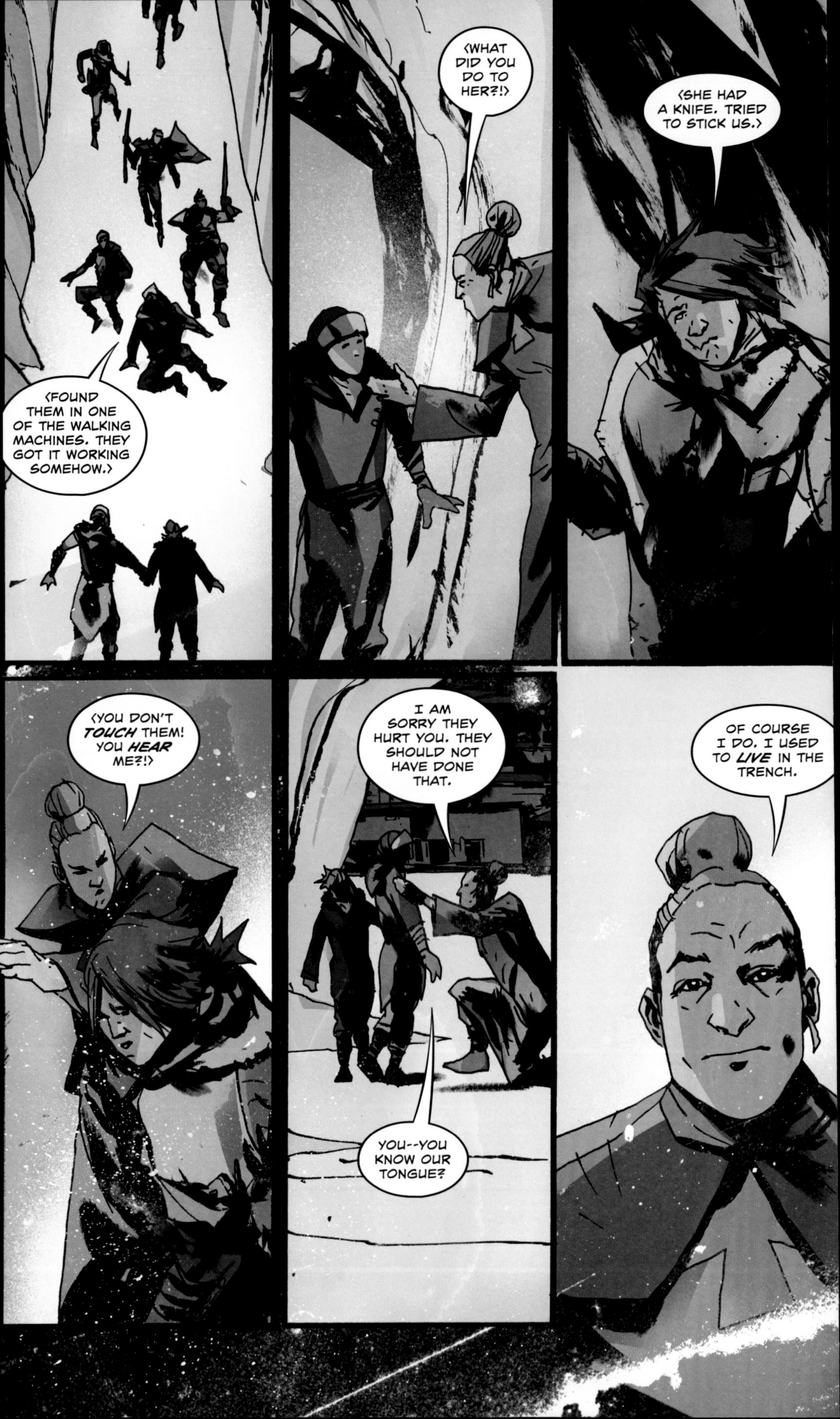

‹FOUND THEM IN ONE OF THE WALKING MACHINES. THEY GOT IT WORKING SOMEHOW.›
‹WHAT DID YOU DO TO HER?!›
‹SHE HAD A KNIFE. TRIED TO STICK US.›
‹YOU DON'T TOUCH THEM! YOU HEAR ME?!›
I AM SORRY THEY HURT YOU. THEY SHOULD NOT HAVE DONE THAT.
YOU--YOU KNOW OUR TONGUE?
OF COURSE I DO. I USED TO LIVE IN THE TRENCH.

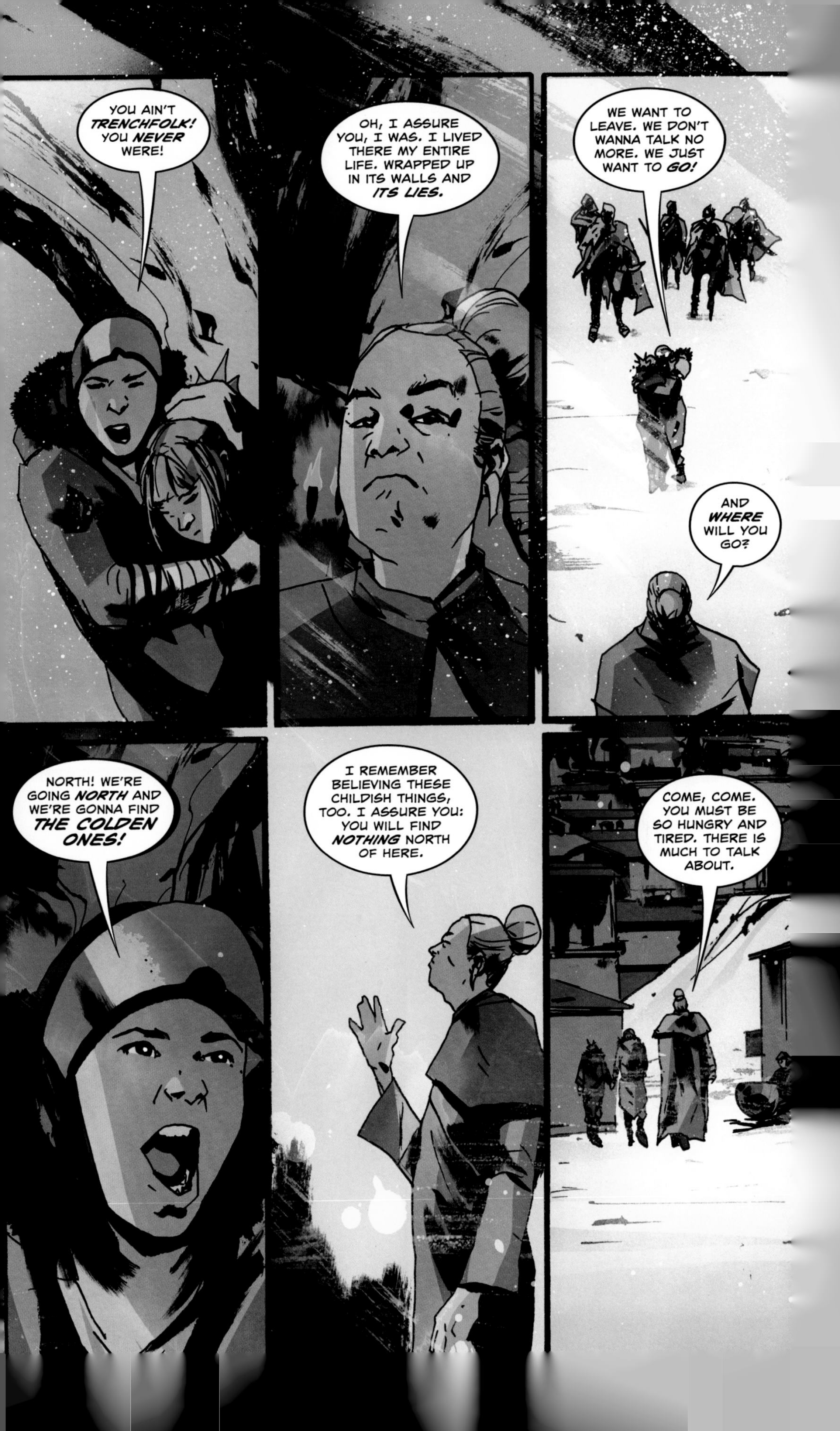
YOU AIN'T TRENCHFOLK! YOU NEVER WERE!
OH, I ASSURE YOU, I WAS. I LIVED THERE MY ENTIRE LIFE. WRAPPED UP IN ITS WALLS AND ITS LIES.
WE WANT TO LEAVE. WE DON'T WANNA TALK NO MORE. WE JUST WANT TO GO!
AND WHERE WILL YOU GO?
NORTH! WE'RE GOING NORTH AND WE'RE GONNA FIND THE COLDEN ONES!
I REMEMBER BELIEVING THESE CHILDISH THINGS, TOO. I ASSURE YOU: YOU WILL FIND NOTHING NORTH OF HERE.
COME, COME. YOU MUST BE SO HUNGRY AND TIRED. THERE IS MUCH TO TALK ABOUT.

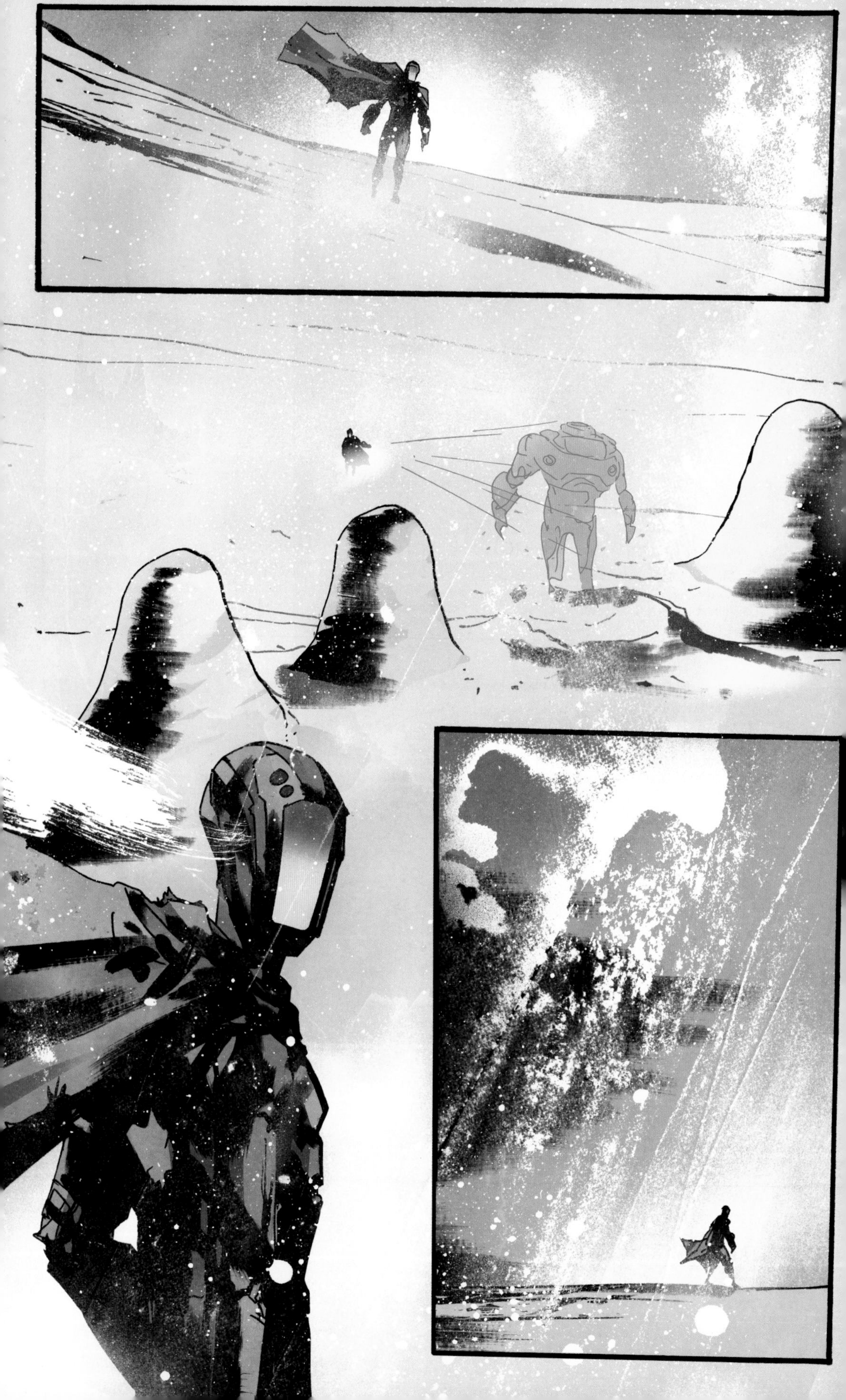

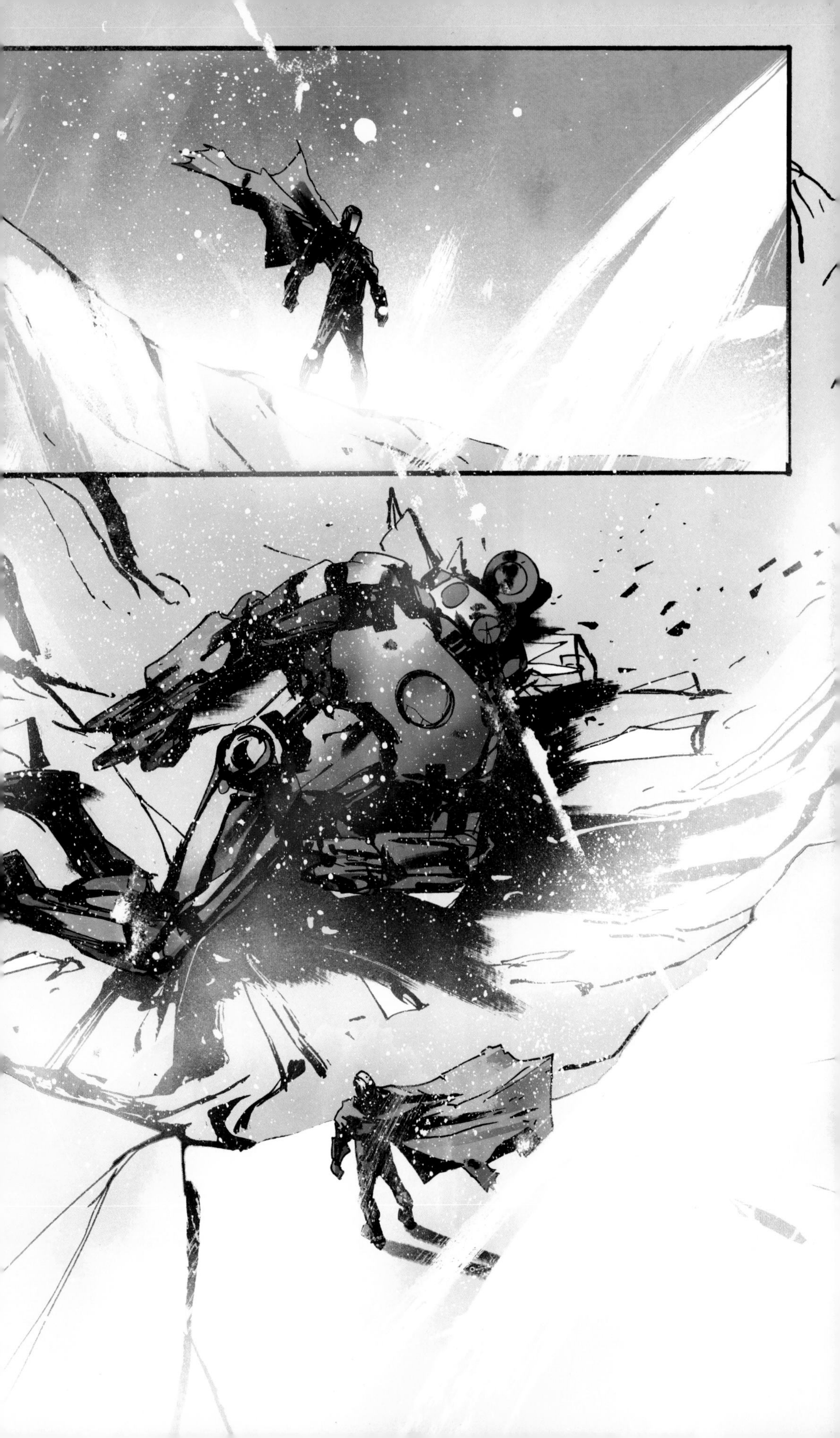

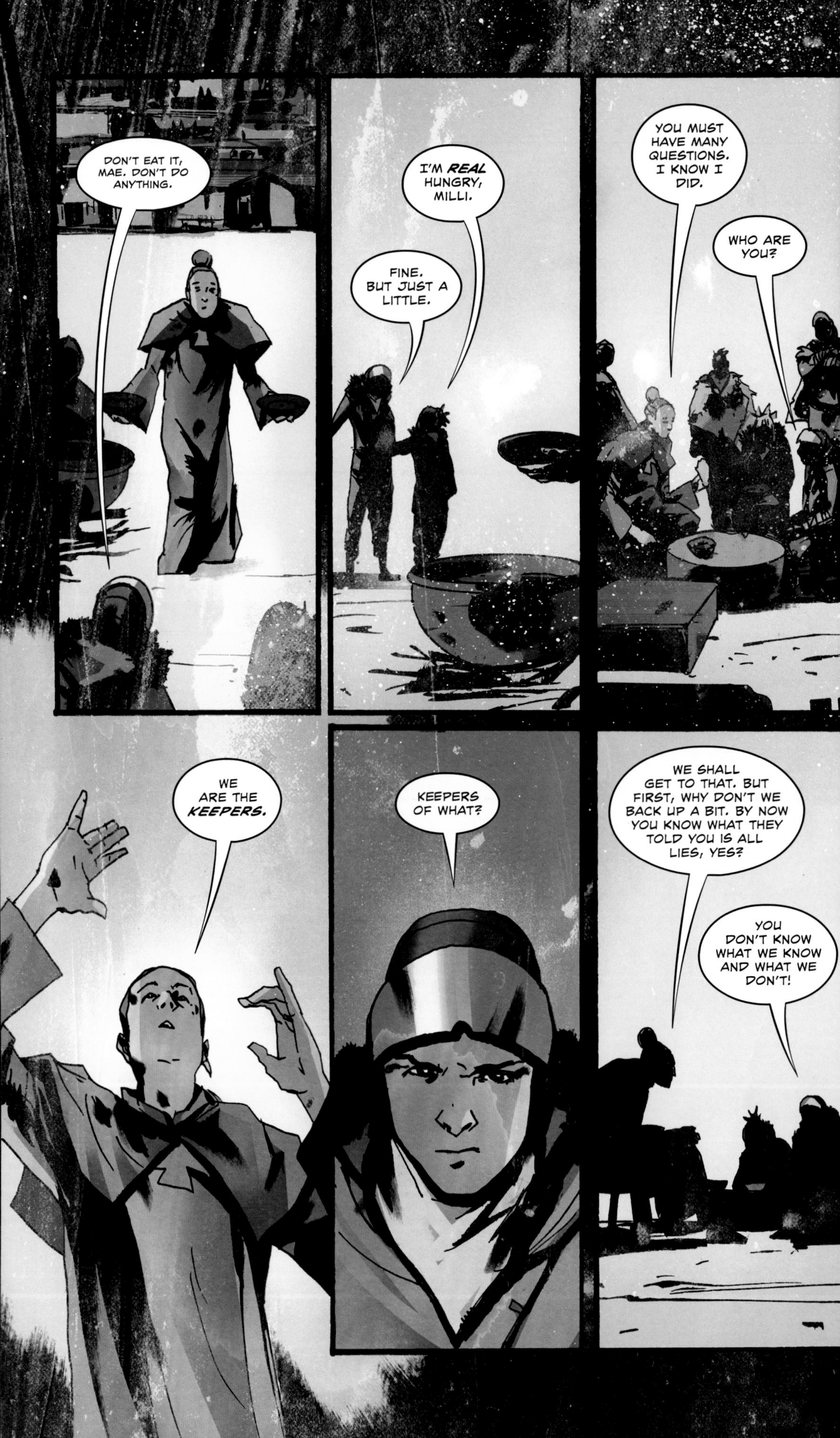
DON'T EAT IT, MAE. DON'T DO ANYTHING.
I'M REAL HUNGRY, MILLI.
FINE. BUT JUST A LITTLE.
YOU MUST HAVE MANY QUESTIONS. I KNOW I DID.
WHO ARE YOU?
WE ARE THE KEEPERS.
KEEPERS OF WHAT?
WE SHALL GET TO THAT. BUT FIRST, WHY DON'T WE BACK UP A BIT. BY NOW YOU KNOW WHAT THEY TOLD YOU IS ALL LIES, YES?
YOU DON'T KNOW WHAT WE KNOW AND WHAT WE DON'T!

THE THREE RULES OF THE TRENCH.

FIRST: *YOU MUST NEVER LEAVE THE TRENCH.* THERE IS ONLY DEATH OUTSIDE OF THE TRENCH AND NOTHING BUT ICE IN EVERY DIRECTION. WE KNOW THAT ONE IS FALSE, YES?

SECOND: *THE TRENCH PROVIDES.* ALL YOU NEED TO SUSTAIN YOU CAN BE FOUND GROWING IN THE TRENCH'S SNOWY WALLS, SWIMMING IN THE FRIGID WATERS UNDER ITS ICY FLOOR, OR IN THE "GIFTS" LEFT BEHIND BY THE COLDEN ONES.

THIS IS ALSO A LIE. THE THINGS LEFT BEHIND. THE MACHINES...THEY ARE *NOT* FROM THE COLDEN ONES.

ARE, TOO! YOU DON'T KNOW *NOTHING!*

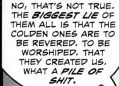

I KNOW MORE THAN YOU CAN IMAGINE, CHILD. AND SOON YOU WILL TOO, IF YOU STOP AND LISTEN.

THE THIRD AND FINAL RULE: *THE TRENCH IS ENDLESS.* IT STRETCHES TO INFINITY IN EITHER DIRECTION. TO TRY TO FIND THE END OF THE TRENCH WILL BRING ONLY MADNESS.

THE *BIGGEST LIE* OF THEM ALL, YES?

NO, THAT'S NOT TRUE. THE *BIGGEST LIE* OF THEM ALL IS THAT THE COLDEN ONES ARE TO BE REVERED. TO BE WORSHIPED. THAT THEY CREATED US. WHAT A *PILE OF SHIT.*

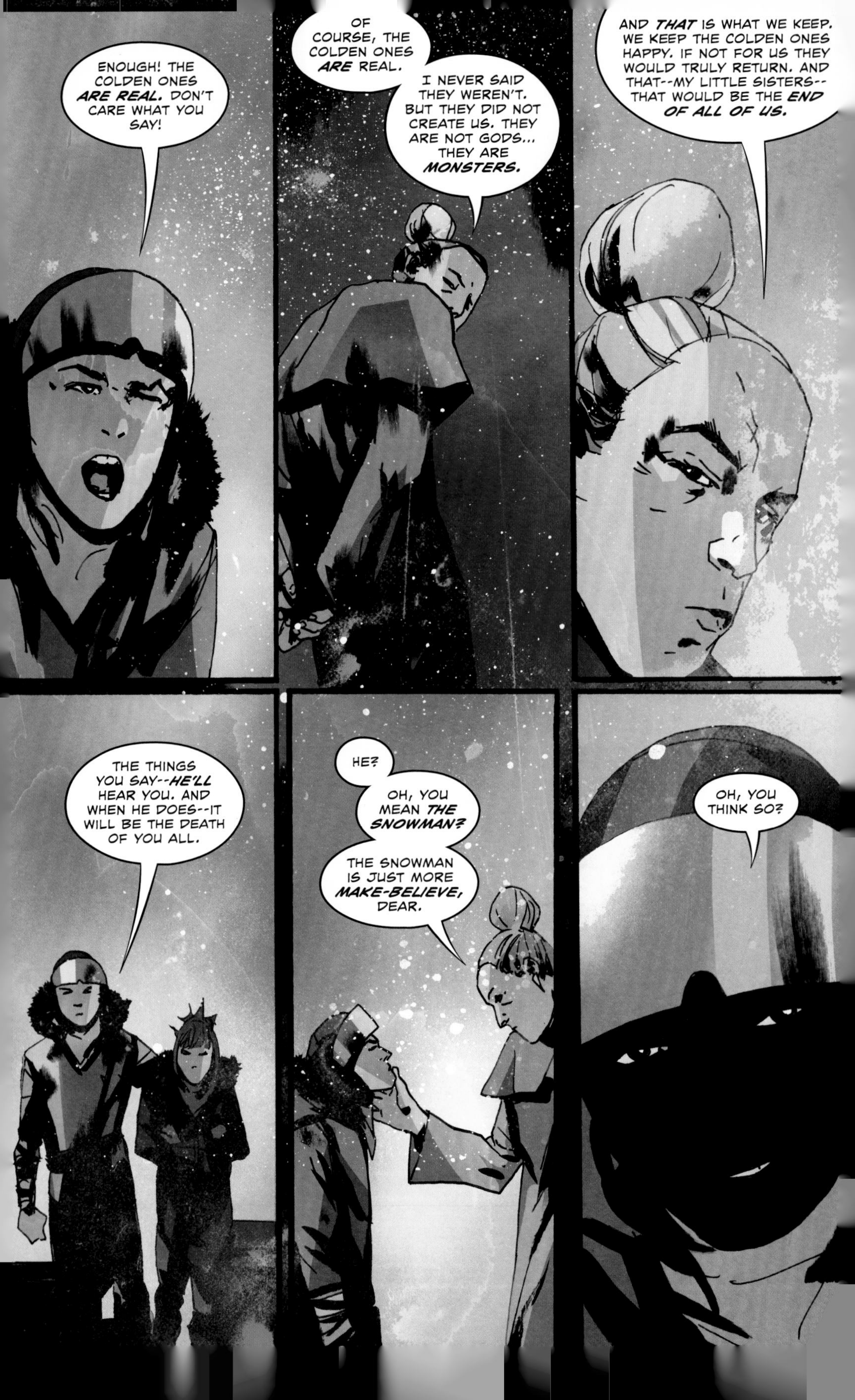
ENOUGH! THE COLDEN ONES ARE REAL. DON'T CARE WHAT YOU SAY!
OF COURSE, THE COLDEN ONES ARE REAL.
I NEVER SAID THEY WEREN'T. BUT THEY DID NOT CREATE US. THEY ARE NOT GODS... THEY ARE MONSTERS.
AND THAT IS WHAT WE KEEP. WE KEEP THE COLDEN ONES HAPPY. IF NOT FOR US THEY WOULD TRULY RETURN. AND THAT--MY LITTLE SISTERS--THAT WOULD BE THE END OF ALL OF US.
THE THINGS YOU SAY--HE'LL HEAR YOU. AND WHEN HE DOES--IT WILL BE THE DEATH OF YOU ALL.
HE?
OH, YOU MEAN THE SNOWMAN?
THE SNOWMAN IS JUST MORE MAKE-BELIEVE, DEAR.
OH, YOU THINK SO?

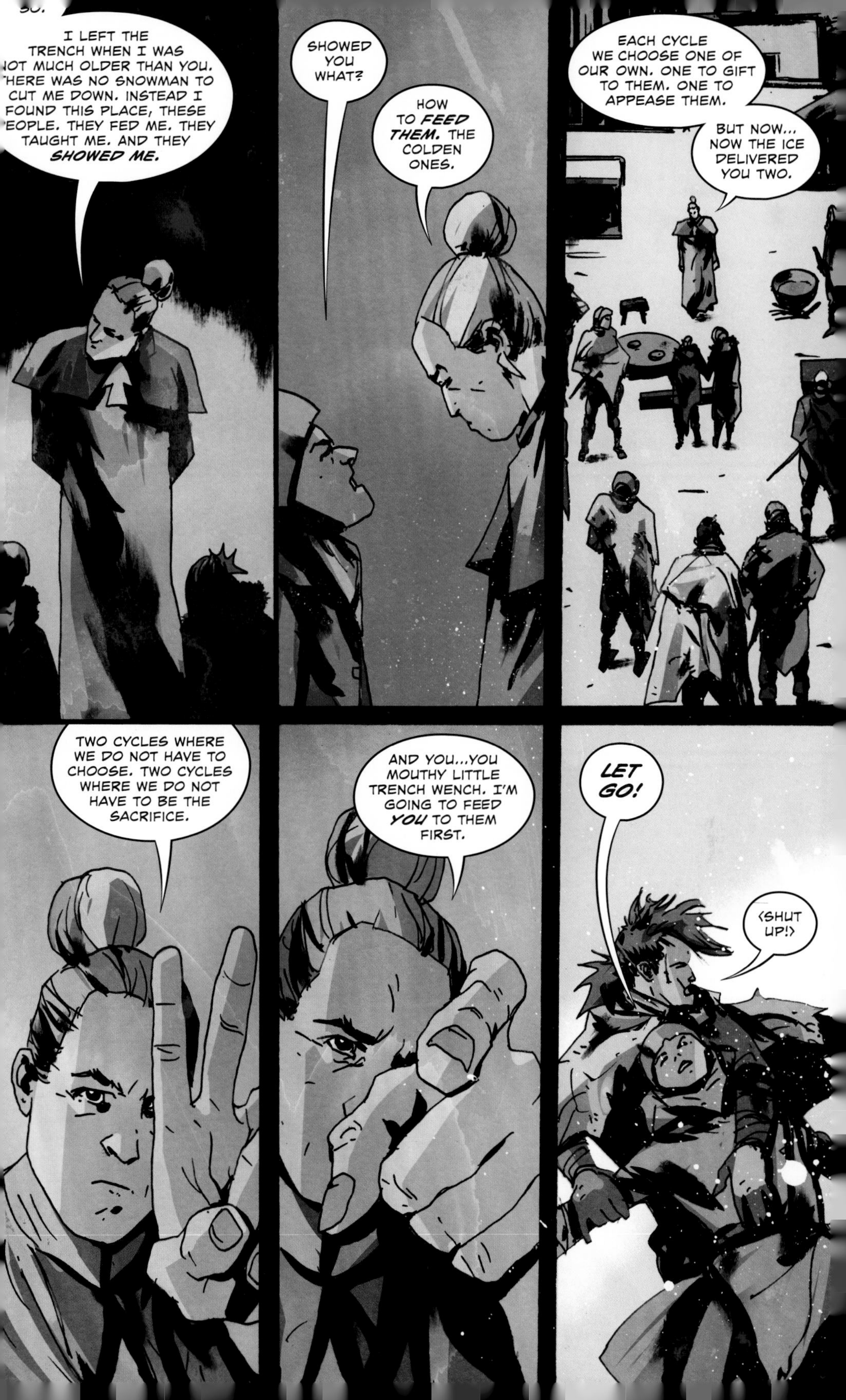
I LEFT THE TRENCH WHEN I WAS NOT MUCH OLDER THAN YOU. THERE WAS NO SNOWMAN TO CUT ME DOWN. INSTEAD I FOUND THIS PLACE, THESE PEOPLE. THEY FED ME. THEY TAUGHT ME. AND THEY *SHOWED ME.*
SHOWED YOU WHAT?
HOW TO *FEED THEM.* THE COLDEN ONES.
EACH CYCLE WE CHOOSE ONE OF OUR OWN. ONE TO GIFT TO THEM. ONE TO APPEASE THEM.
BUT NOW... NOW THE ICE DELIVERED YOU TWO.
TWO CYCLES WHERE WE DO NOT HAVE TO CHOOSE. TWO CYCLES WHERE WE DO NOT HAVE TO BE THE SACRIFICE.
AND YOU...YOU MOUTHY LITTLE TRENCH WENCH. I'M GOING TO FEED *YOU* TO THEM FIRST.
LET GO!
<SHUT UP!>

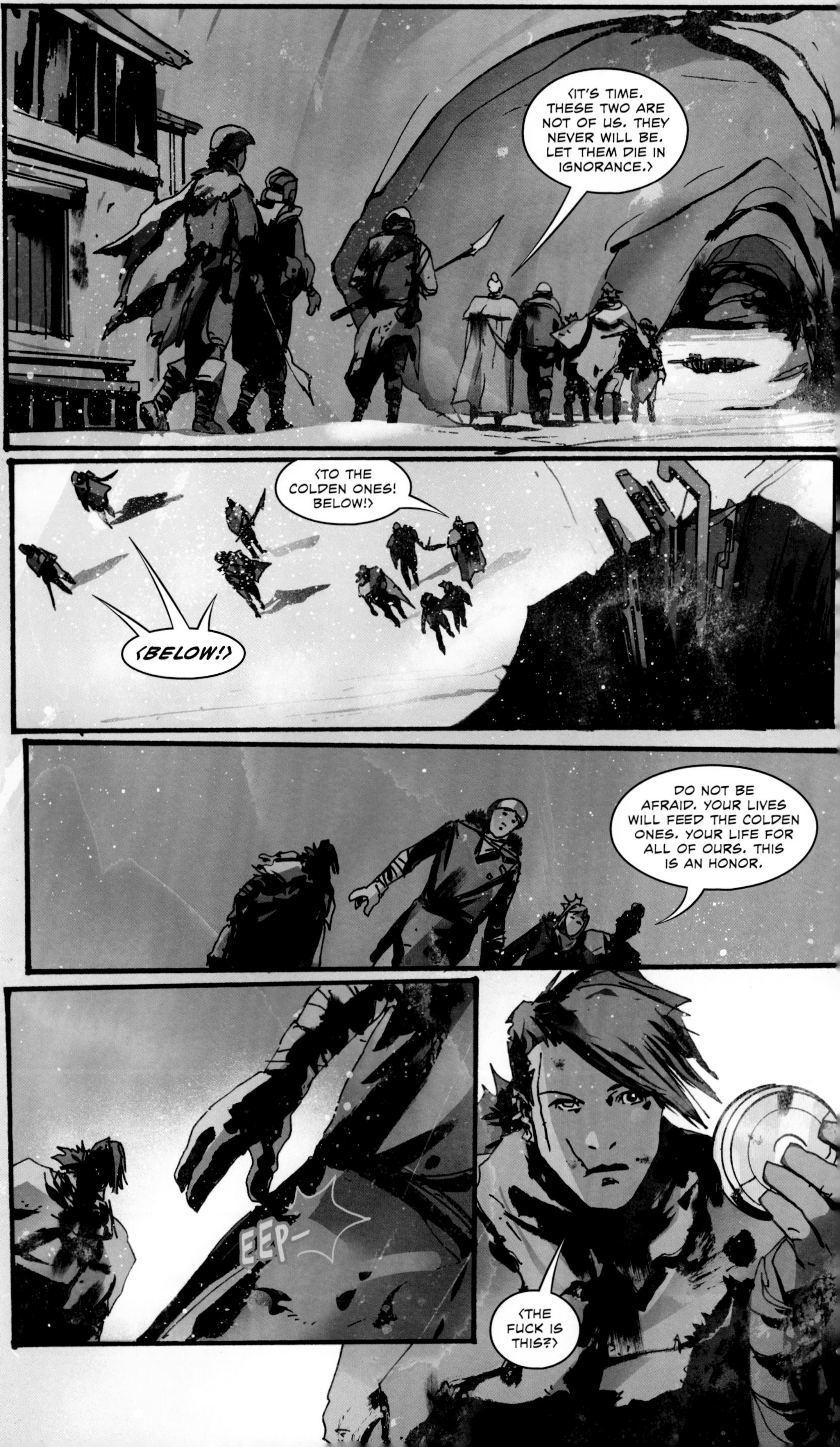

<IT'S TIME. THESE TWO ARE NOT OF US. THEY NEVER WILL BE. LET THEM DIE IN IGNORANCE.>
<TO THE COLDEN ONES! BELOW!>
<BELOW!>
DO NOT BE AFRAID. YOUR LIVES WILL FEED THE COLDEN ONES. YOUR LIFE FOR ALL OF OURS. THIS IS AN HONOR.
EEP-
<THE FUCK IS THIS?>

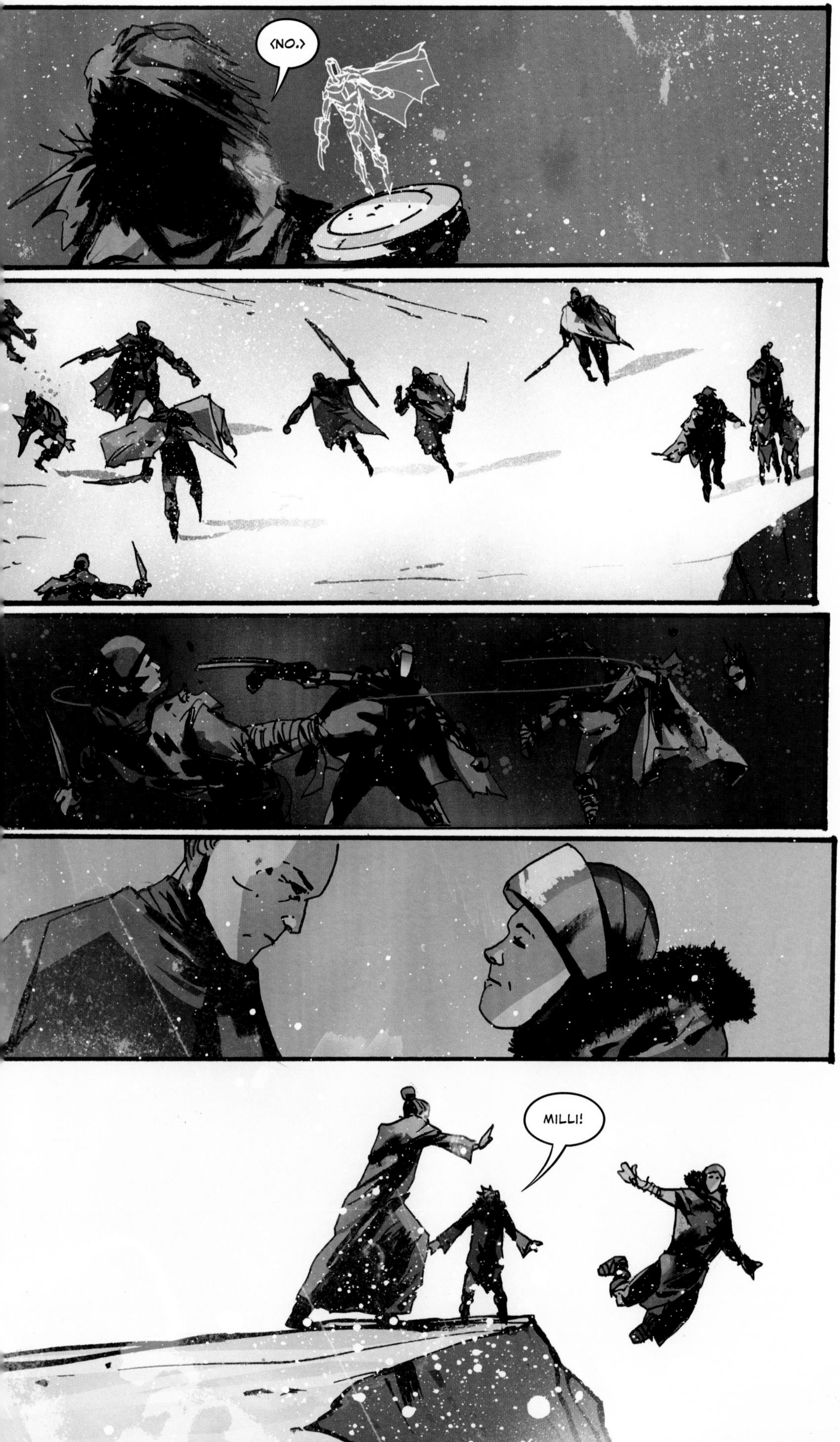

‹NO.›
MILLI!

NO!

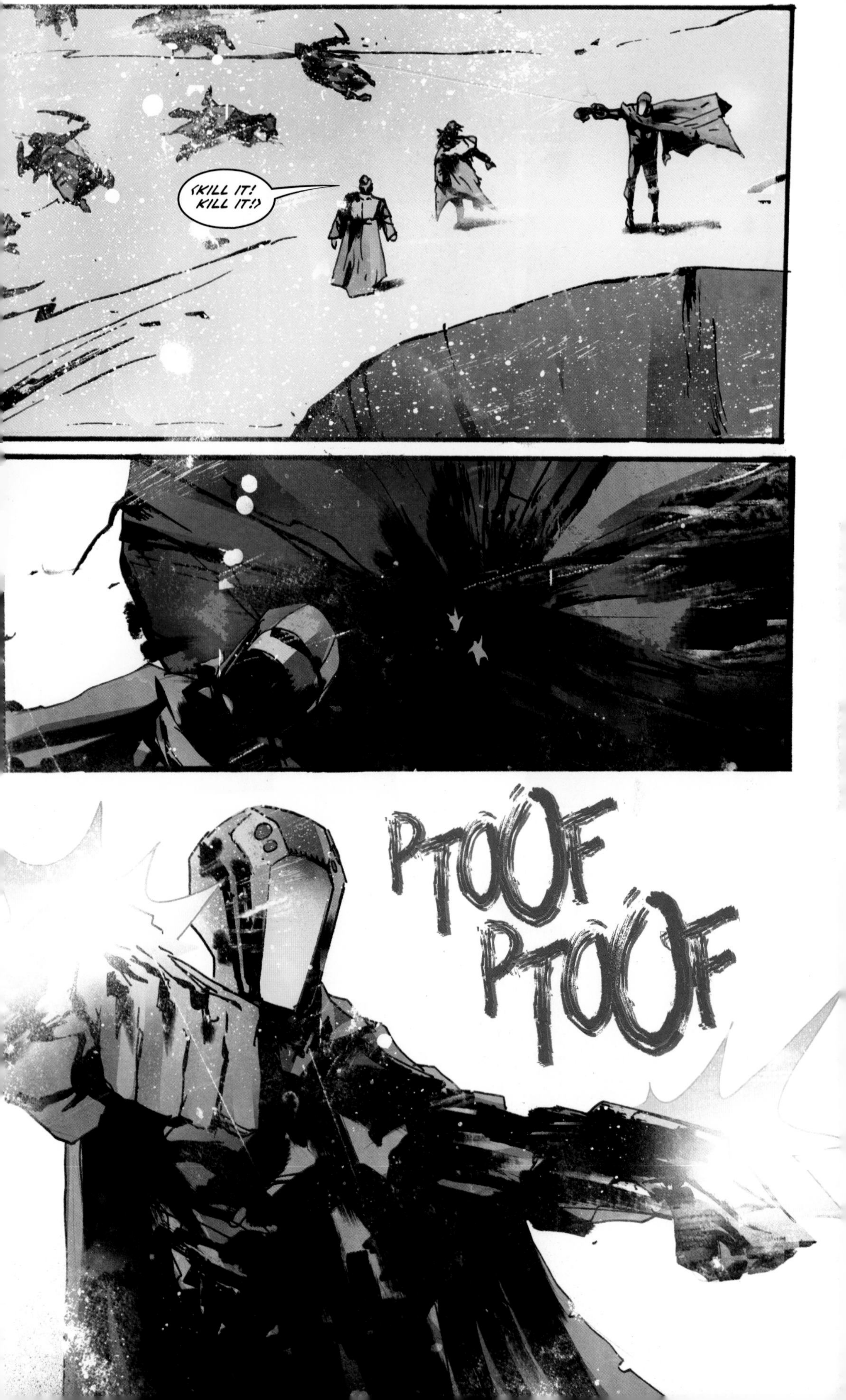
‹KILL IT! KILL IT!›
PTOOF
PTOOF

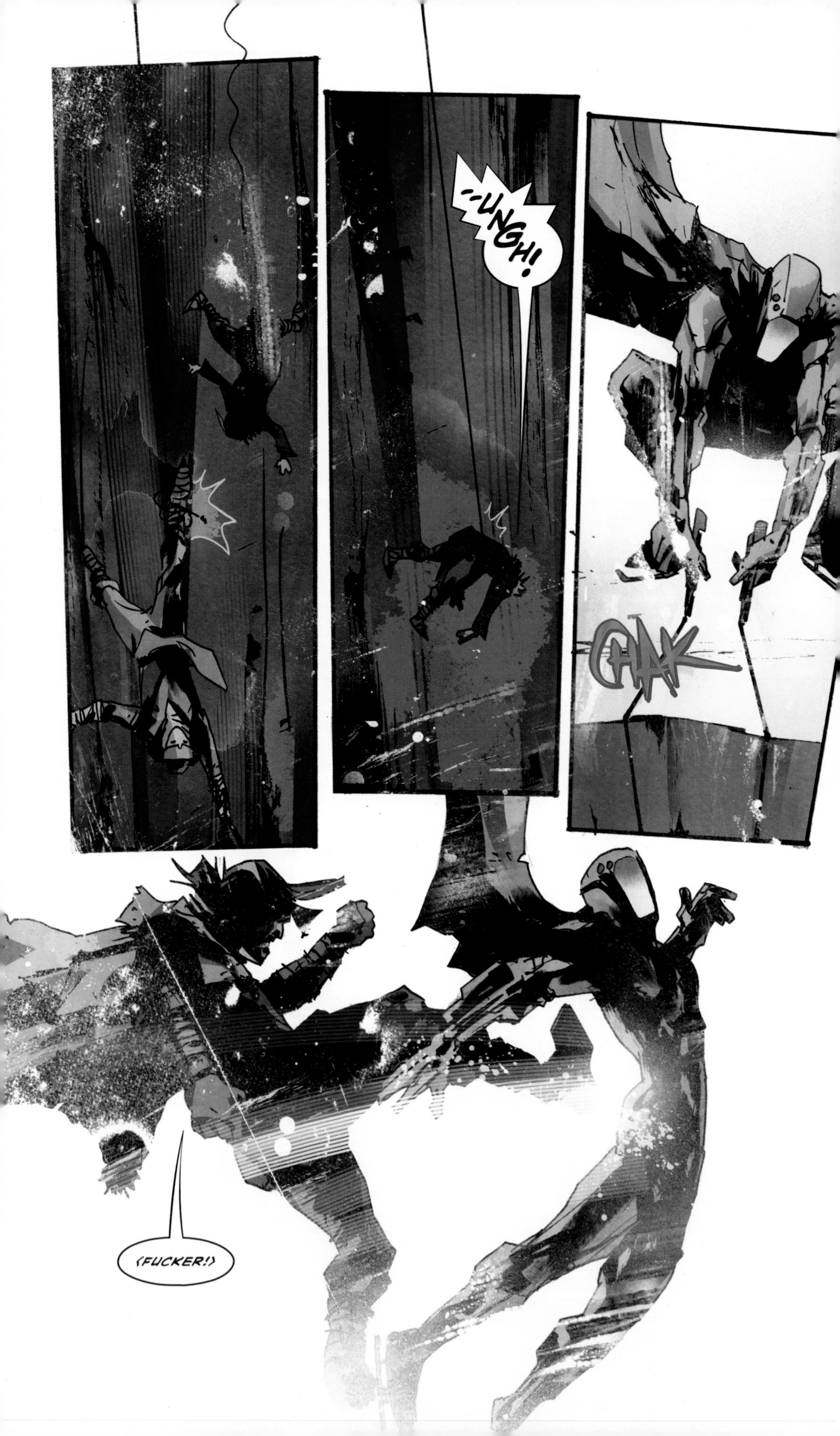
--UNGH!
CHAK
(FUCKER!)

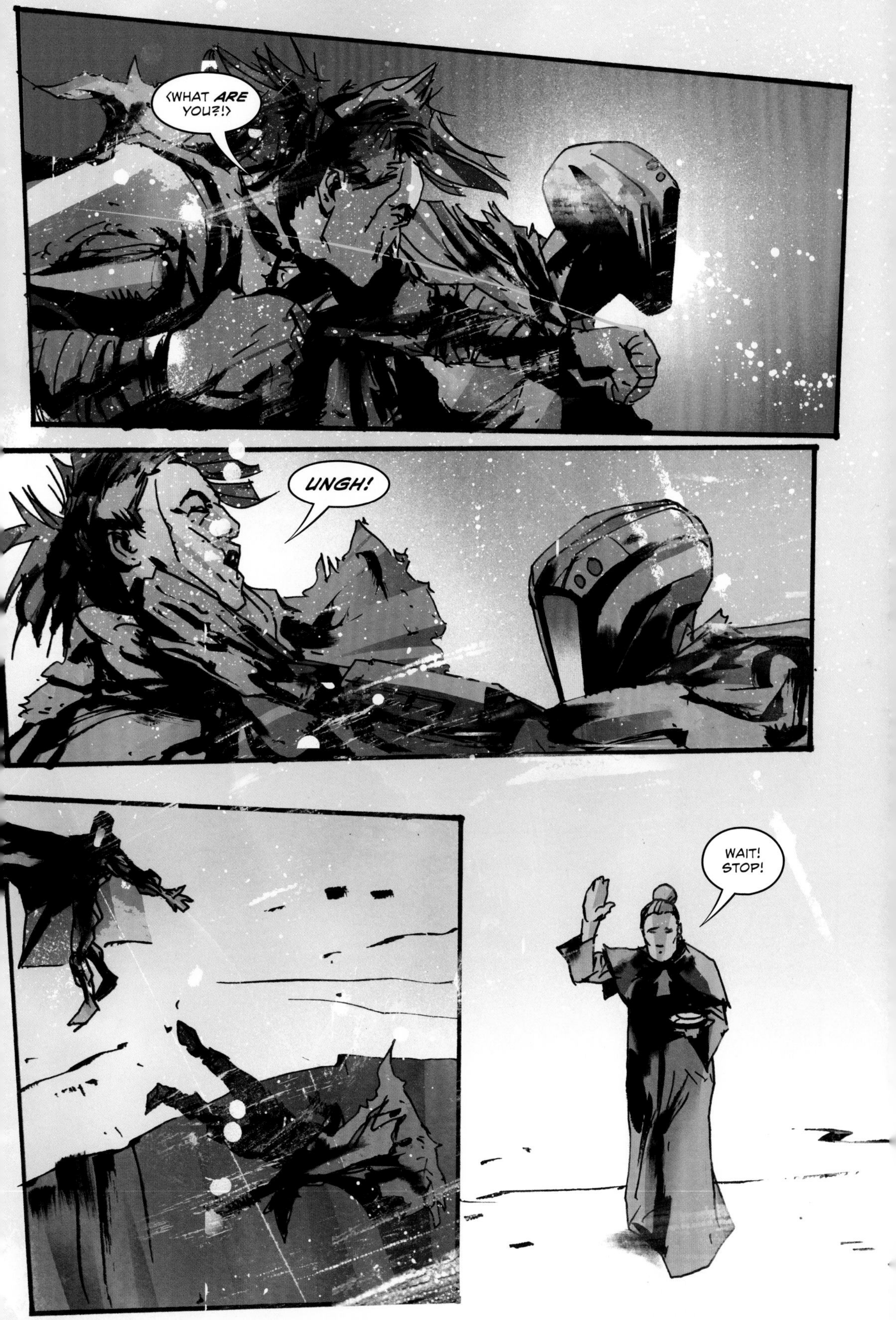
⟨WHAT ARE YOU?!⟩
UNGH!
WAIT! STOP!

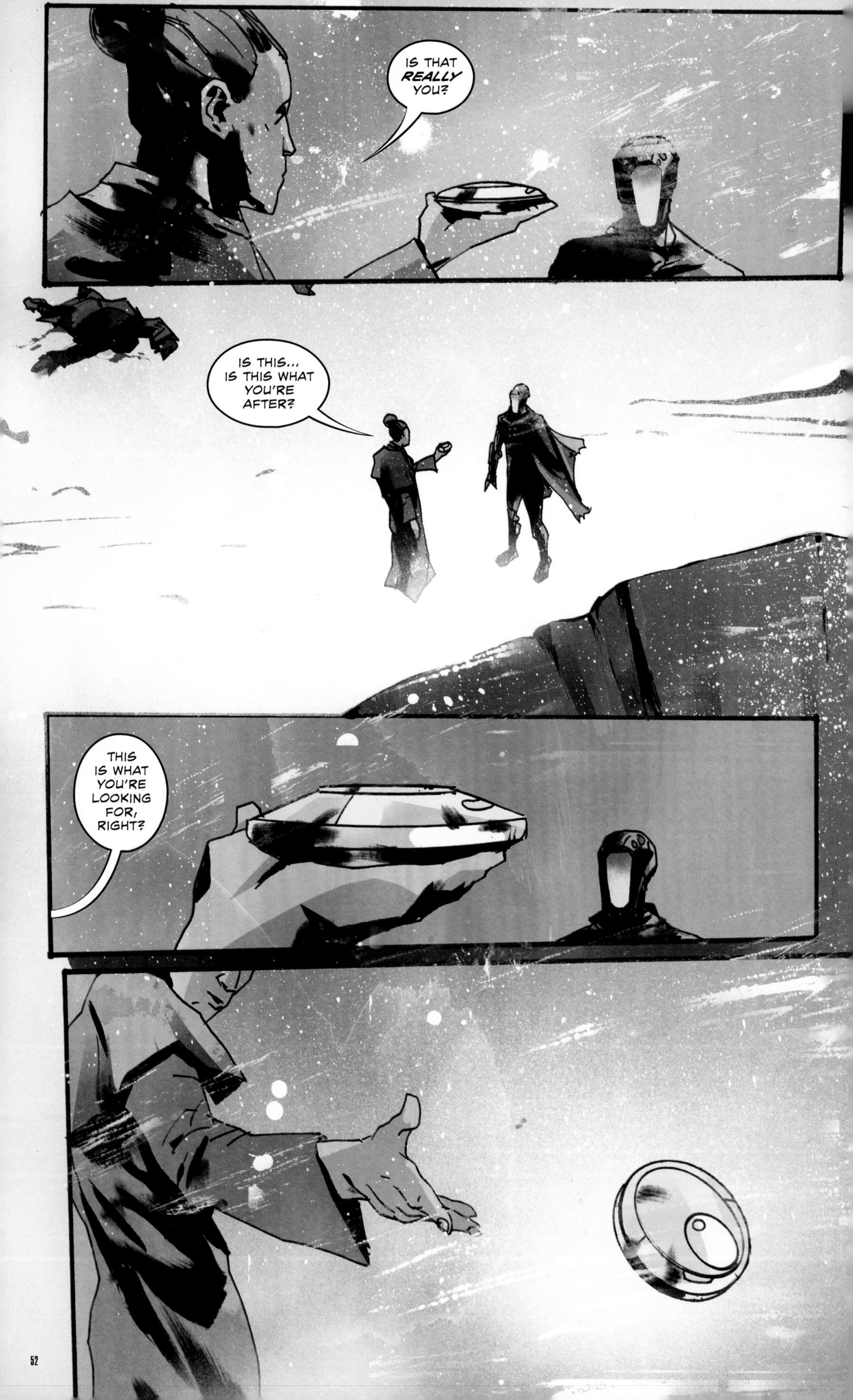
IS THAT *REALLY* YOU?
IS THIS... IS THIS WHAT YOU'RE AFTER?
THIS IS WHAT YOU'RE LOOKING FOR, RIGHT?

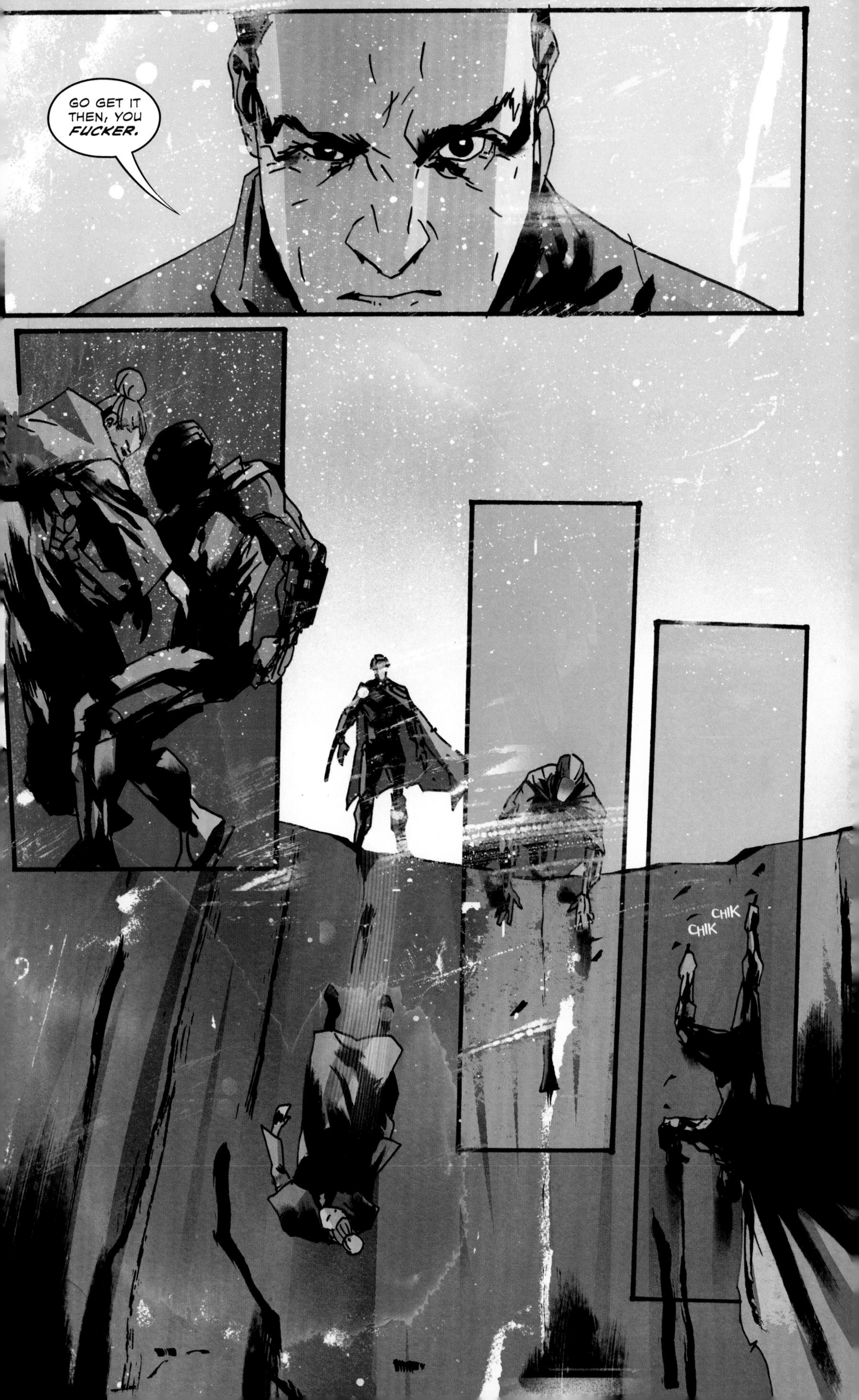
GO GET IT THEN, YOU FUCKER.
CHIK
CHIK

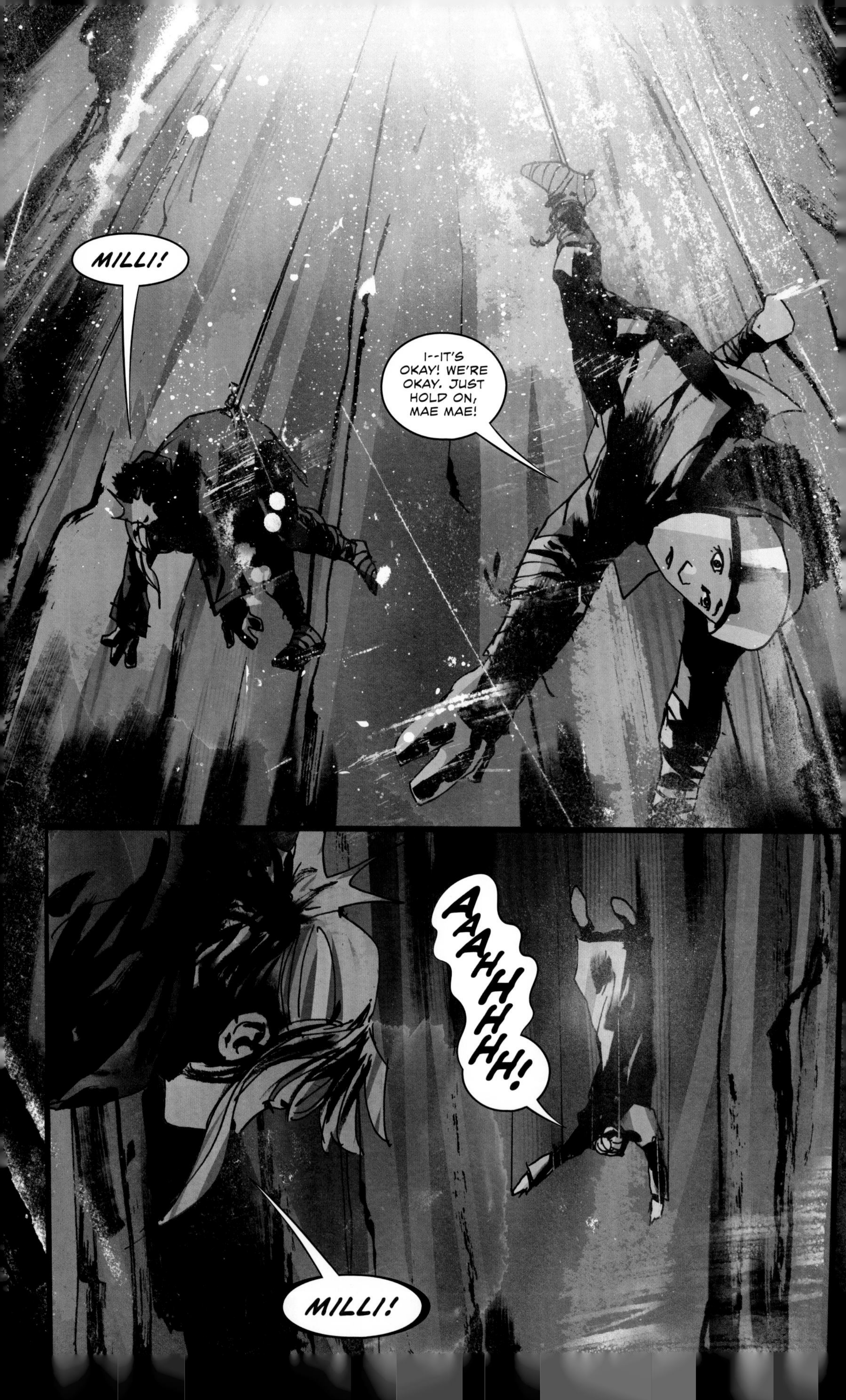
MILLI!
I--IT'S OKAY! WE'RE OKAY. JUST HOLD ON, MAE MAE!
AAAHHHHH!
MILLI!

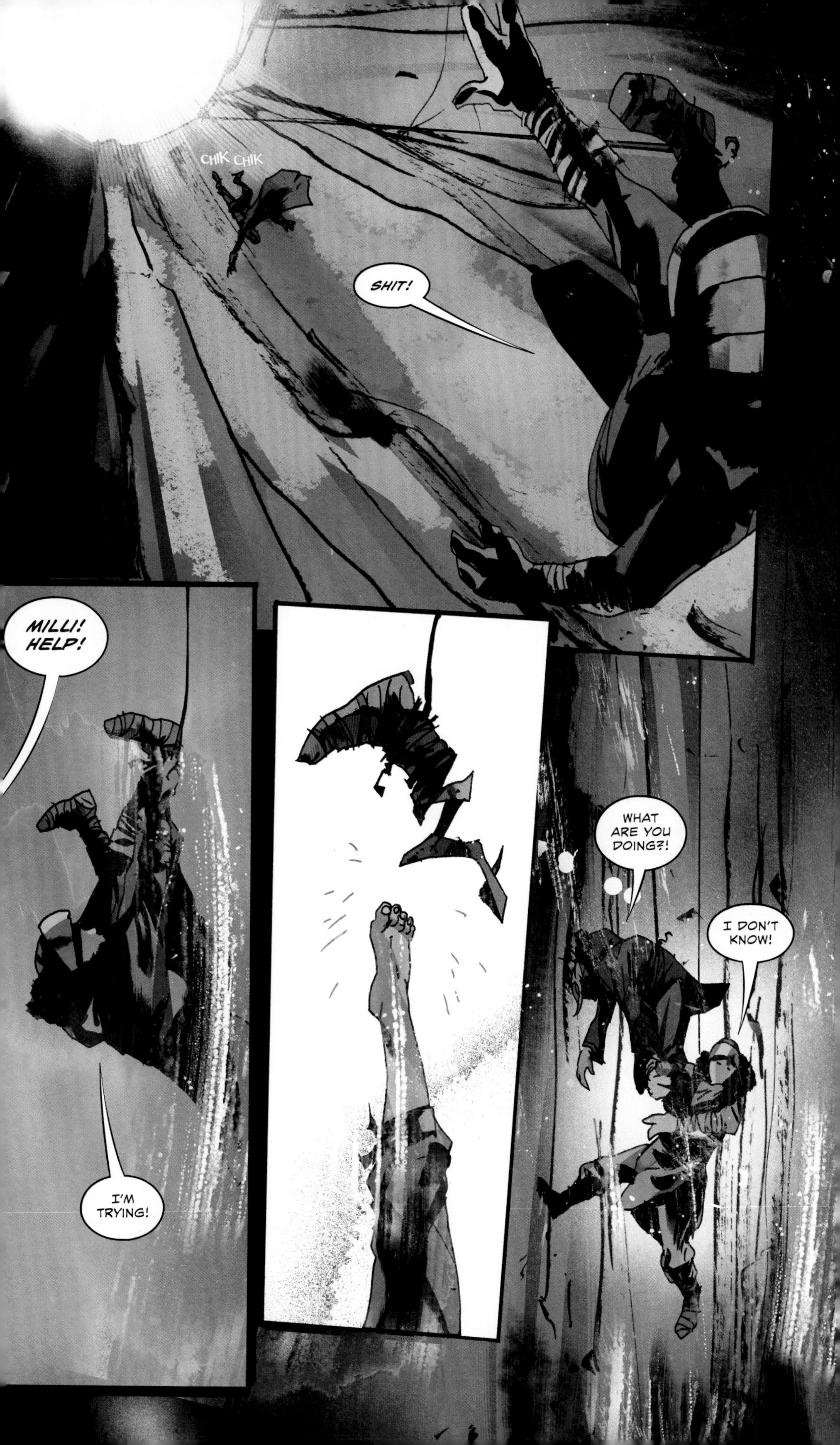
CHIK CHIK
SHIT!
MILLI! HELP!
I'M TRYING!
WHAT ARE YOU DOING?!
I DON'T KNOW!

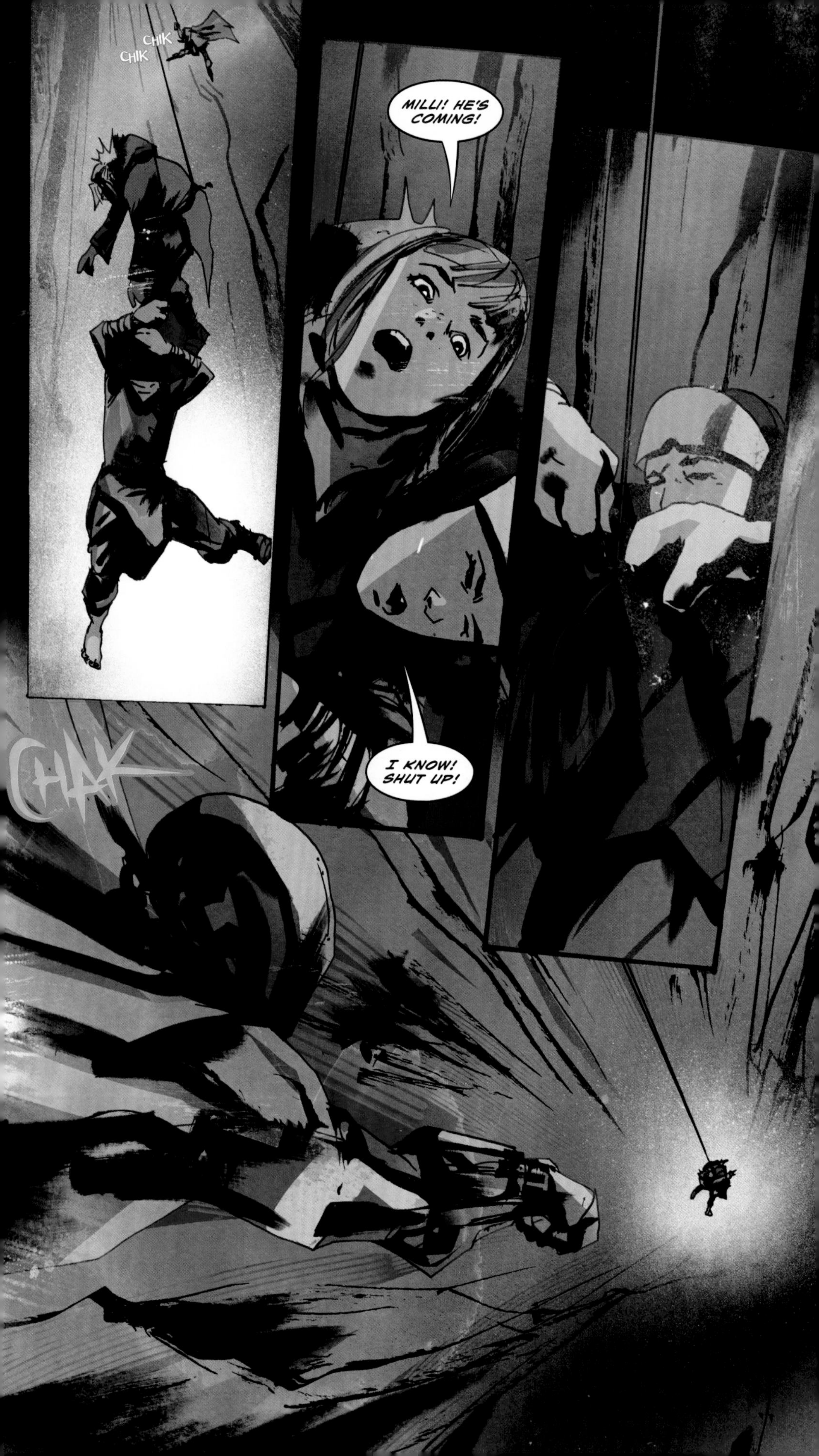
CHIK
CHIK
MILLI! HE'S COMING!
I KNOW! SHUT UP!
CHAK

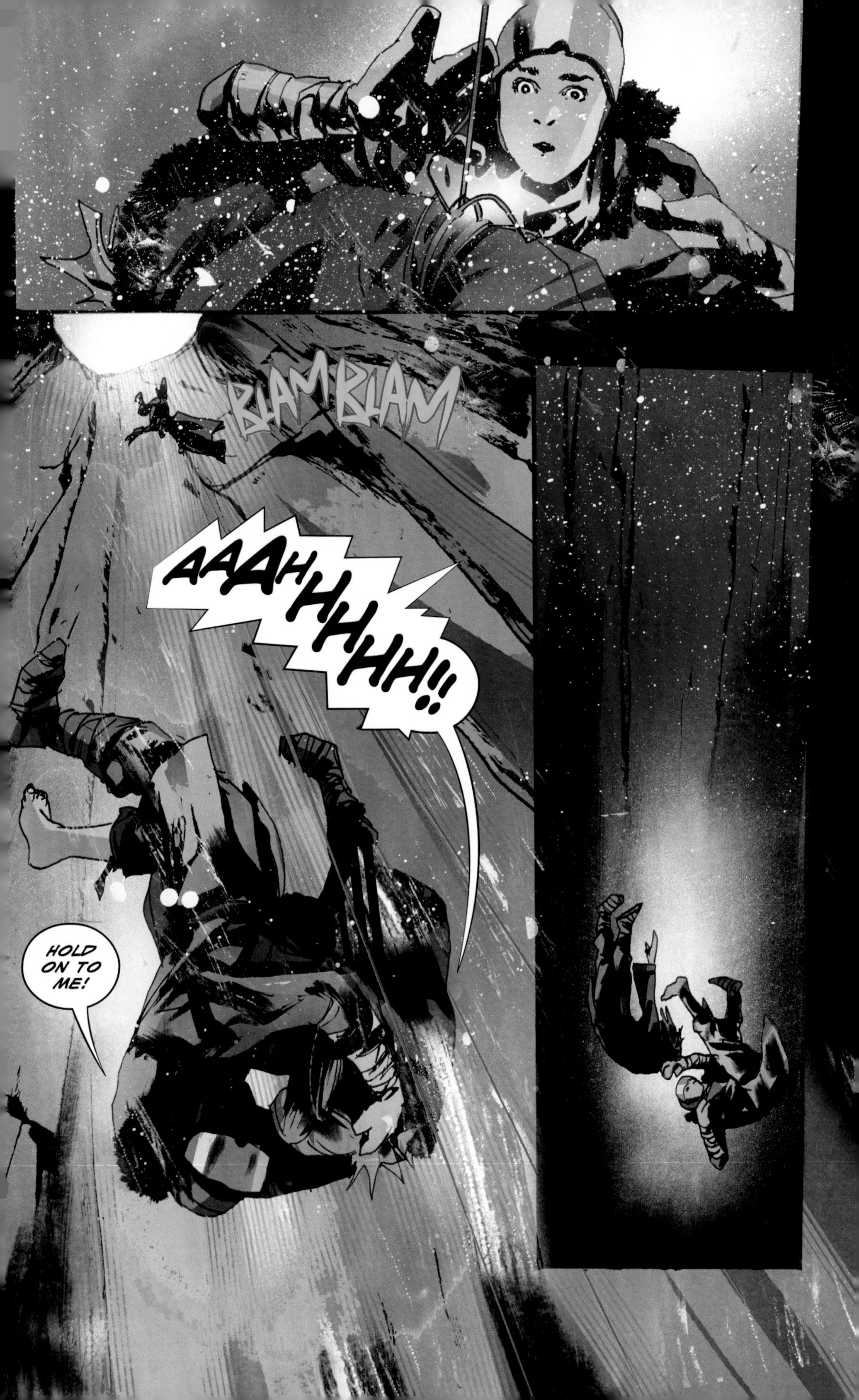
BLAM BLAM
AAAHHHHH!!
HOLD ON TO ME!

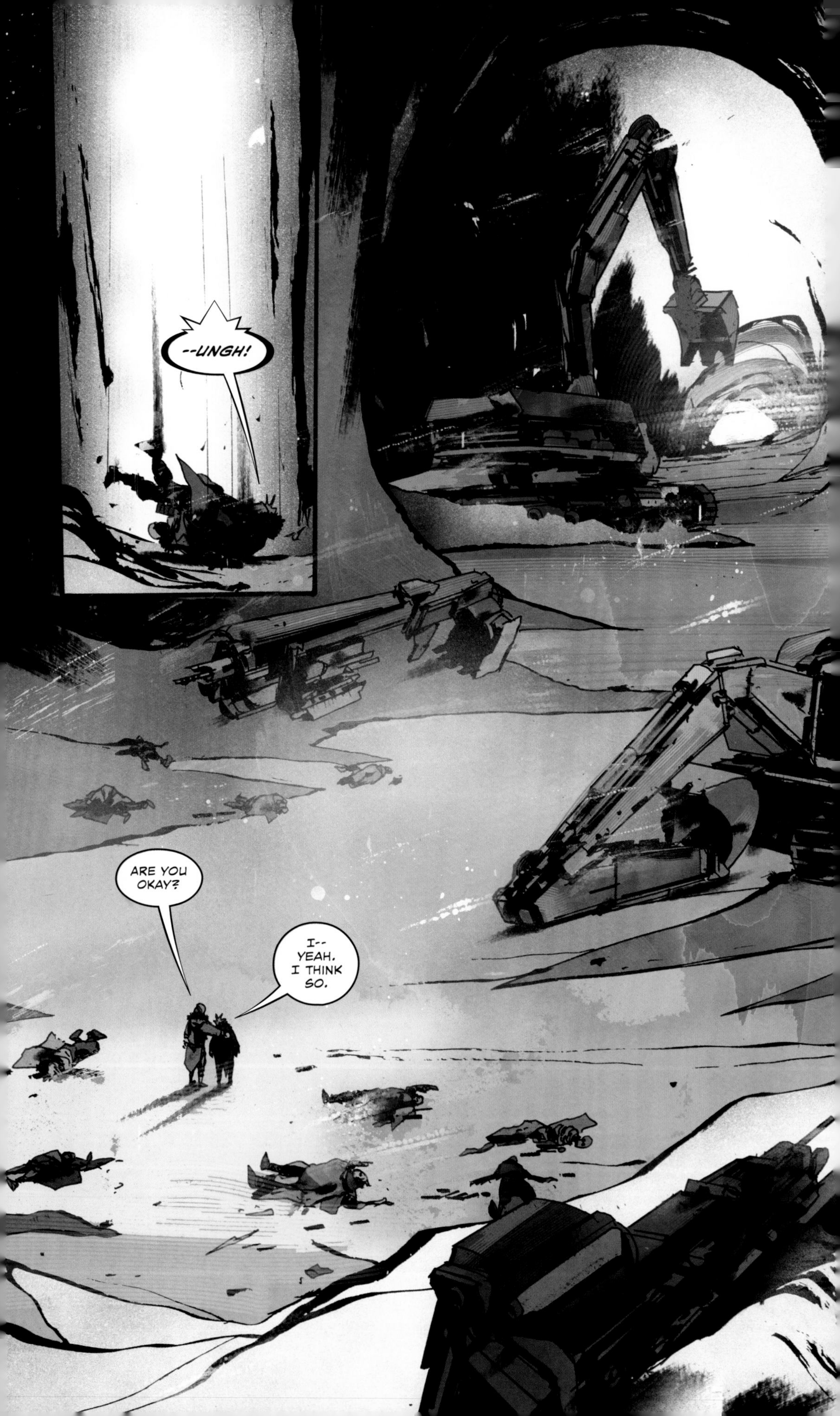
--UNGH!
ARE YOU OKAY?
I-- YEAH. I THINK SO.

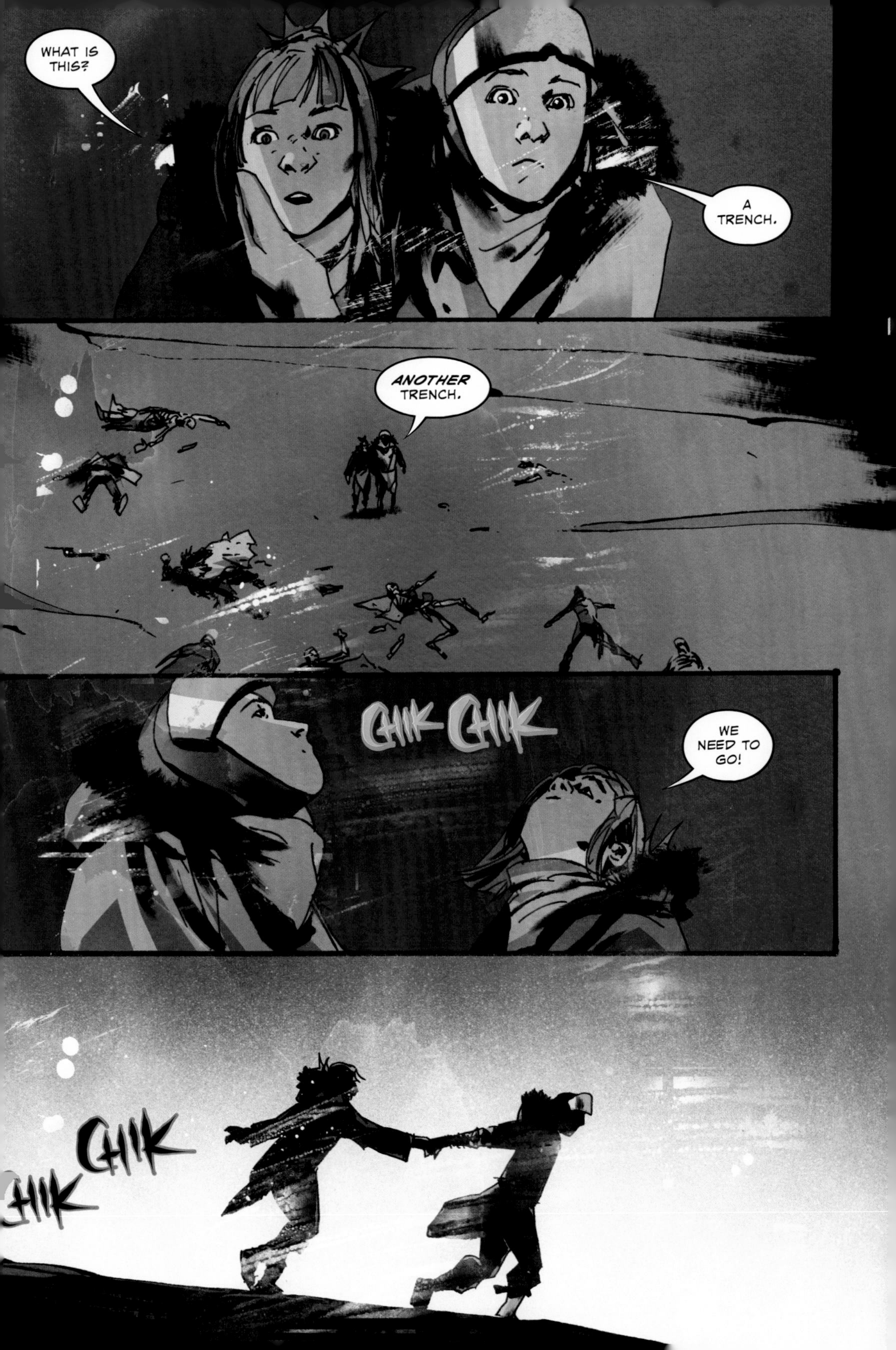
WHAT IS THIS?
A TRENCH.
ANOTHER TRENCH.
CHIK CHIK
WE NEED TO GO!
CHIK
CHIK

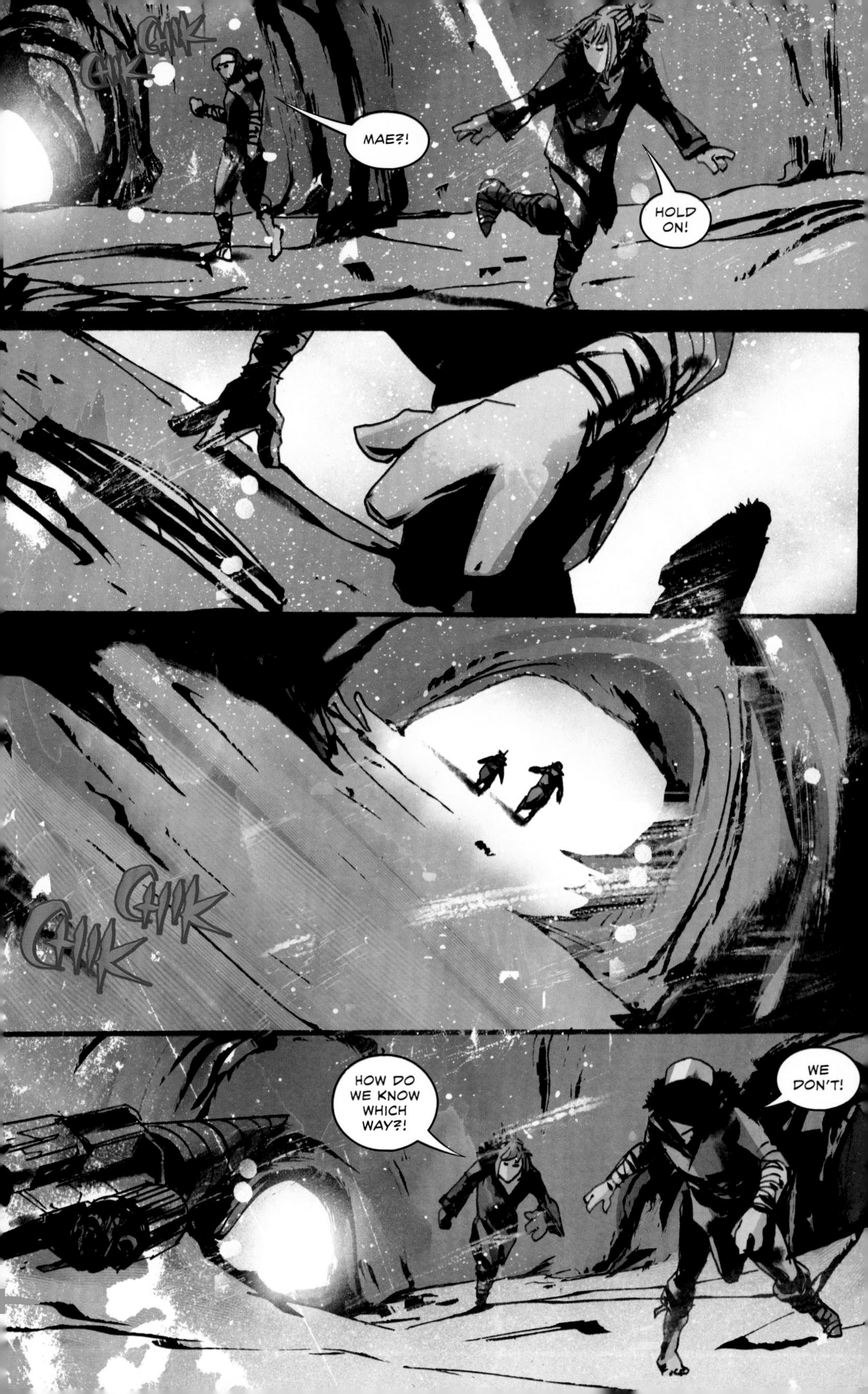
CHIK
CHIK
MAE?!
HOLD ON!
CHIK
CHIK
HOW DO WE KNOW WHICH WAY?!
WE DON'T!

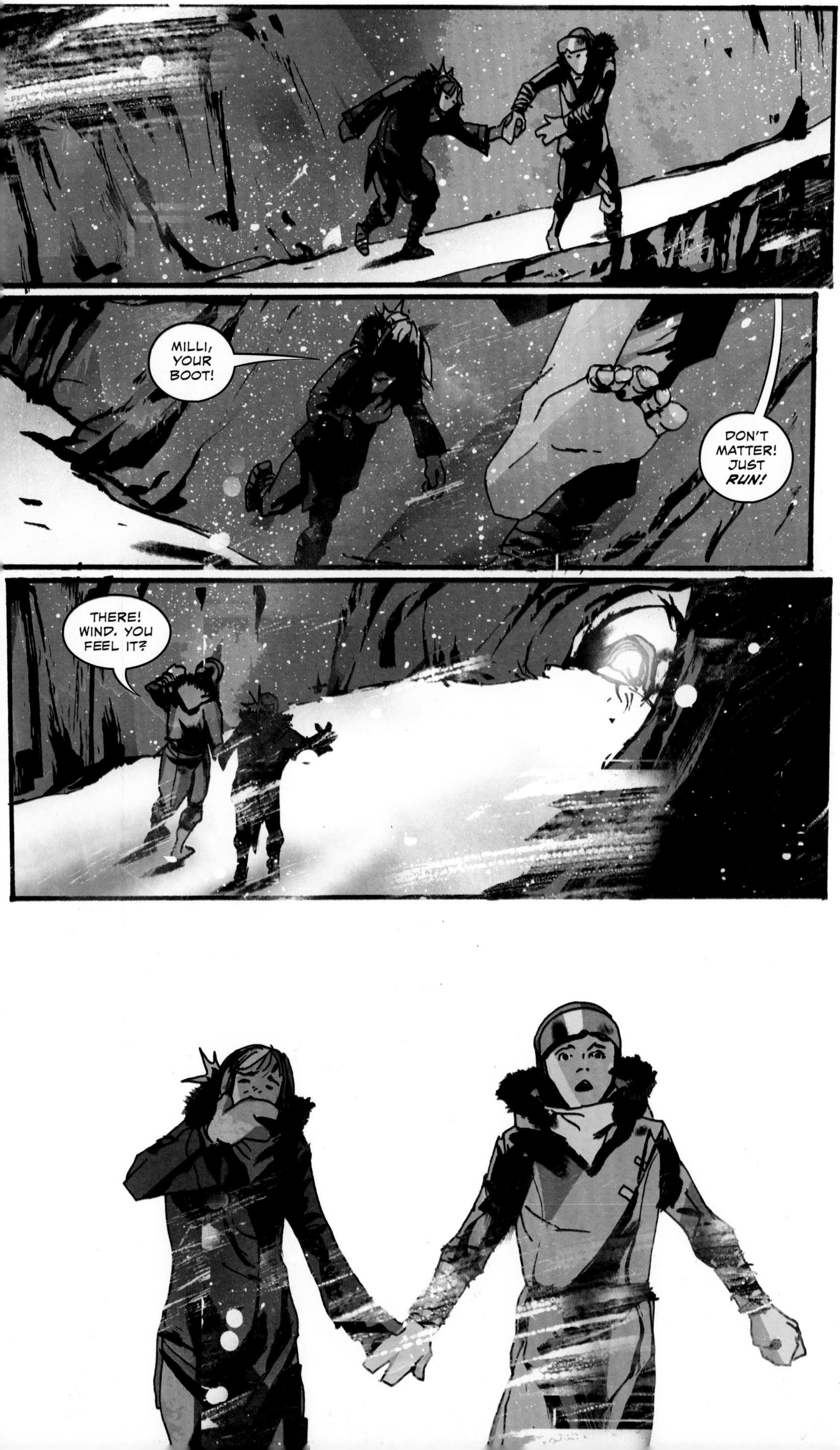
MILLI, YOUR BOOT!
DON'T MATTER! JUST *RUN!*
THERE! WIND. YOU FEEL IT?

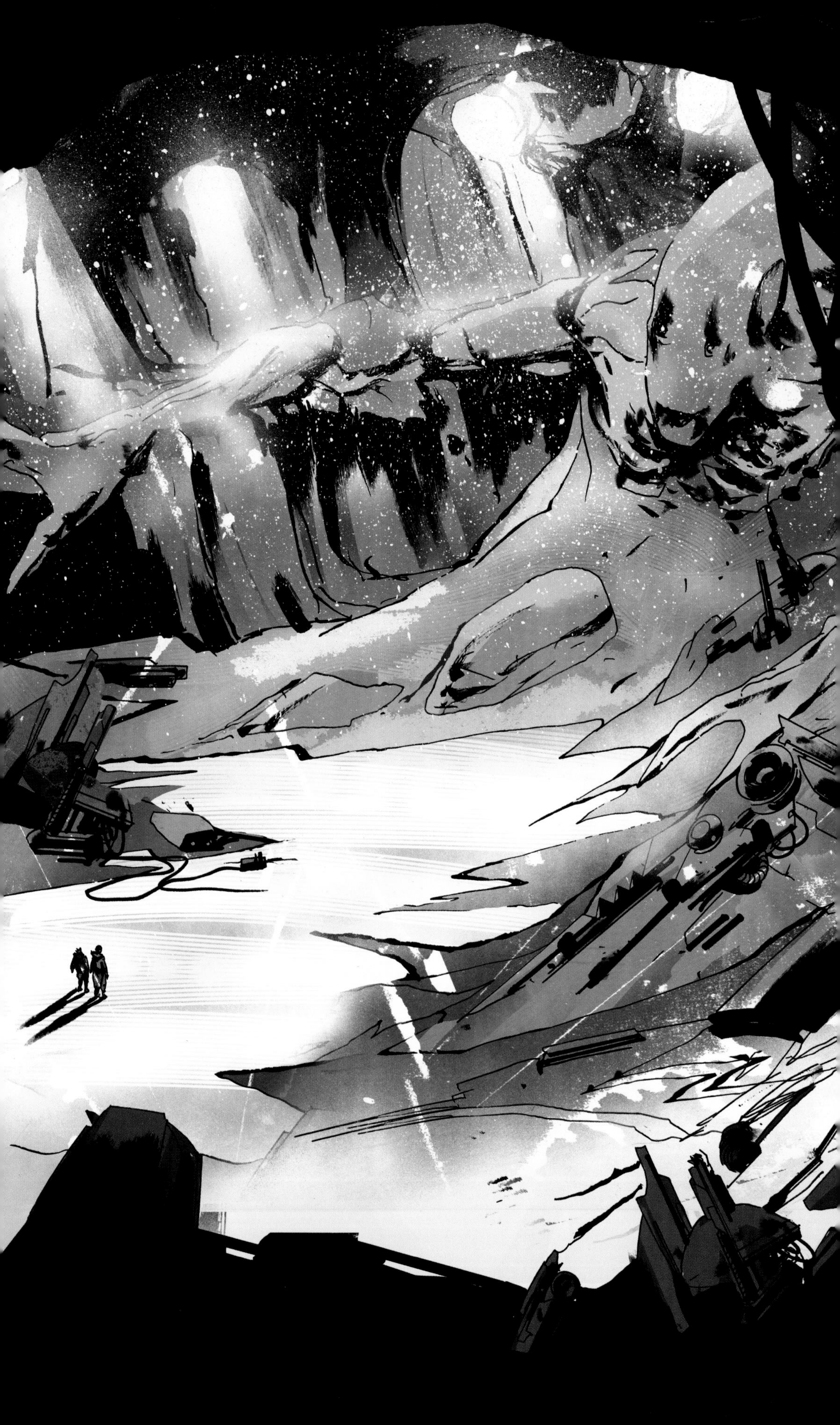

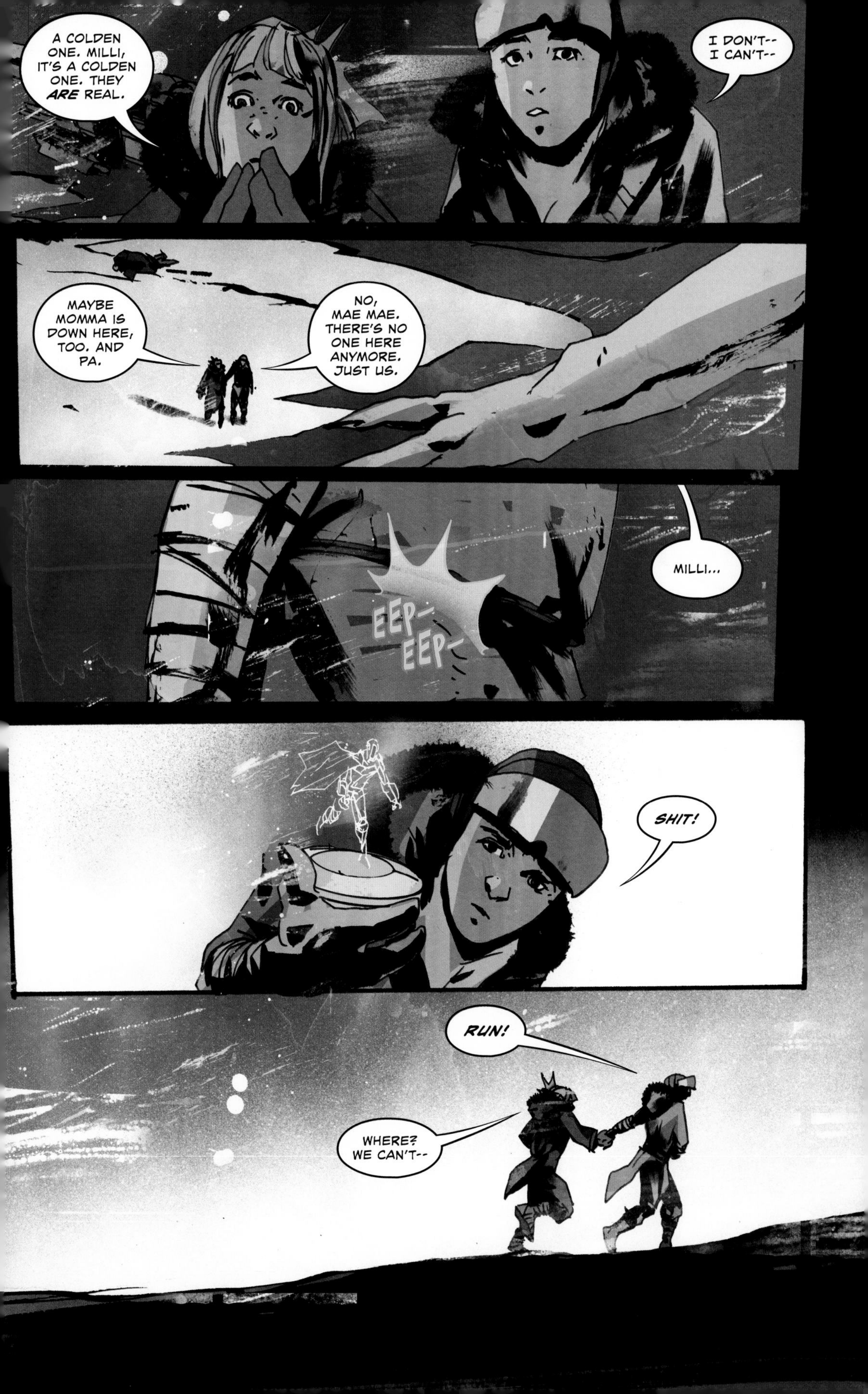
A COLDEN ONE. MILLI, IT'S A COLDEN ONE. THEY ARE REAL.
I DON'T-- I CAN'T--
MAYBE MOMMA IS DOWN HERE, TOO. AND PA.
NO, MAE MAE. THERE'S NO ONE HERE ANYMORE. JUST US.
MILLI...
EEP- EEP-
SHIT!
RUN!
WHERE? WE CAN'T--

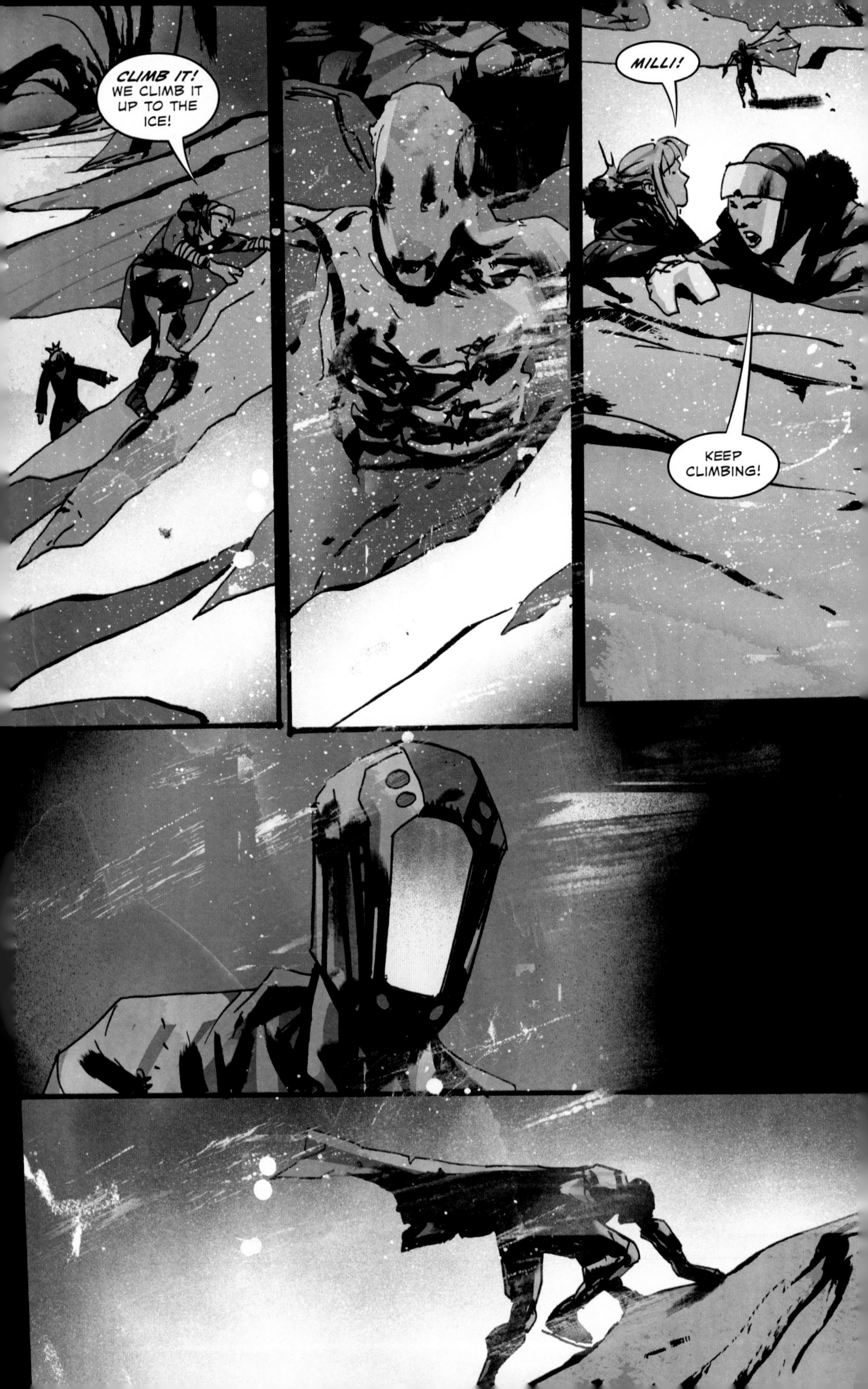
CLIMB IT! WE CLIMB IT UP TO THE ICE!
MILLI!
KEEP CLIMBING!

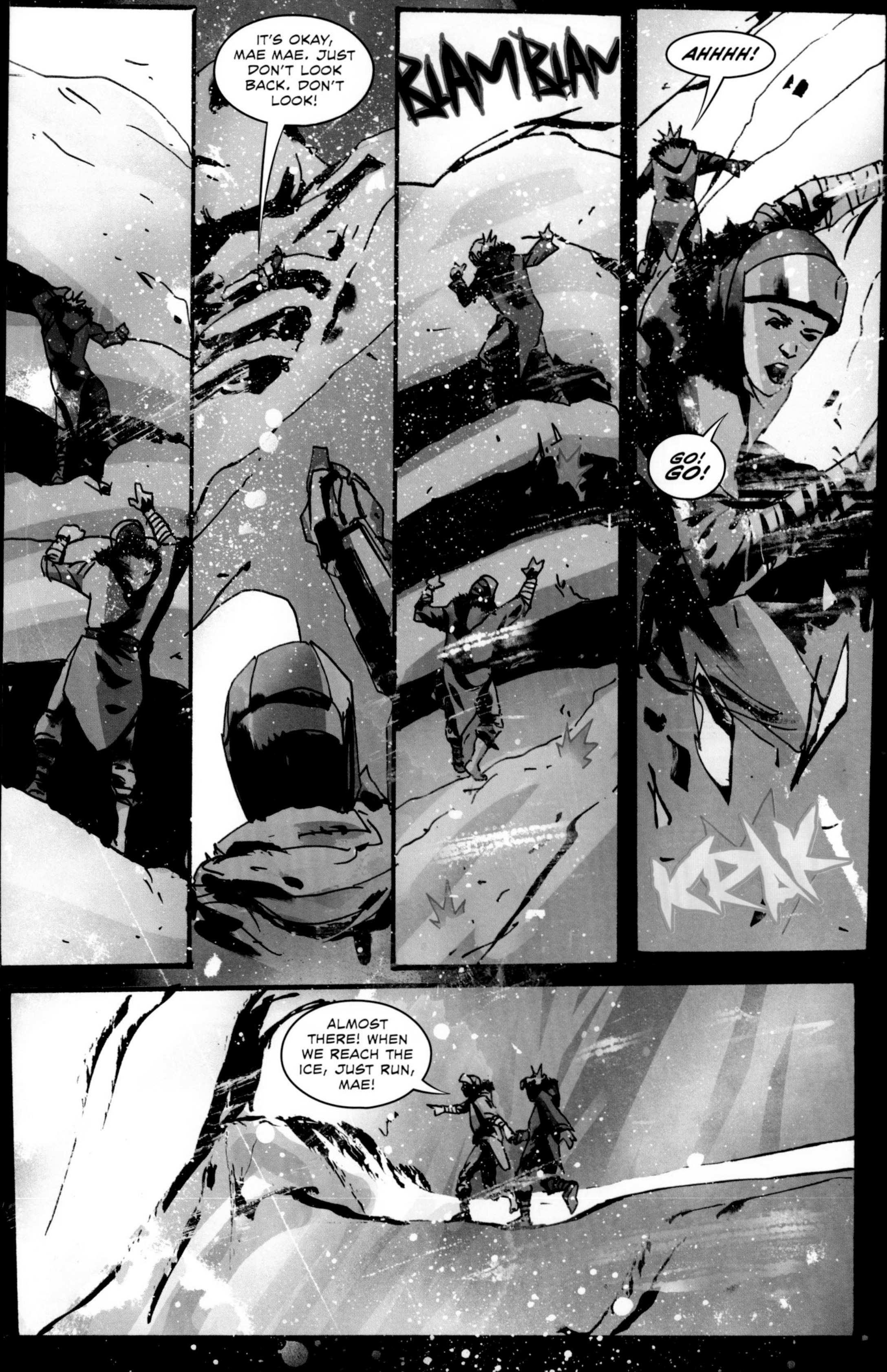
IT'S OKAY, MAE MAE. JUST DON'T LOOK BACK. DON'T LOOK!
BLAM BLAM
AHHHH!
GO! GO!
KRAK
ALMOST THERE! WHEN WE REACH THE ICE, JUST RUN, MAE!

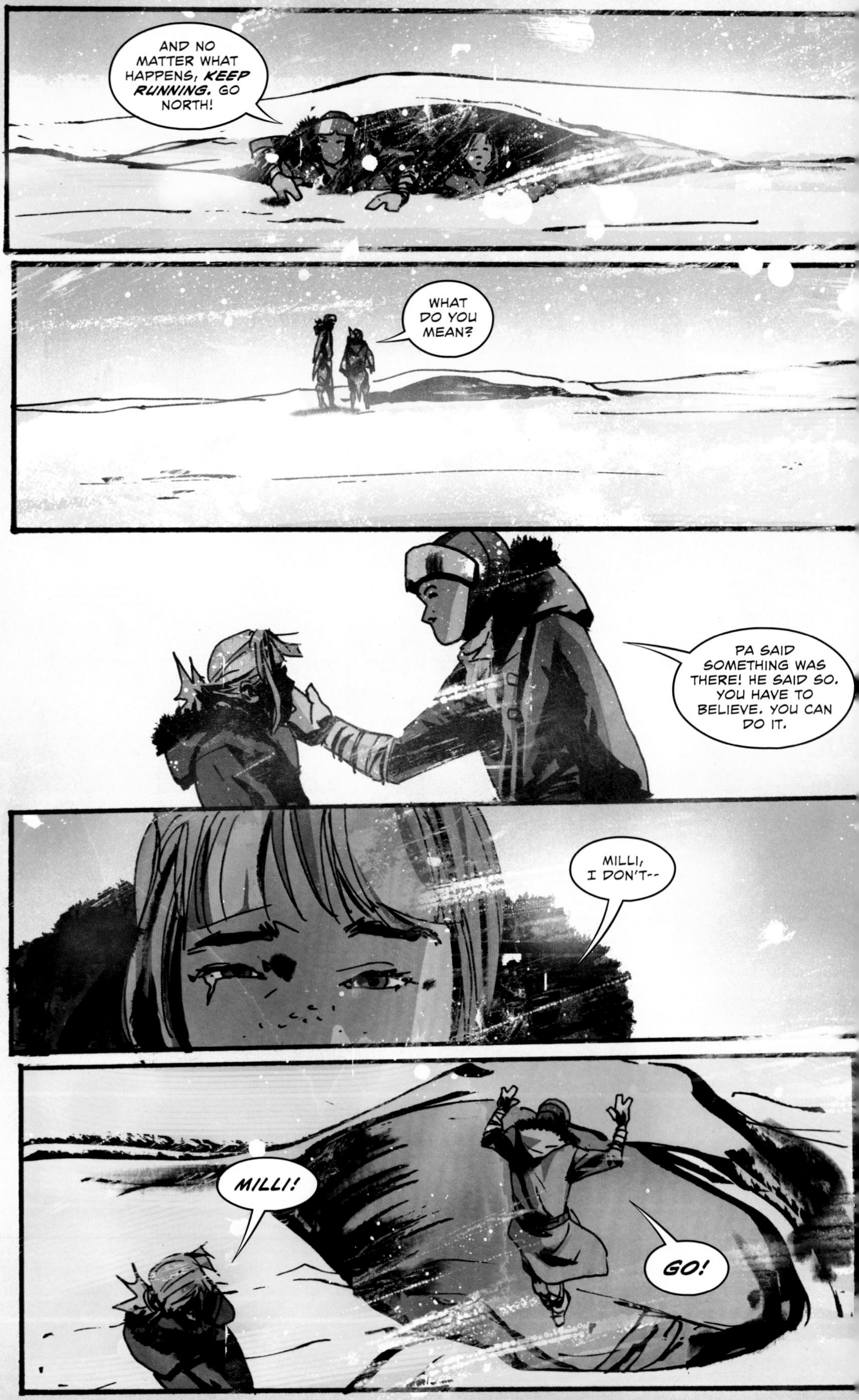
AND NO MATTER WHAT HAPPENS, ***KEEP RUNNING.*** GO NORTH!
WHAT DO YOU MEAN?
PA SAID SOMETHING WAS THERE! HE SAID SO. YOU HAVE TO BELIEVE. YOU CAN DO IT.
MILLI, I DON'T--
MILLI!
GO!

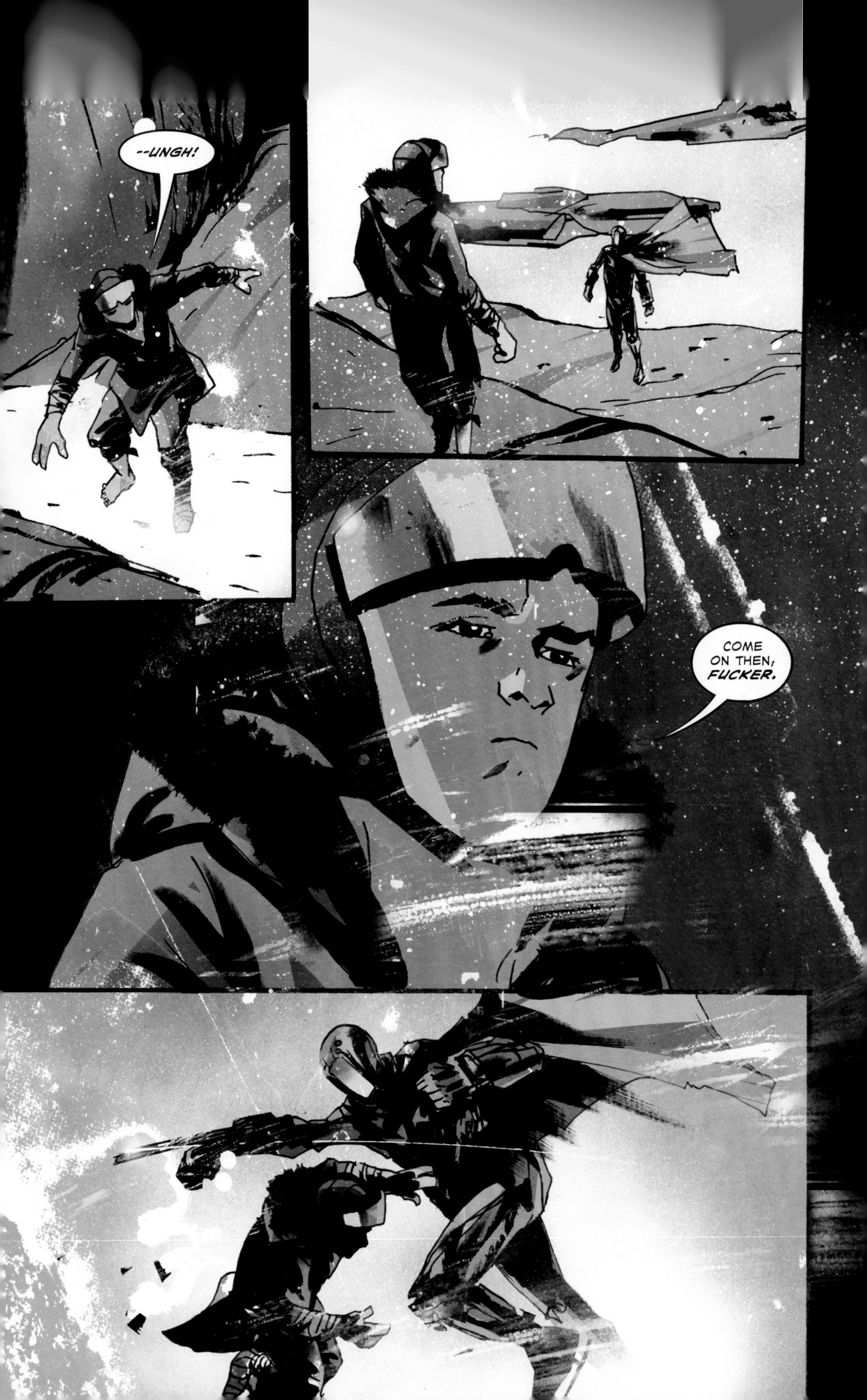
--UNGH!
COME ON THEN, FUCKER.

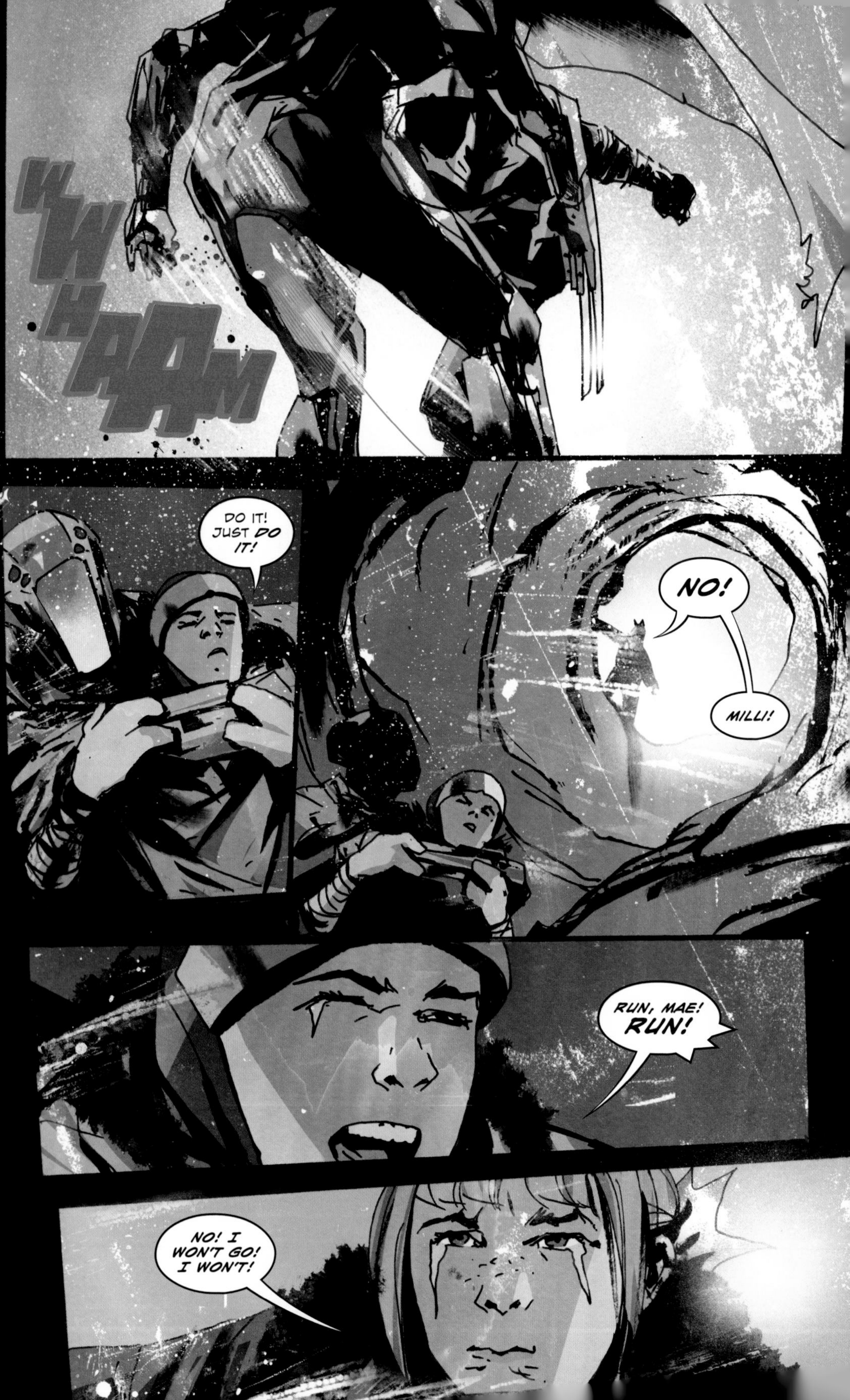

WHRAAM
DO IT! JUST DO IT!
NO!
MILLI!
RUN, MAE! RUN!
NO! I WON'T GO! I WON'T!

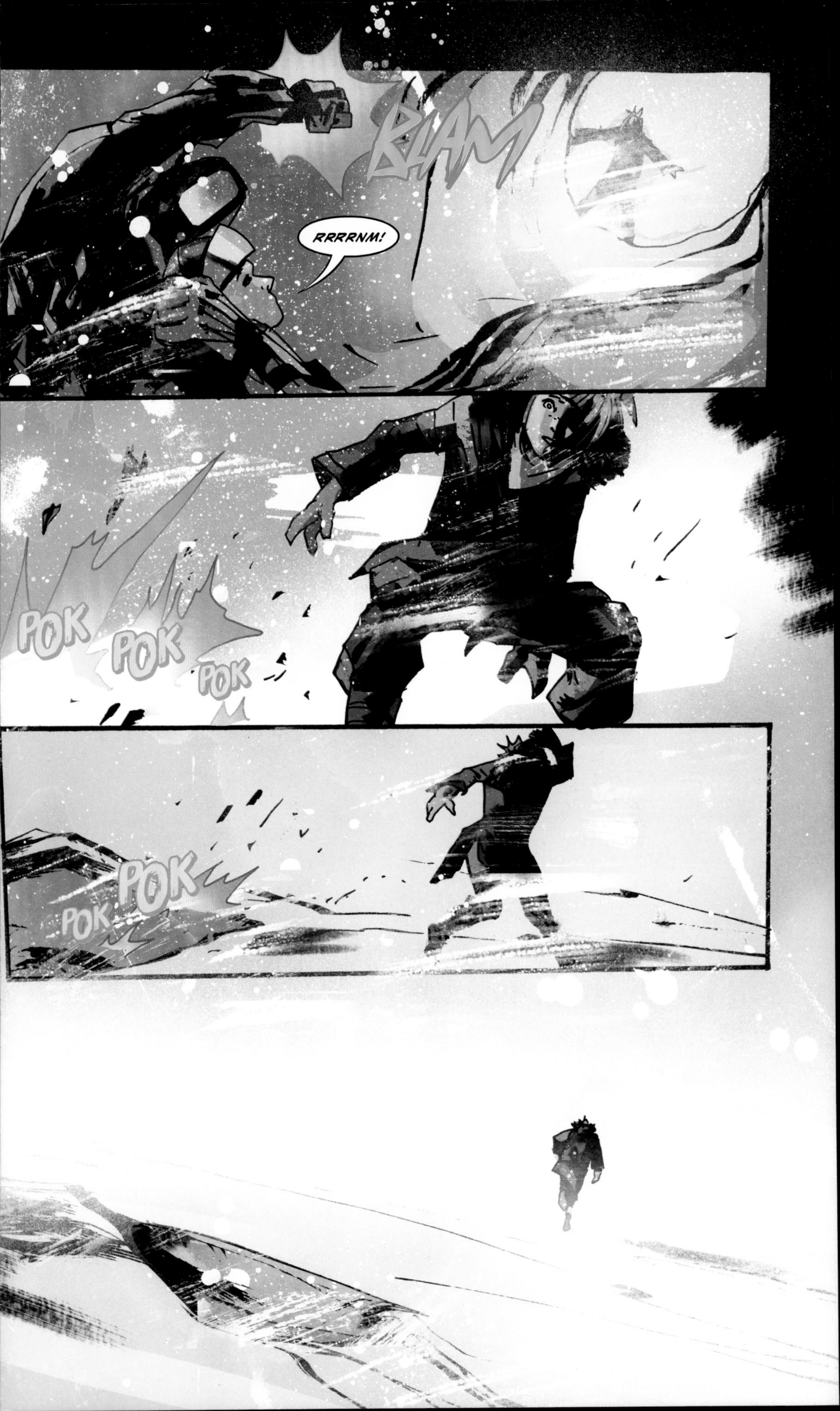
BLAM
RRRRNM!
POK
POK
POK
POK
POK

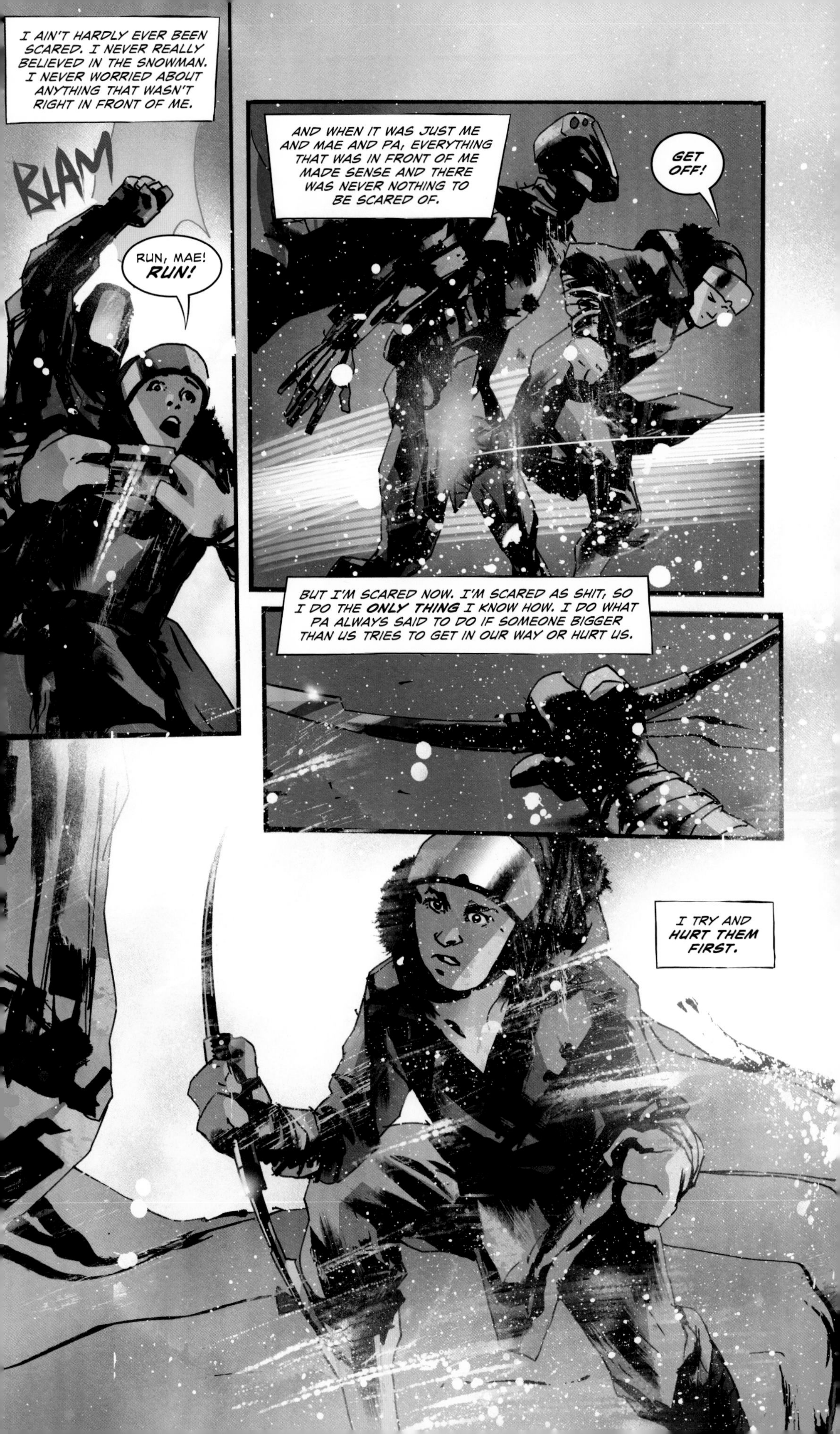
I AIN'T HARDLY EVER BEEN SCARED. I NEVER REALLY BELIEVED IN THE SNOWMAN. I NEVER WORRIED ABOUT ANYTHING THAT WASN'T RIGHT IN FRONT OF ME.
BLAM
RUN, MAE! ***RUN!***
AND WHEN IT WAS JUST ME AND MAE AND PA, EVERYTHING THAT WAS IN FRONT OF ME MADE SENSE AND THERE WAS NEVER NOTHING TO BE SCARED OF.
GET OFF!
BUT I'M SCARED NOW. I'M SCARED AS SHIT, SO I DO THE **ONLY THING** I KNOW HOW. I DO WHAT PA ALWAYS SAID TO DO IF SOMEONE BIGGER THAN US TRIES TO GET IN OUR WAY OR HURT US.
I TRY AND **HURT THEM FIRST.**

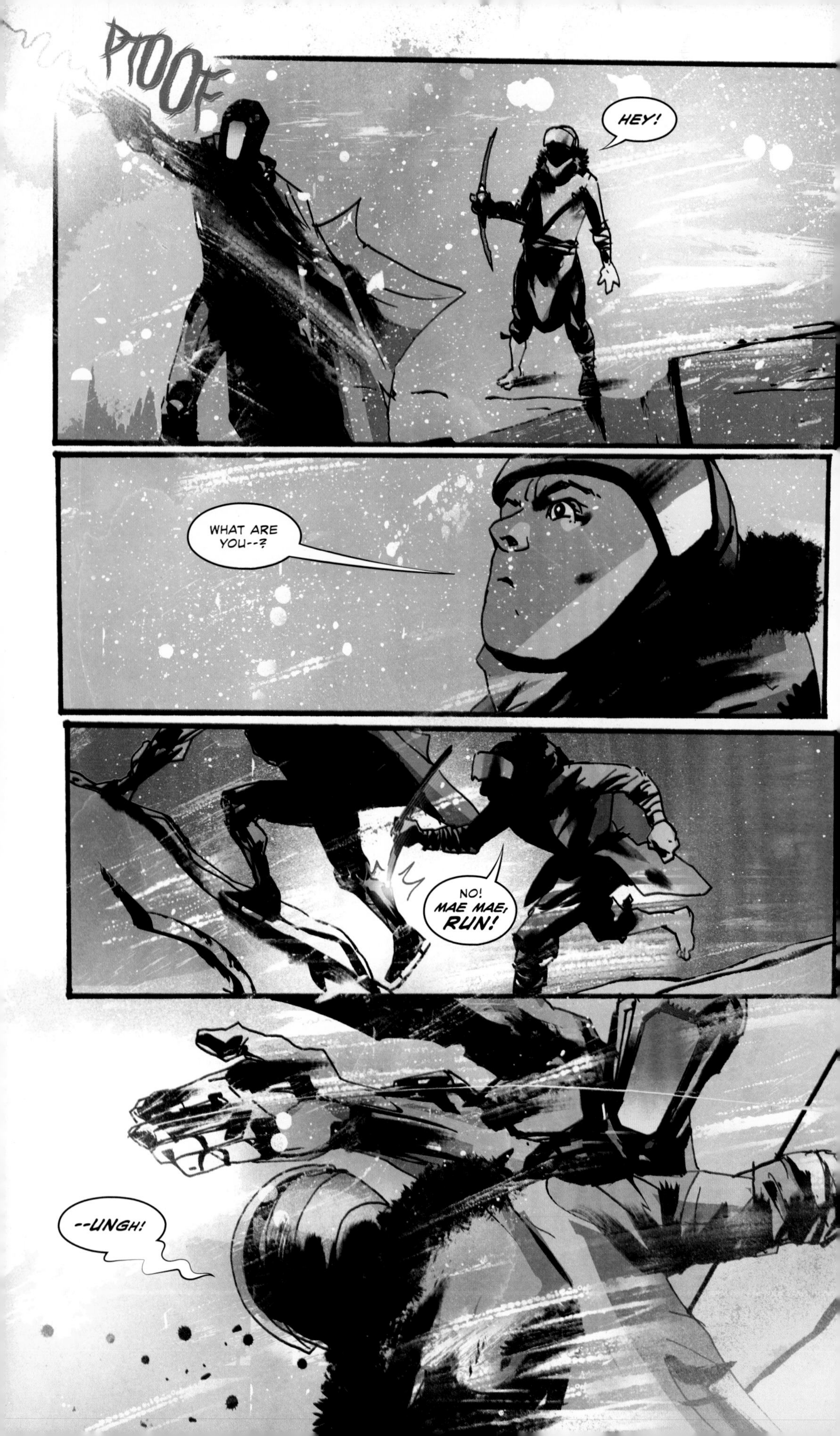
PTOOF
HEY!
WHAT ARE YOU--?
NO! MAE MAE, RUN!
--UNGH!

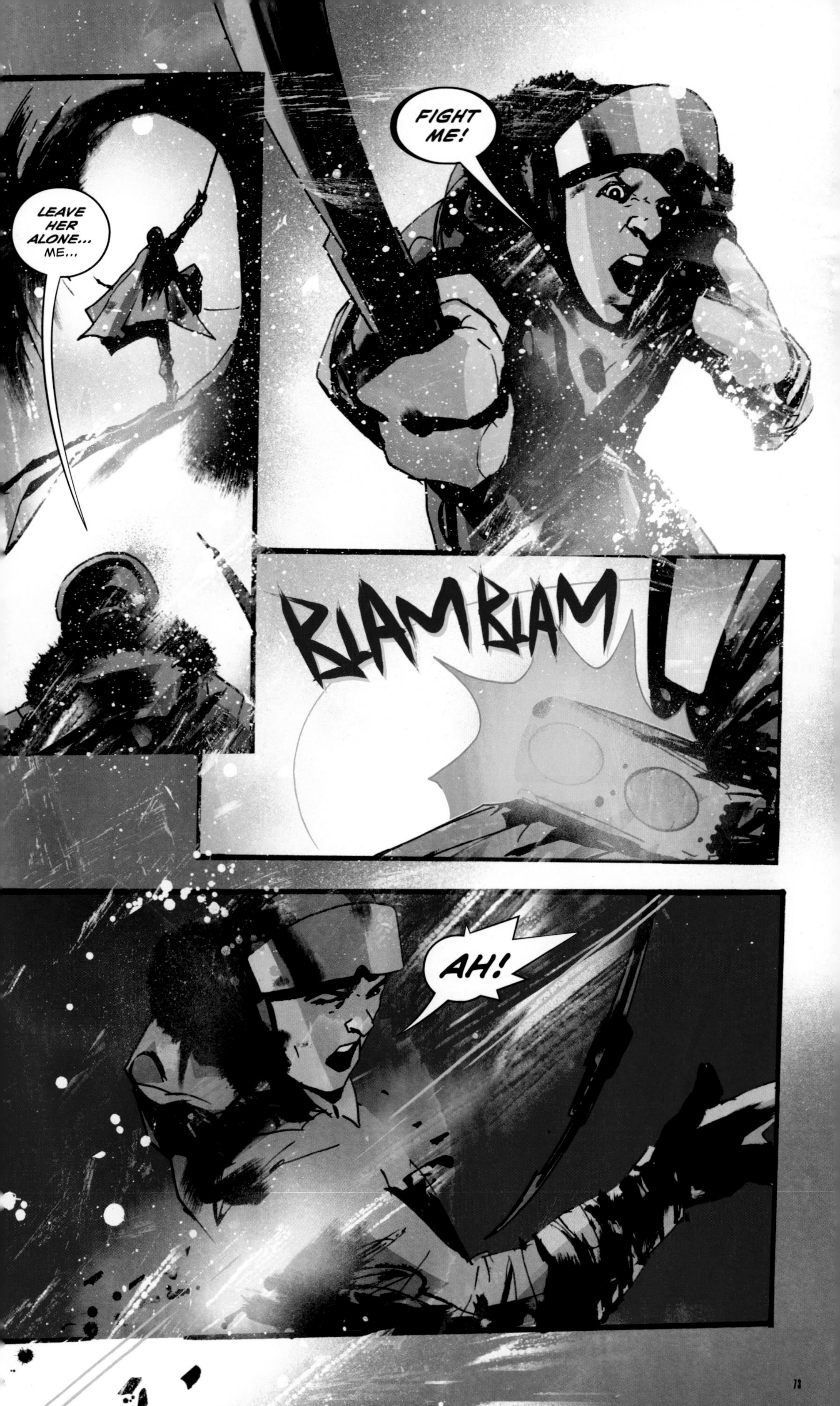
LEAVE HER ALONE... ME...
FIGHT ME!
BLAM BLAM
AH!

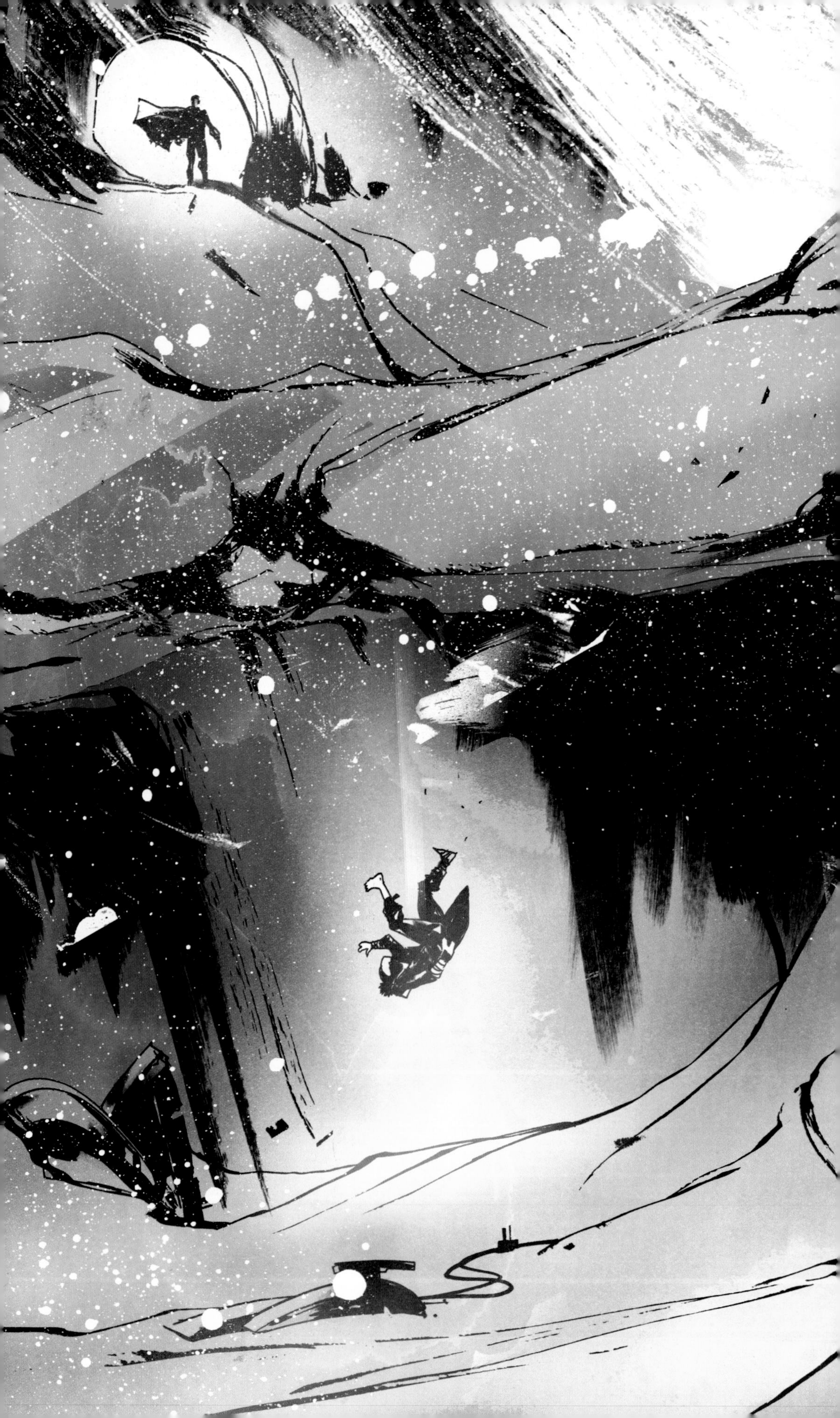

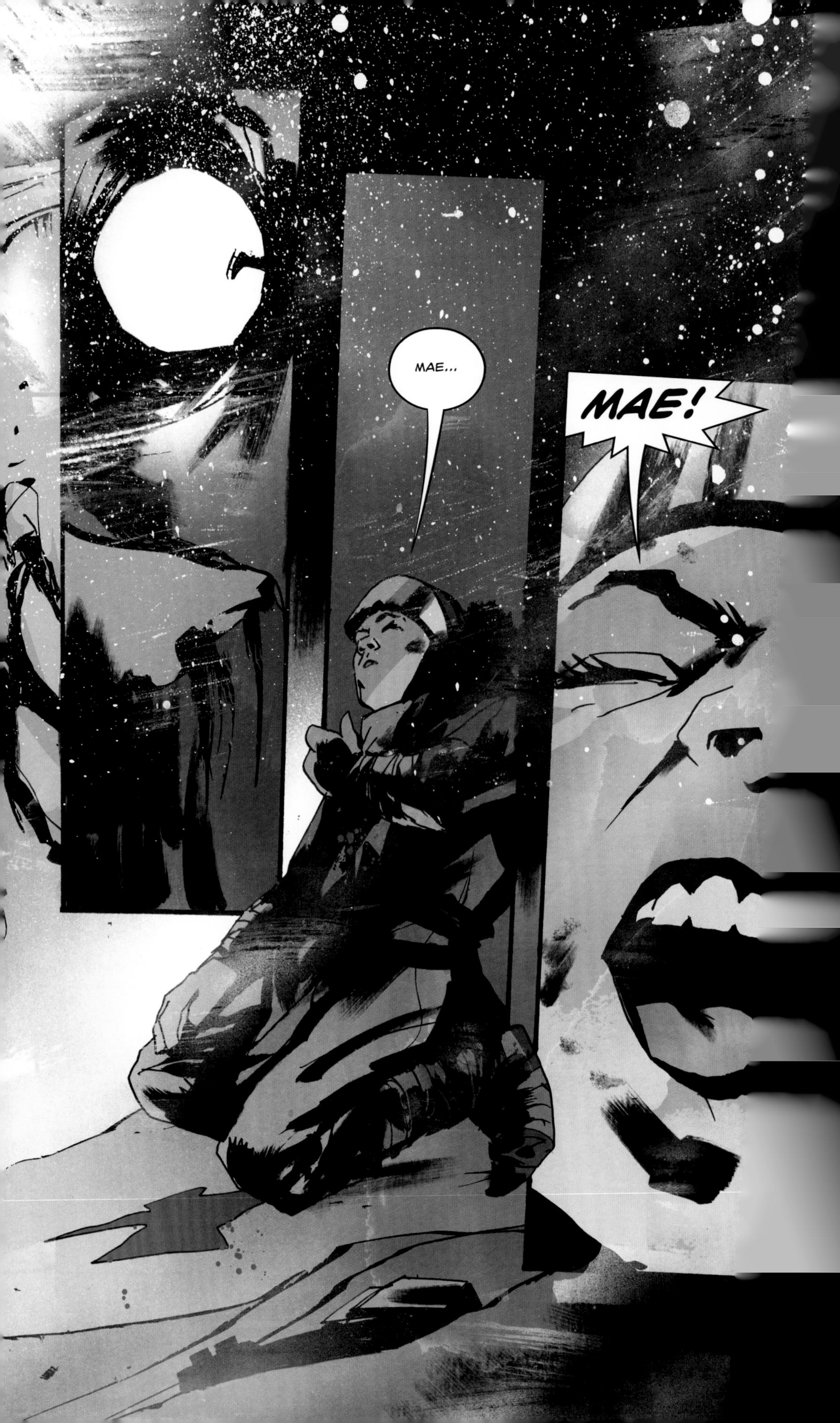
MAE...
MAE!

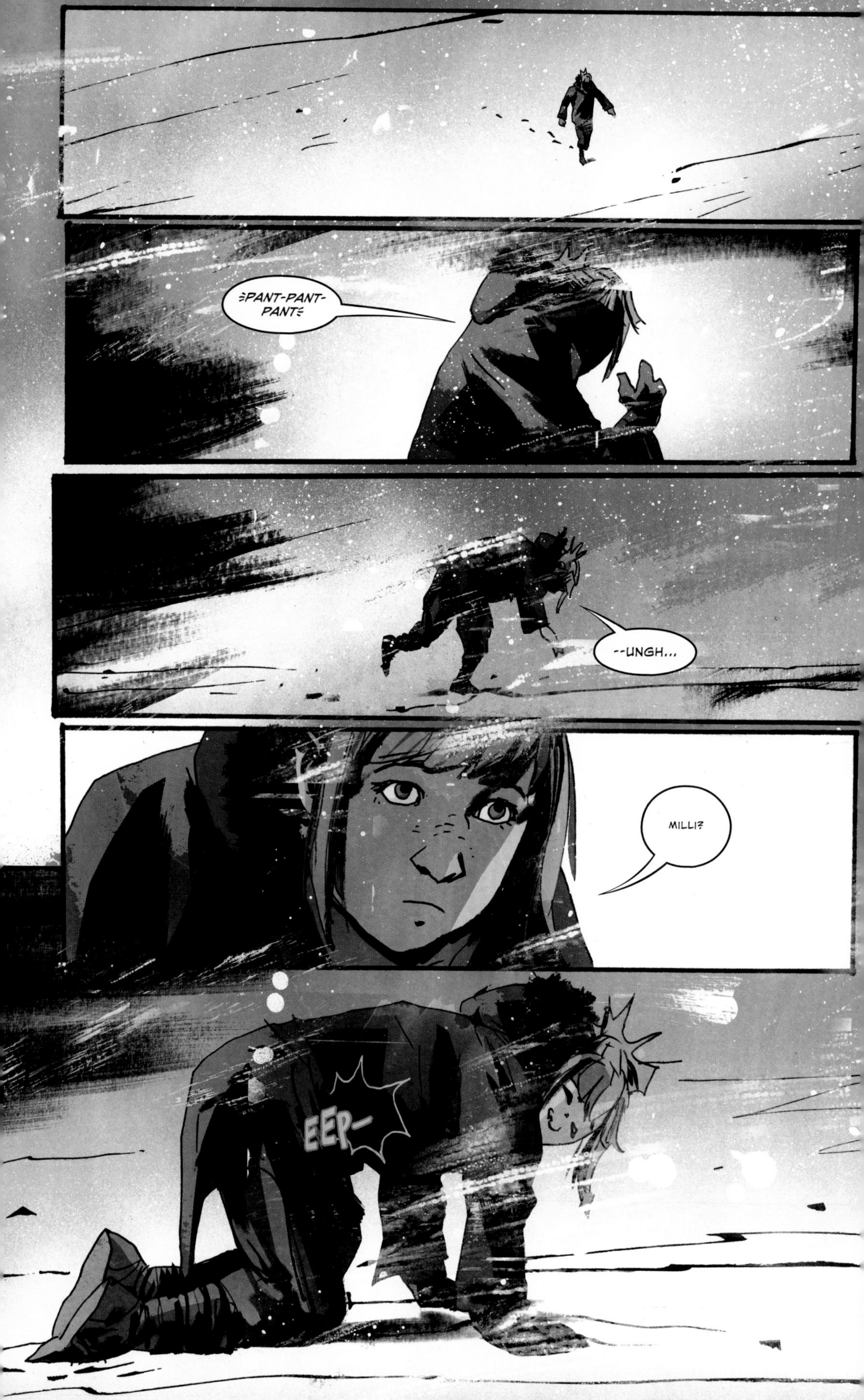
PANT-PANT-PANT
--UNGH...
MILLI?
EEP-

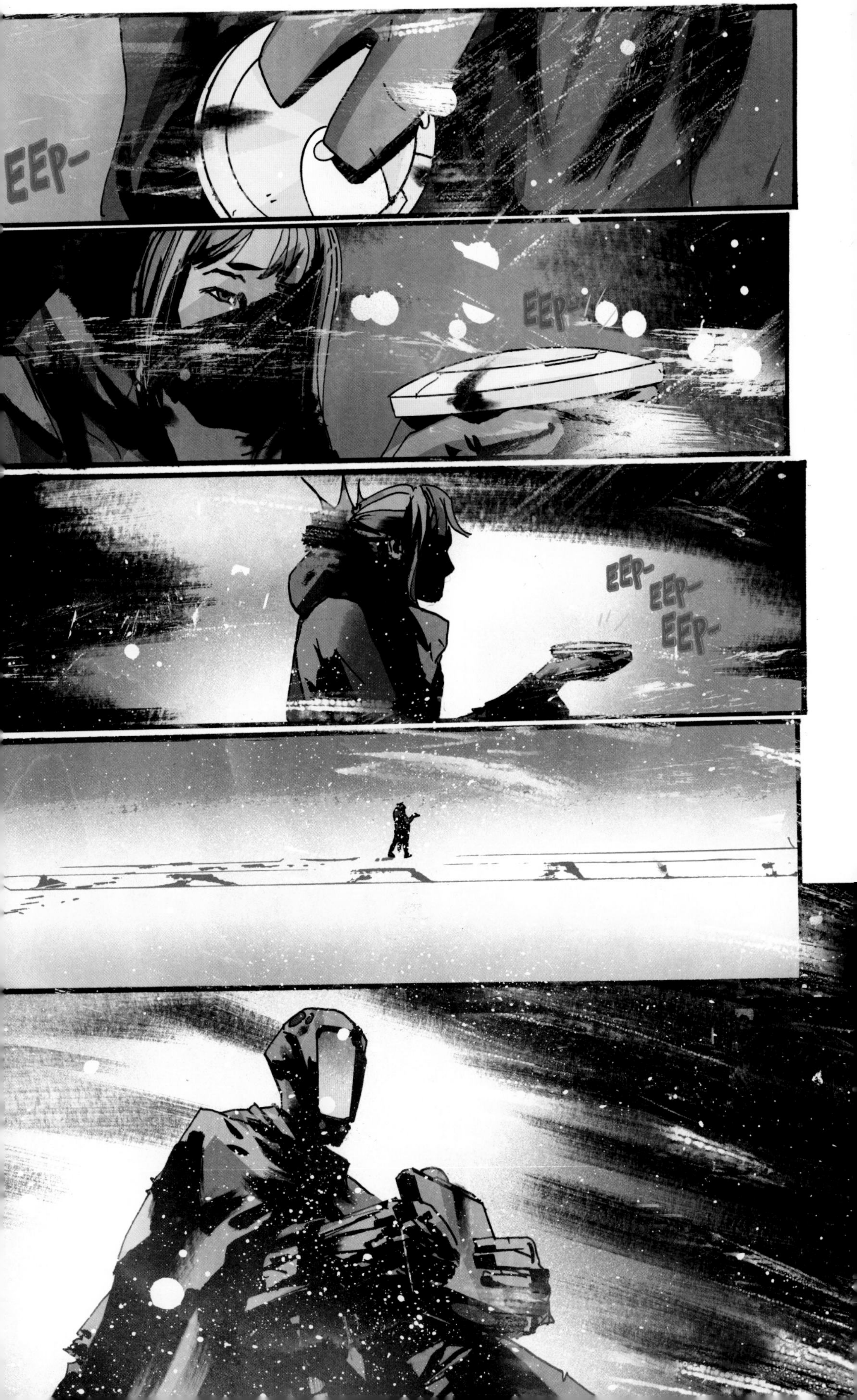
EEP-
EEP-
EEP-
EEP-
EEP-

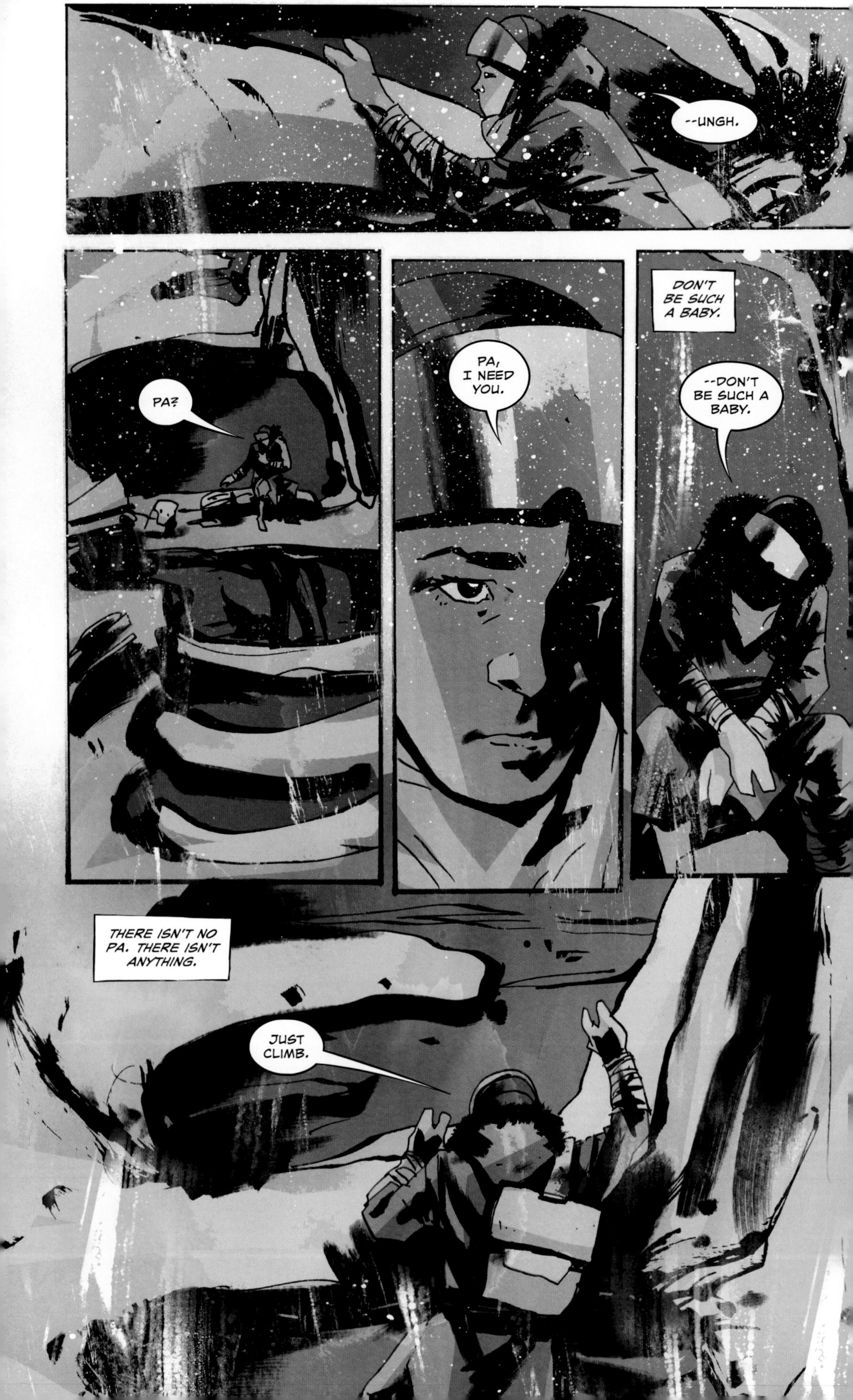
--UNGH.
PA?
PA, I NEED YOU.
DON'T BE SUCH A BABY.
--DON'T BE SUCH A BABY.
THERE ISN'T NO PA. THERE ISN'T ANYTHING.
JUST CLIMB.

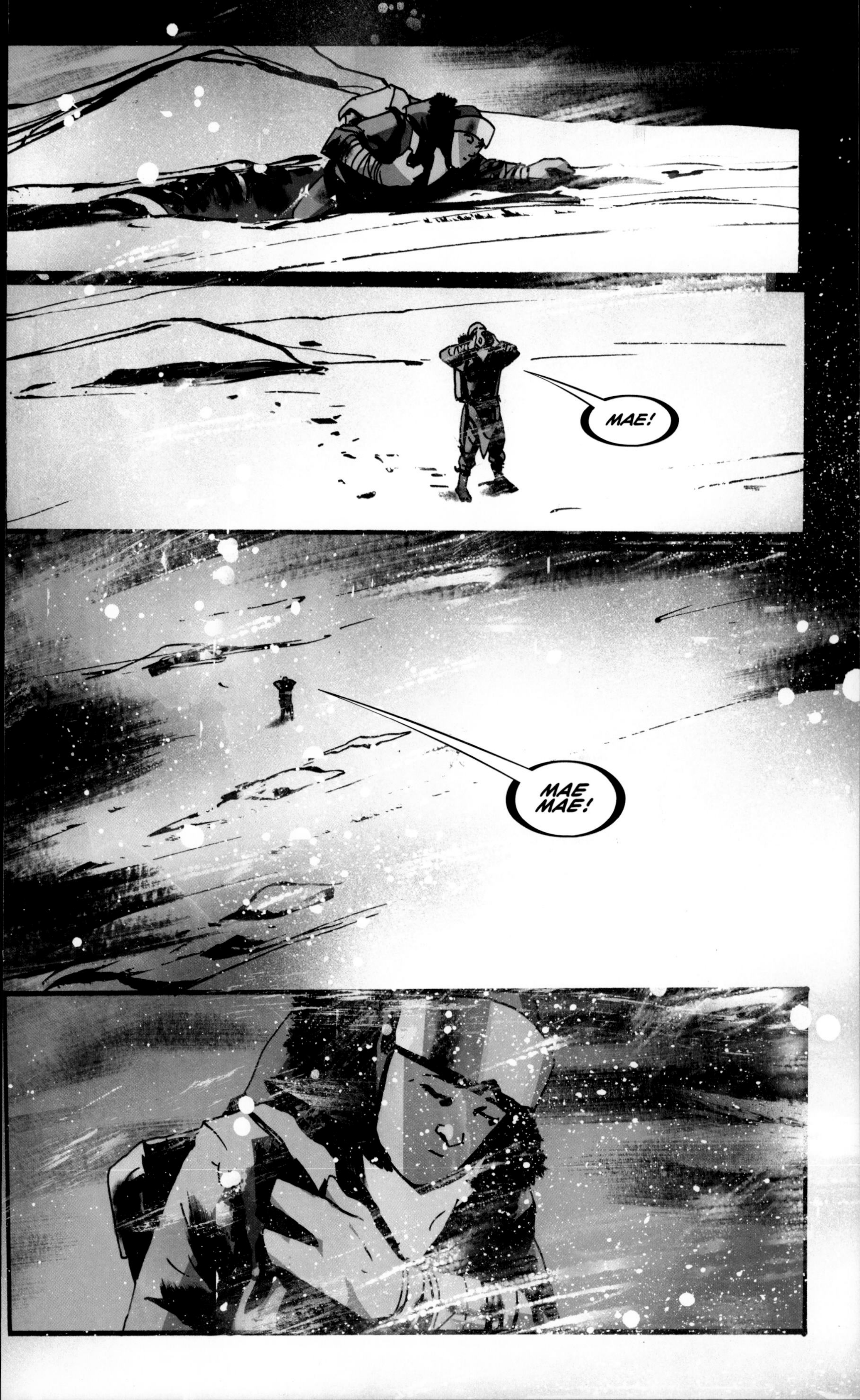
MAE!
MAE MAE!

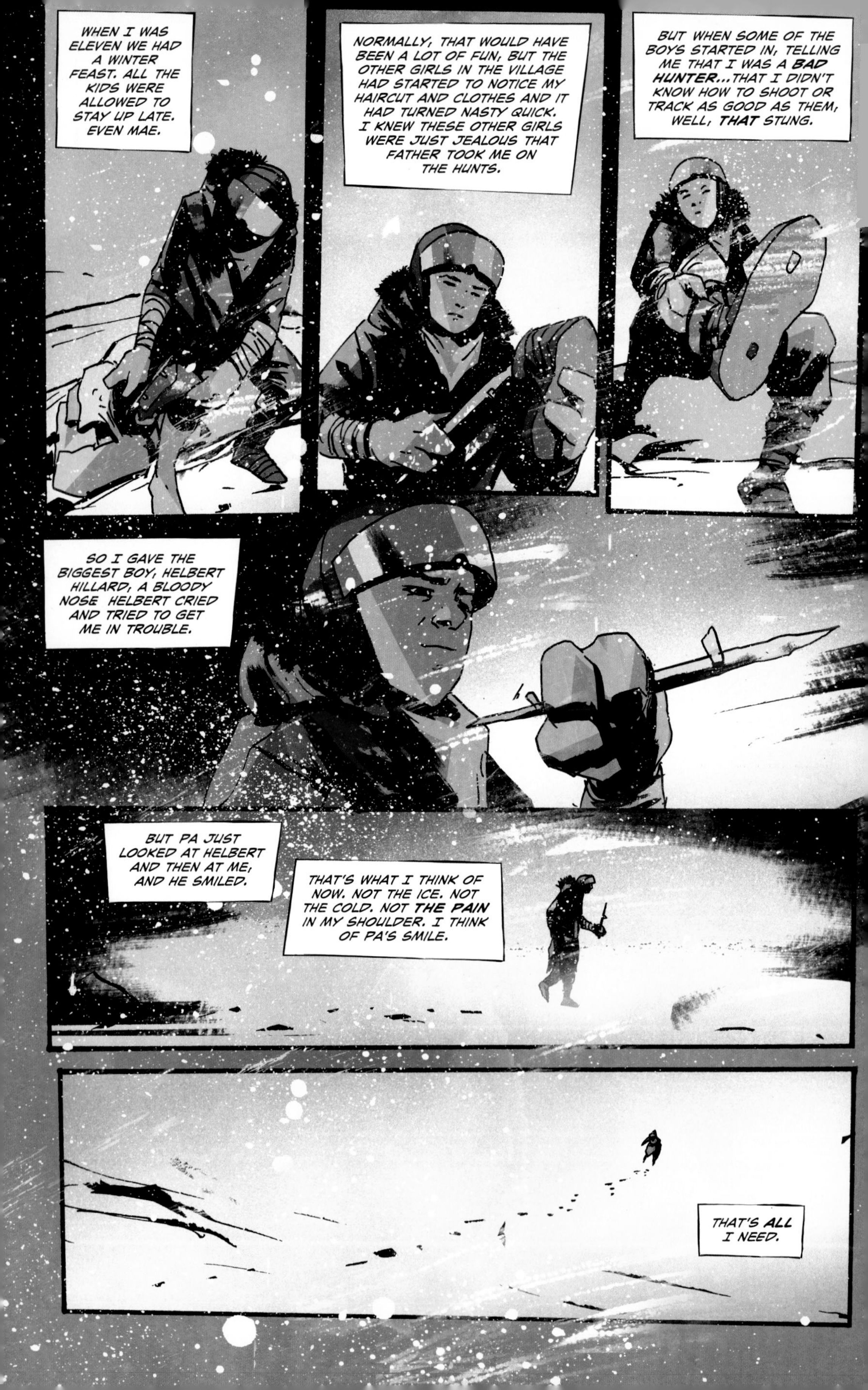
WHEN I WAS ELEVEN WE HAD A WINTER FEAST. ALL THE KIDS WERE ALLOWED TO STAY UP LATE. EVEN MAE.
NORMALLY, THAT WOULD HAVE BEEN A LOT OF FUN, BUT THE OTHER GIRLS IN THE VILLAGE HAD STARTED TO NOTICE MY HAIRCUT AND CLOTHES AND IT HAD TURNED NASTY QUICK. I KNEW THESE OTHER GIRLS WERE JUST JEALOUS THAT FATHER TOOK ME ON THE HUNTS.
BUT WHEN SOME OF THE BOYS STARTED IN, TELLING ME THAT I WAS A **BAD HUNTER**...THAT I DIDN'T KNOW HOW TO SHOOT OR TRACK AS GOOD AS THEM, WELL, **THAT** STUNG.
SO I GAVE THE BIGGEST BOY, HELBERT HILLARD, A BLOODY NOSE HELBERT CRIED AND TRIED TO GET ME IN TROUBLE.
BUT PA JUST LOOKED AT HELBERT AND THEN AT ME, AND HE SMILED.
THAT'S WHAT I THINK OF NOW. NOT THE ICE. NOT THE COLD. NOT **THE PAIN** IN MY SHOULDER. I THINK OF PA'S SMILE.
THAT'S **ALL** I NEED.

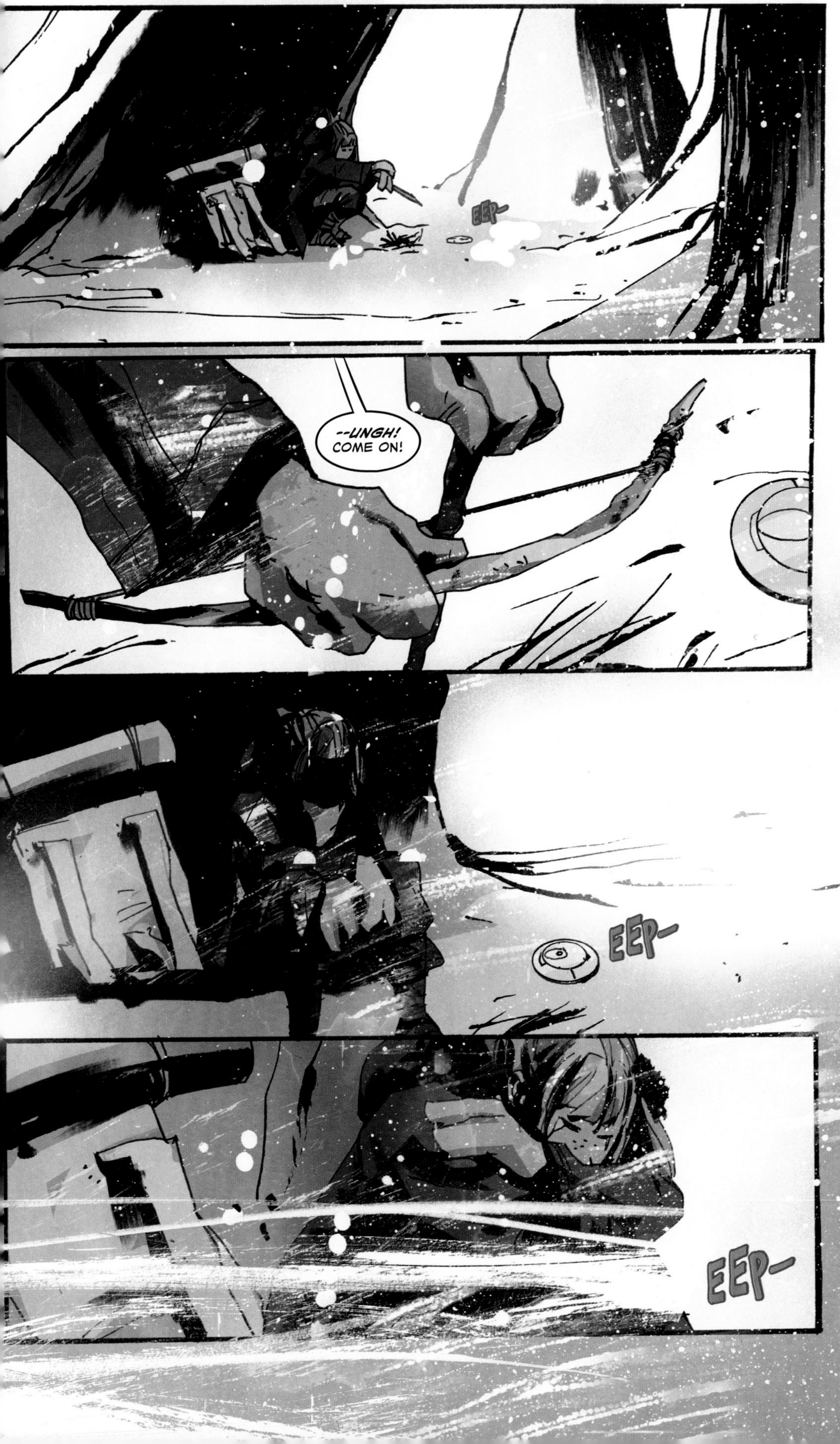
EEP-
--UNGH! COME ON!
EEP-
EEP-

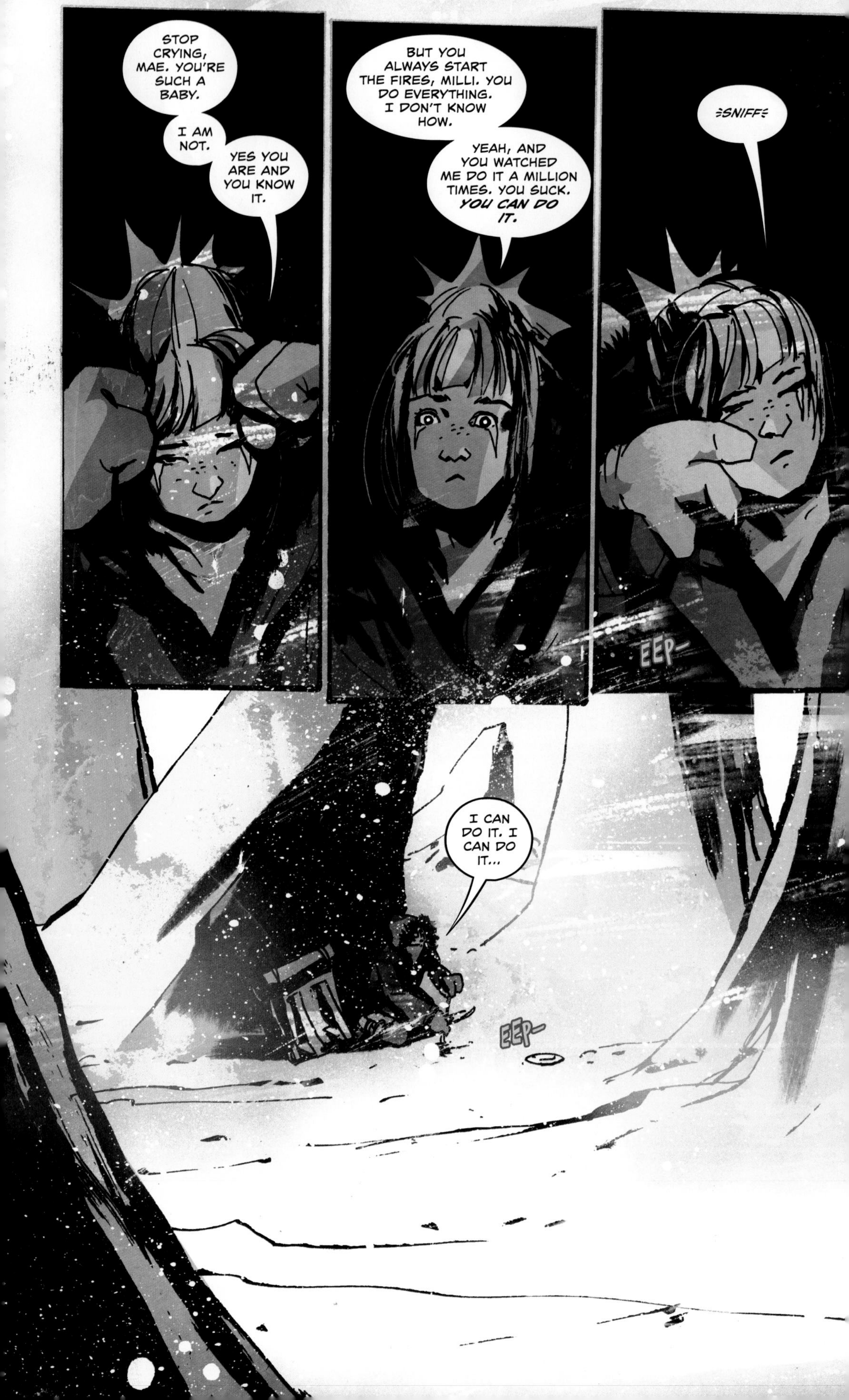
STOP CRYING, MAE. YOU'RE SUCH A BABY.
I AM NOT.
YES YOU ARE AND YOU KNOW IT.
BUT YOU ALWAYS START THE FIRES, MILLI. YOU DO EVERYTHING. I DON'T KNOW HOW.
YEAH, AND YOU WATCHED ME DO IT A MILLION TIMES. YOU SUCK. *YOU CAN DO IT.*
SNIFF
EEP—
I CAN DO IT. I CAN DO IT...
EEP—

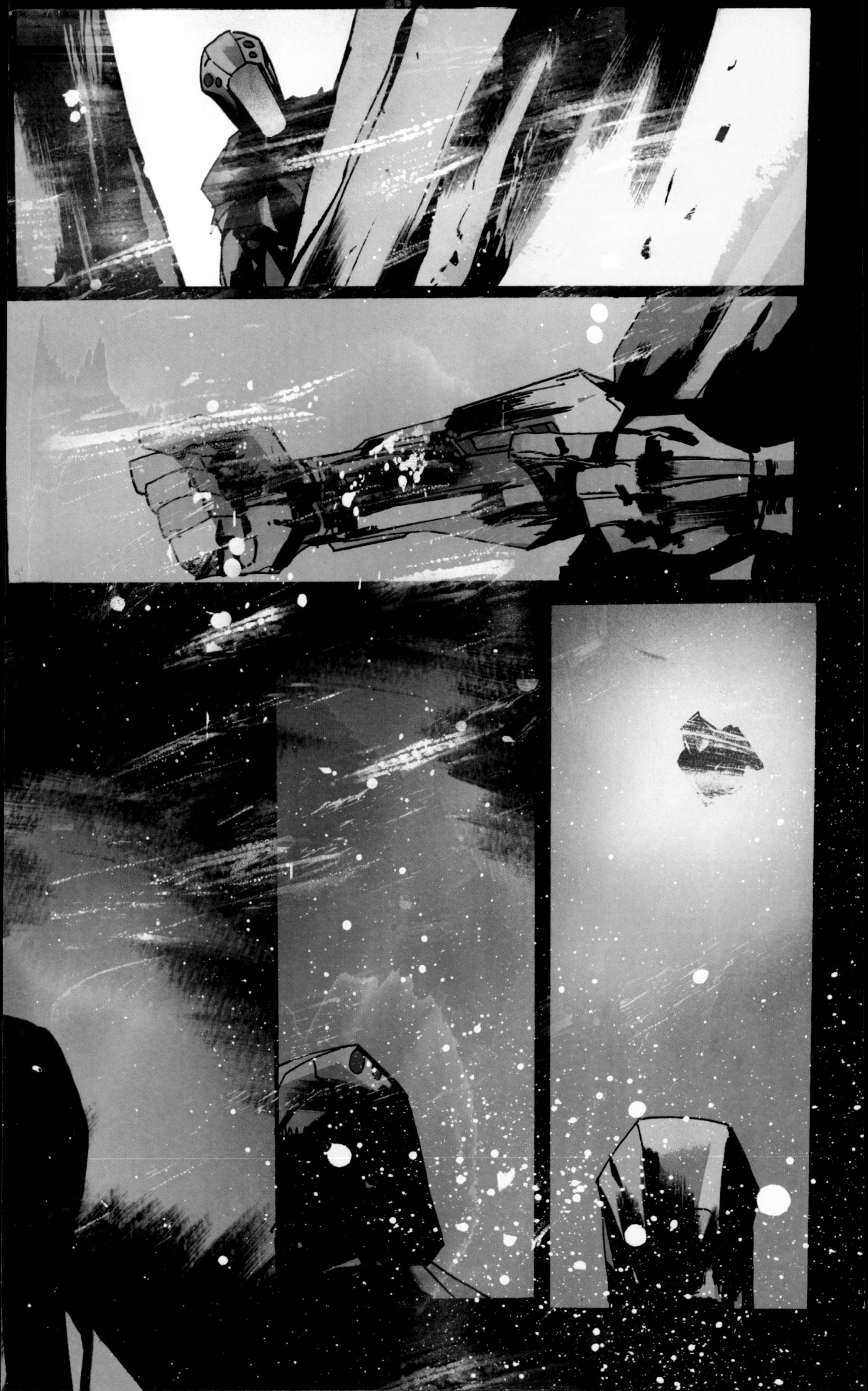

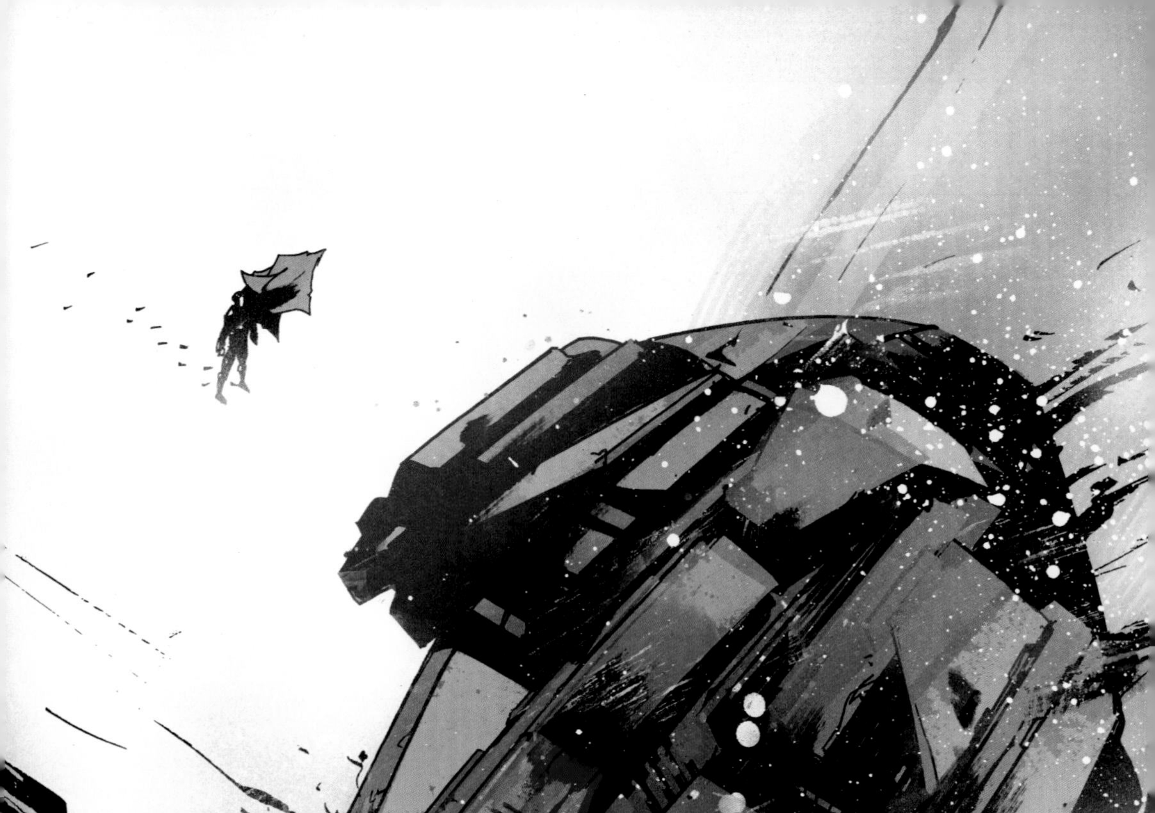
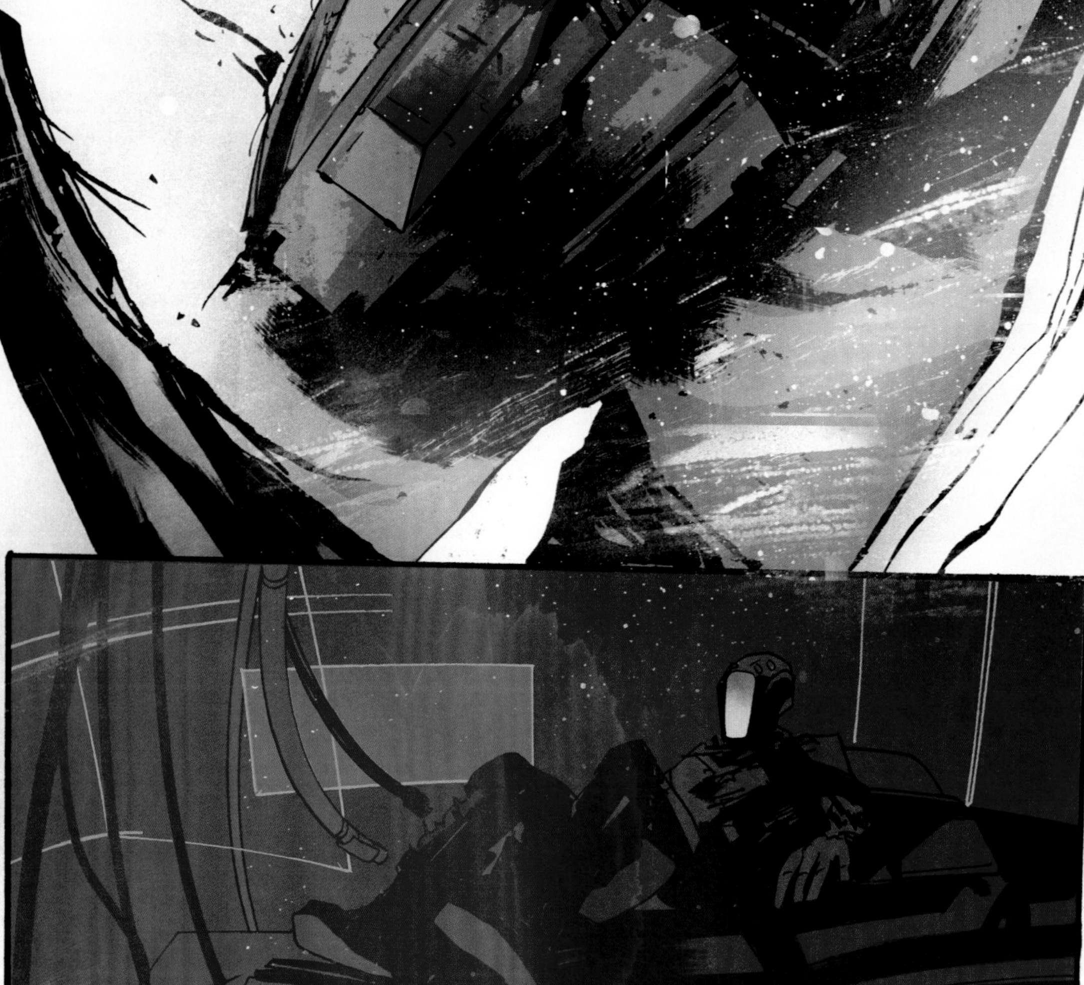

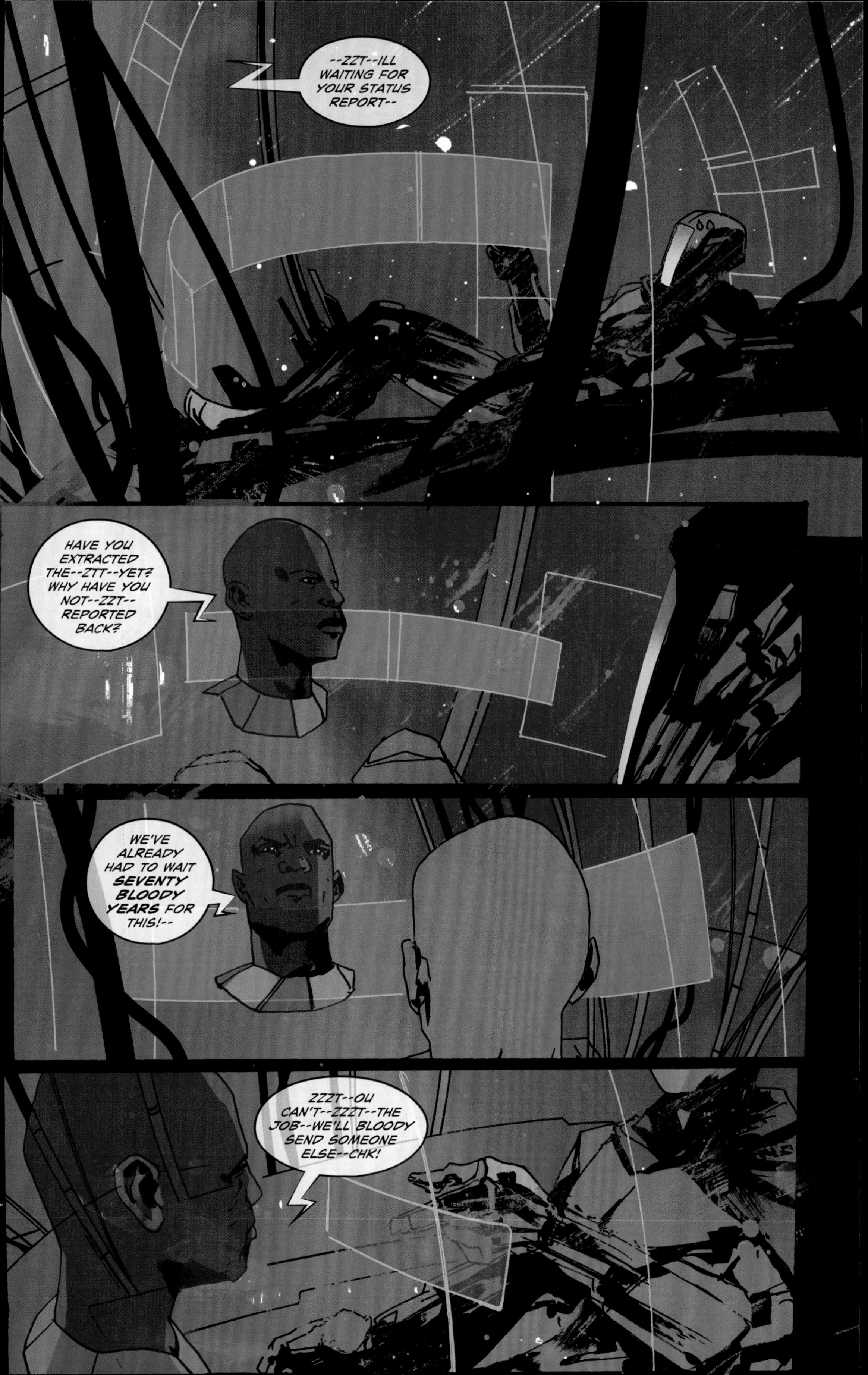
--ZZT--ILL WAITING FOR YOUR STATUS REPORT--
HAVE YOU EXTRACTED THE--ZTT--YET? WHY HAVE YOU NOT--ZZT--REPORTED BACK?
WE'VE ALREADY HAD TO WAIT SEVENTY BLOODY YEARS FOR THIS!--
ZZZT--OU CAN'T--ZZZT--THE JOB--WE'LL BLOODY SEND SOMEONE ELSE--CHK!

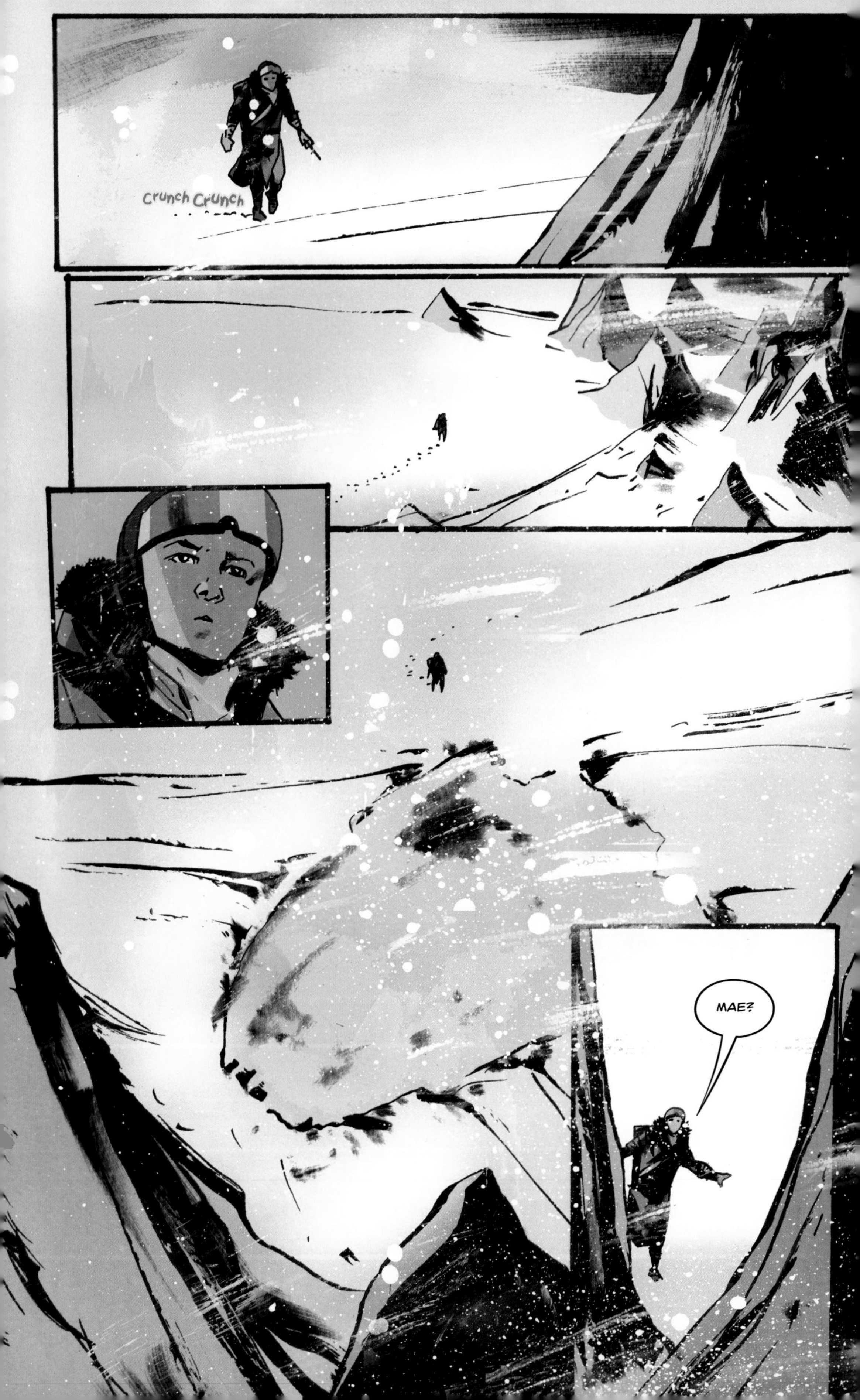
Crunch Crunch
MAE?

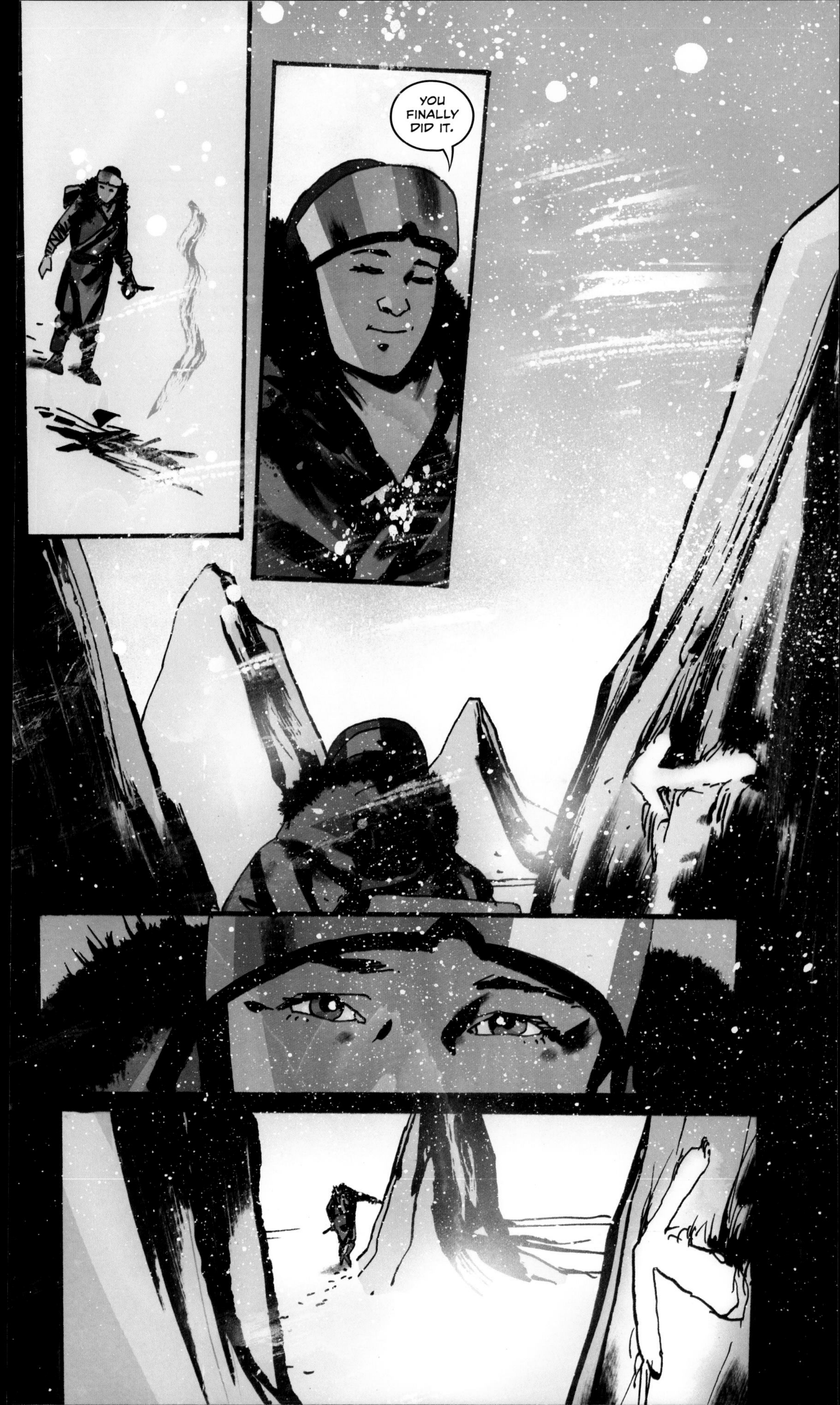
YOU FINALLY DID IT.

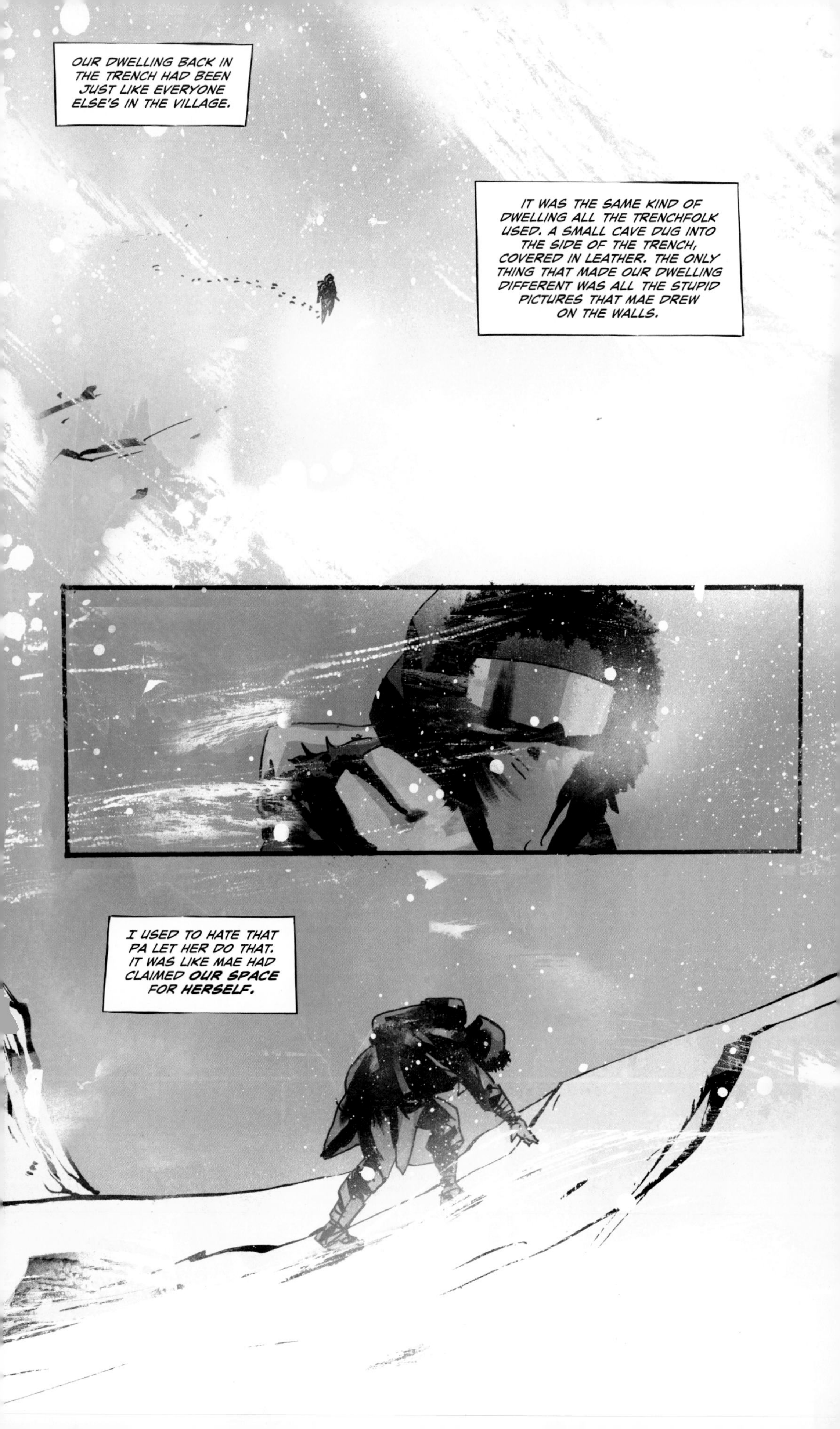
OUR DWELLING BACK IN THE TRENCH HAD BEEN JUST LIKE EVERYONE ELSE'S IN THE VILLAGE.
IT WAS THE SAME KIND OF DWELLING ALL THE TRENCHFOLK USED. A SMALL CAVE DUG INTO THE SIDE OF THE TRENCH, COVERED IN LEATHER. THE ONLY THING THAT MADE OUR DWELLING DIFFERENT WAS ALL THE STUPID PICTURES THAT MAE DREW ON THE WALLS.
I USED TO HATE THAT PA LET HER DO THAT. IT WAS LIKE MAE HAD CLAIMED **OUR SPACE** FOR **HERSELF**.

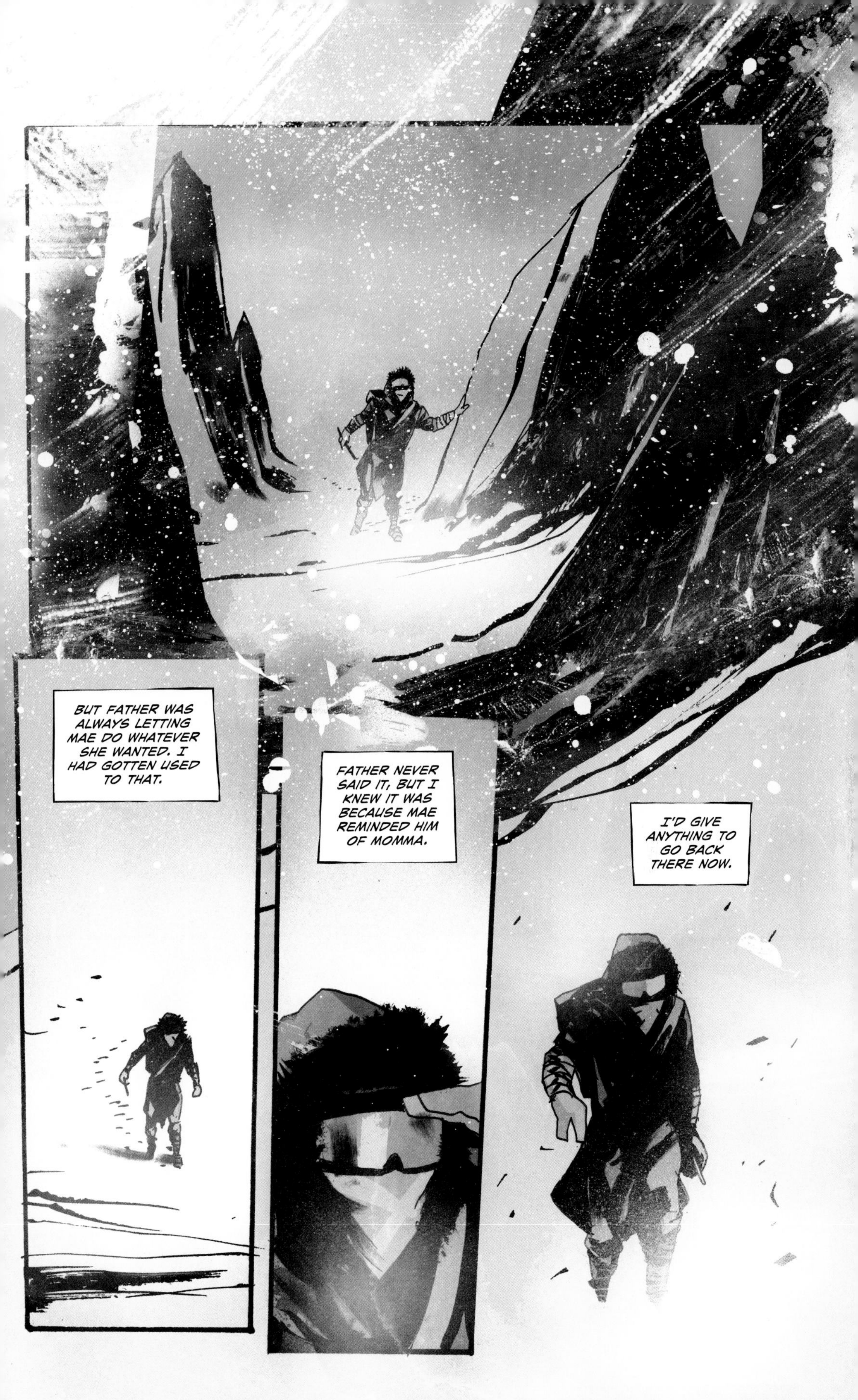
BUT FATHER WAS ALWAYS LETTING MAE DO WHATEVER SHE WANTED. I HAD GOTTEN USED TO THAT.
FATHER NEVER SAID IT, BUT I KNEW IT WAS BECAUSE MAE REMINDED HIM OF MOMMA.
I'D GIVE ANYTHING TO GO BACK THERE NOW.

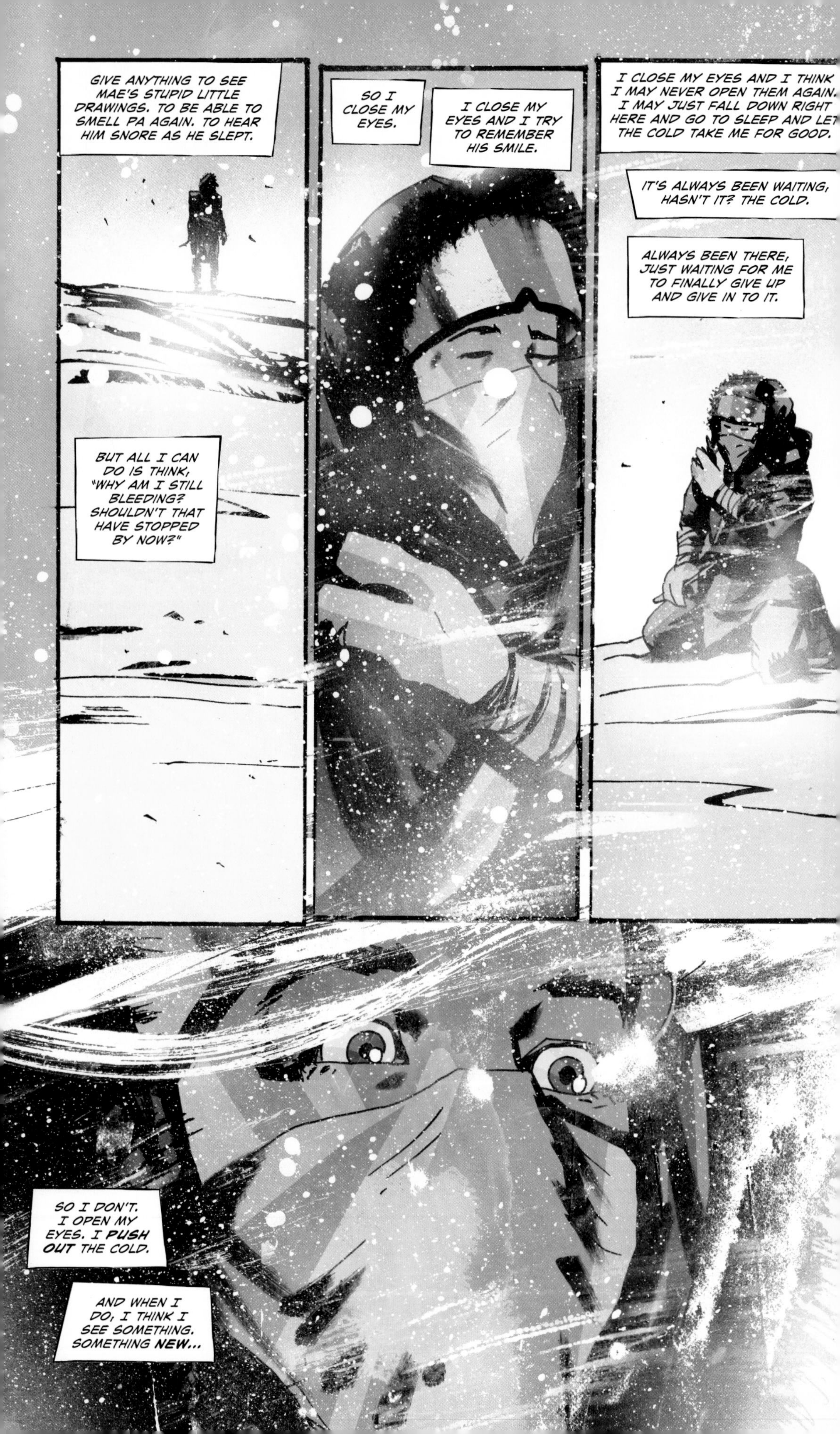
GIVE ANYTHING TO SEE MAE'S STUPID LITTLE DRAWINGS. TO BE ABLE TO SMELL PA AGAIN. TO HEAR HIM SNORE AS HE SLEPT.
BUT ALL I CAN DO IS THINK, "WHY AM I STILL BLEEDING? SHOULDN'T THAT HAVE STOPPED BY NOW?"
SO I CLOSE MY EYES.
I CLOSE MY EYES AND I TRY TO REMEMBER HIS SMILE.
I CLOSE MY EYES AND I THINK I MAY NEVER OPEN THEM AGAIN. I MAY JUST FALL DOWN RIGHT HERE AND GO TO SLEEP AND LET THE COLD TAKE ME FOR GOOD.
IT'S ALWAYS BEEN WAITING, HASN'T IT? THE COLD.
ALWAYS BEEN THERE, JUST WAITING FOR ME TO FINALLY GIVE UP AND GIVE IN TO IT.
SO I DON'T. I OPEN MY EYES. I **PUSH OUT** THE COLD.
AND WHEN I DO, I THINK I SEE SOMETHING. SOMETHING **NEW**...

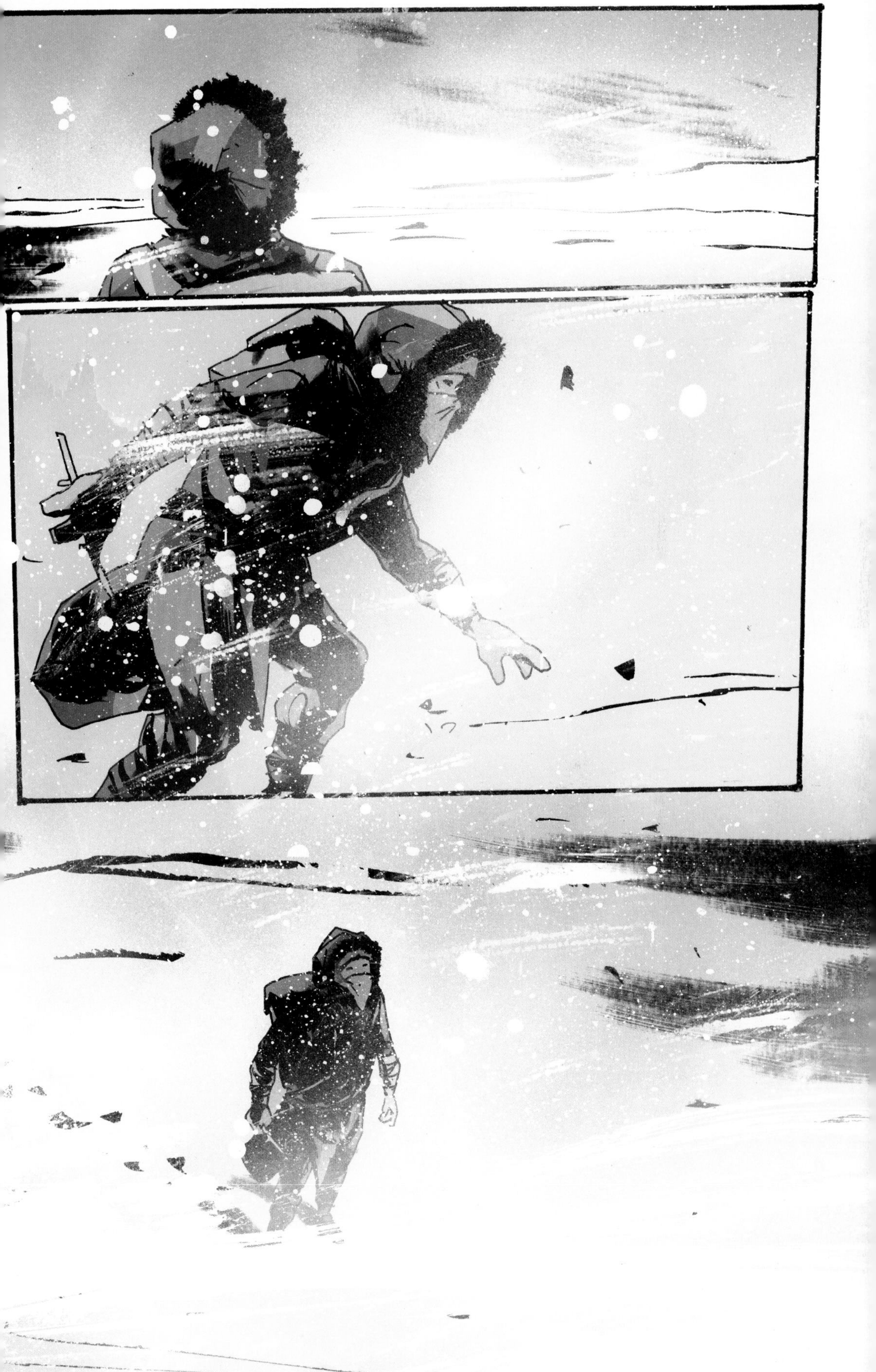

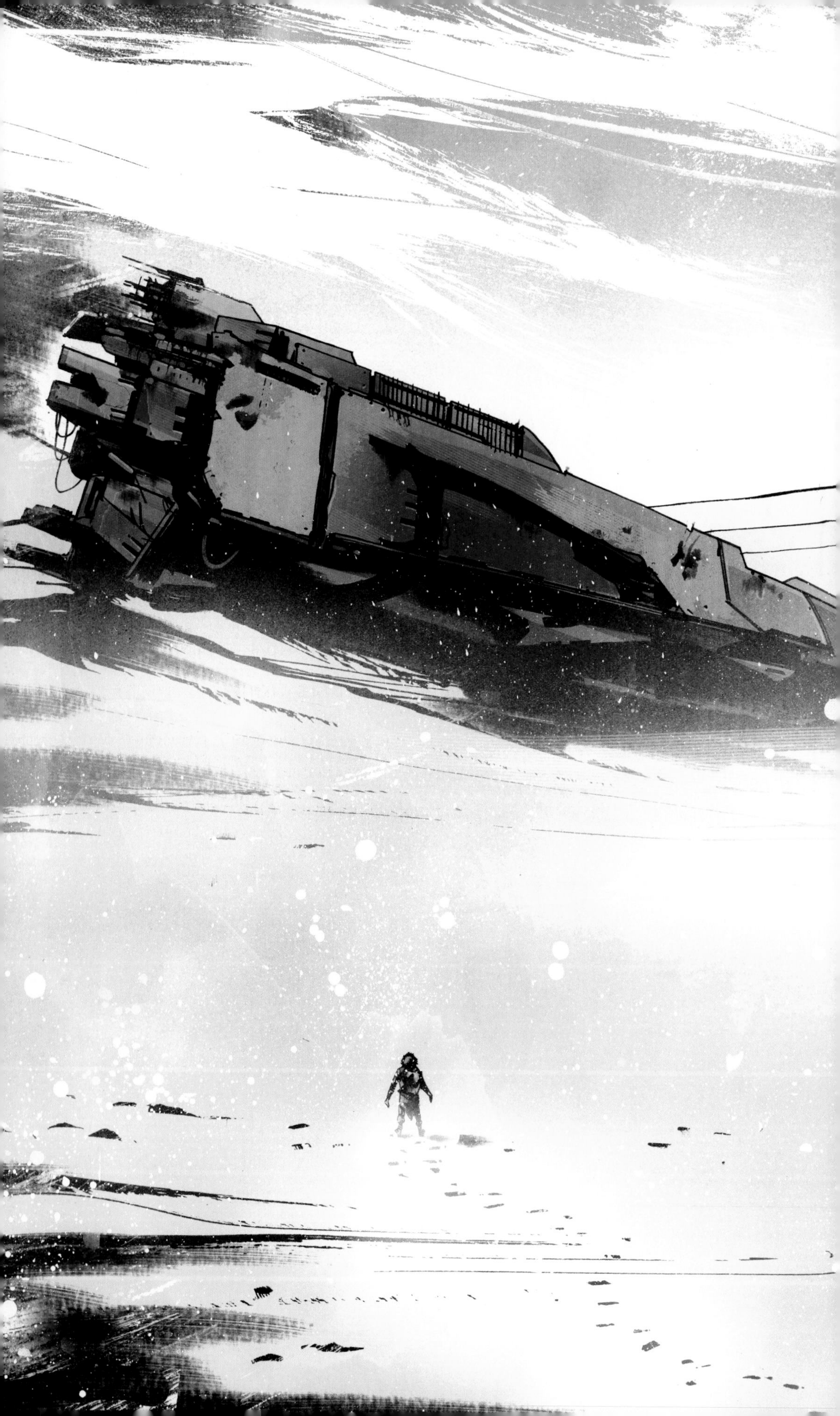

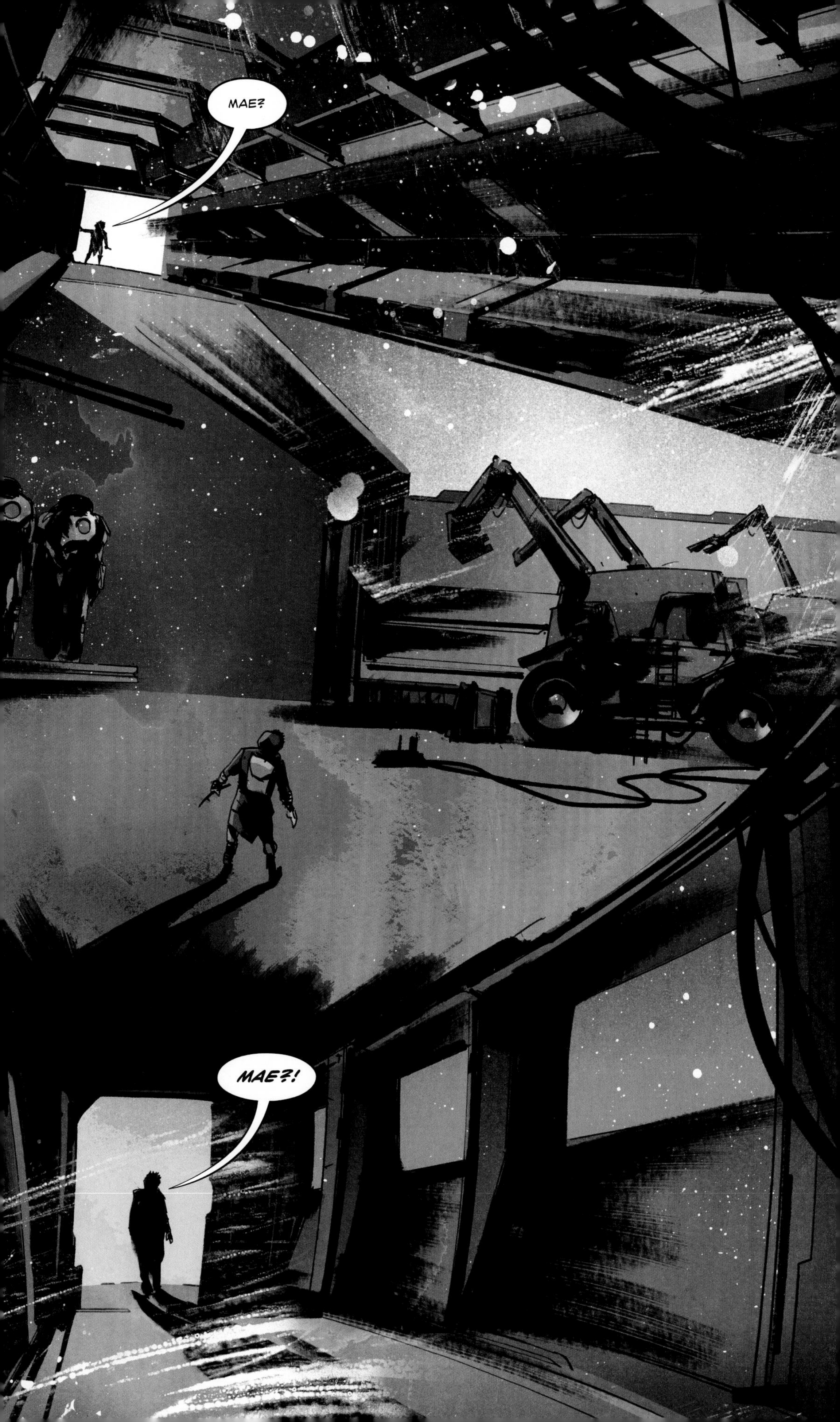
MAE?
MAE?!

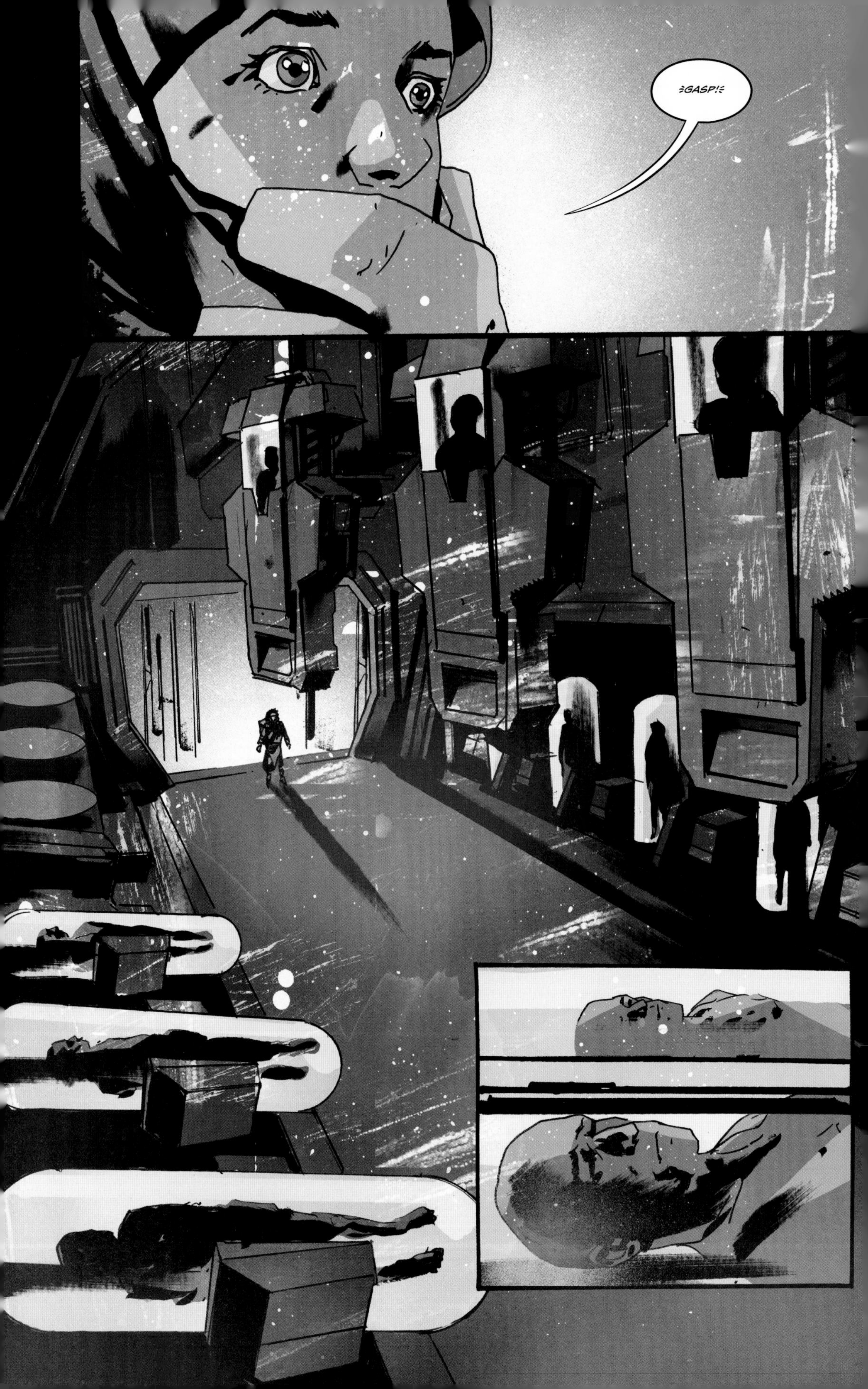
GASP!

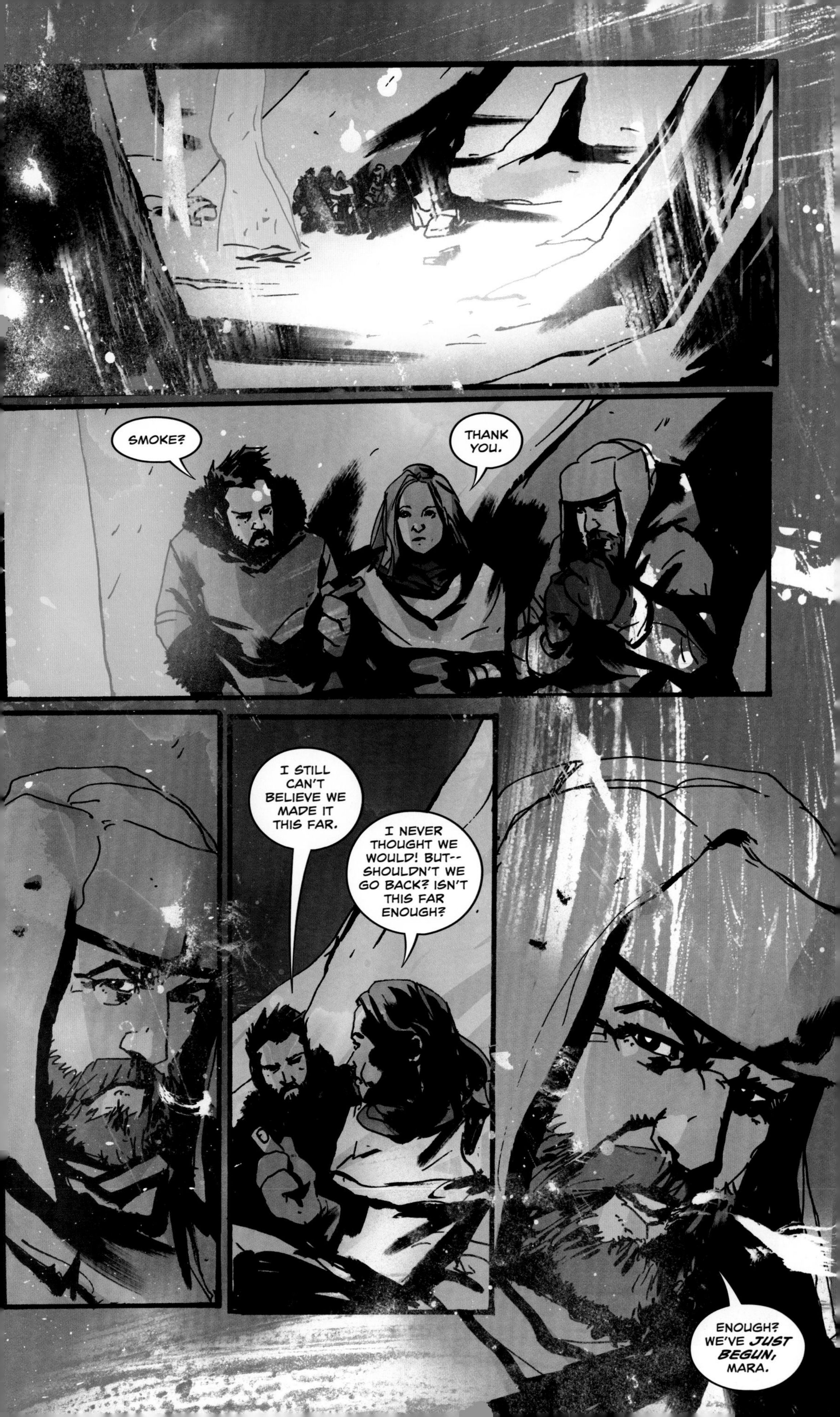
SMOKE?
THANK YOU.
I STILL CAN'T BELIEVE WE MADE IT THIS FAR.
I NEVER THOUGHT WE WOULD! BUT-- SHOULDN'T WE GO BACK? ISN'T THIS FAR ENOUGH?
ENOUGH? WE'VE *JUST BEGUN,* MARA.

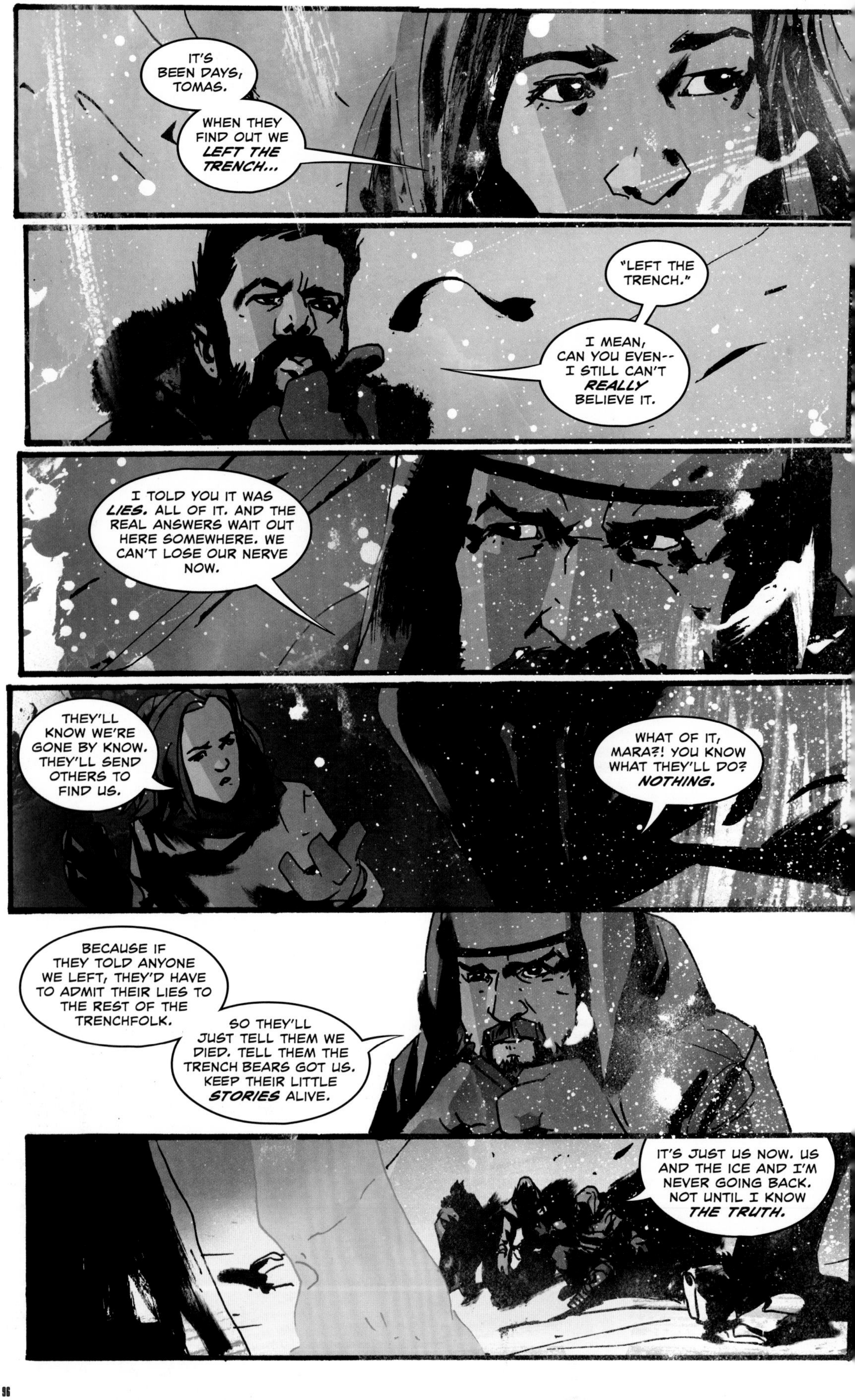
IT'S BEEN DAYS, TOMAS.
WHEN THEY FIND OUT WE LEFT THE TRENCH...
"LEFT THE TRENCH."
I MEAN, CAN YOU EVEN-- I STILL CAN'T REALLY BELIEVE IT.
I TOLD YOU IT WAS LIES. ALL OF IT. AND THE REAL ANSWERS WAIT OUT HERE SOMEWHERE. WE CAN'T LOSE OUR NERVE NOW.
THEY'LL KNOW WE'RE GONE BY KNOW. THEY'LL SEND OTHERS TO FIND US.
WHAT OF IT, MARA?! YOU KNOW WHAT THEY'LL DO? NOTHING.
BECAUSE IF THEY TOLD ANYONE WE LEFT, THEY'D HAVE TO ADMIT THEIR LIES TO THE REST OF THE TRENCHFOLK.
SO THEY'LL JUST TELL THEM WE DIED. TELL THEM THE TRENCH BEARS GOT US. KEEP THEIR LITTLE STORIES ALIVE.
IT'S JUST US NOW. US AND THE ICE AND I'M NEVER GOING BACK. NOT UNTIL I KNOW THE TRUTH.

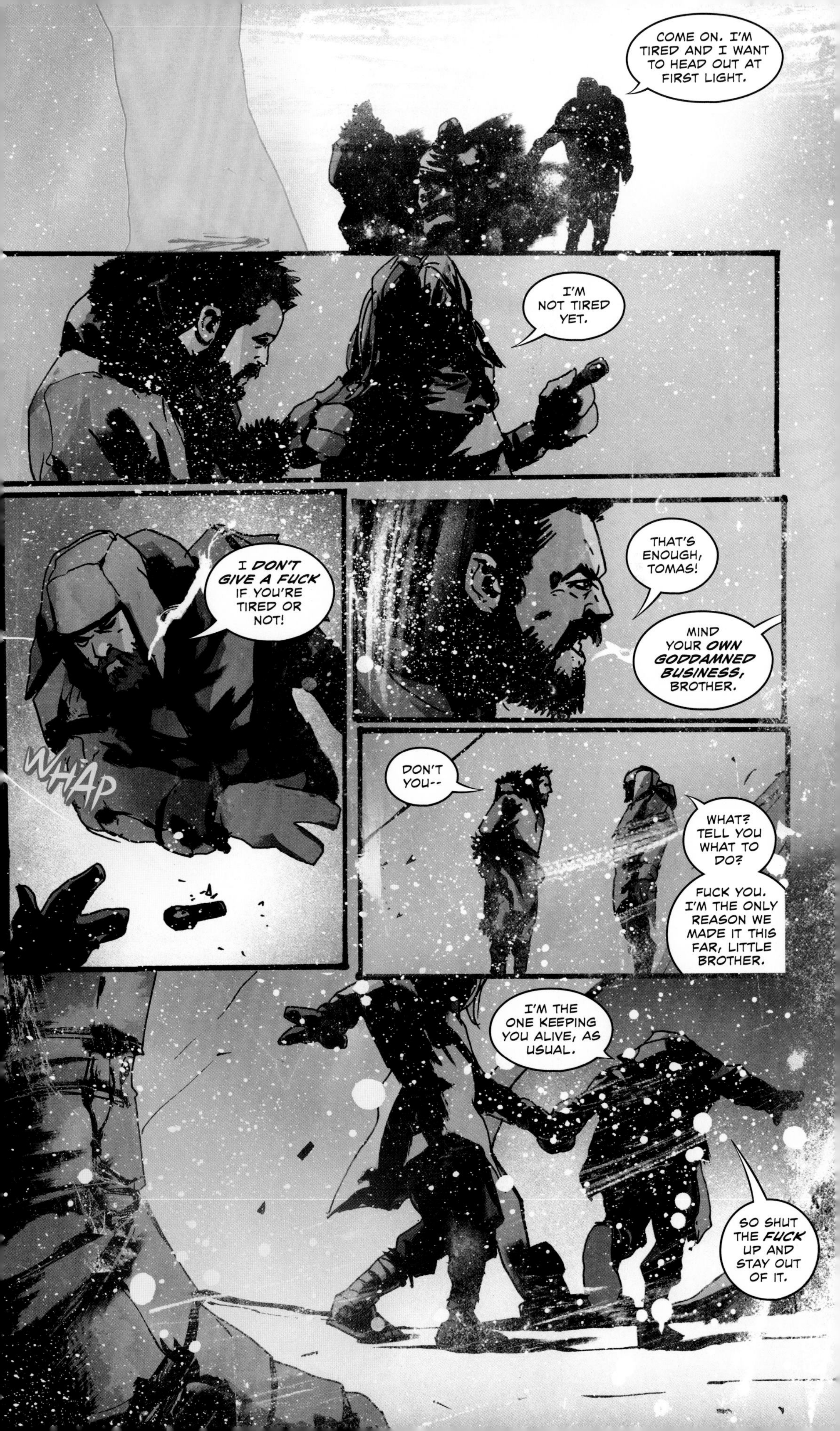
COME ON. I'M TIRED AND I WANT TO HEAD OUT AT FIRST LIGHT.
I'M NOT TIRED YET.
I *DON'T GIVE A FUCK* IF YOU'RE TIRED OR NOT!
WHAP
THAT'S ENOUGH, TOMAS!
MIND YOUR *OWN GODDAMNED BUSINESS,* BROTHER.
DON'T YOU--
WHAT? TELL YOU WHAT TO DO?
FUCK YOU. I'M THE ONLY REASON WE MADE IT THIS FAR, LITTLE BROTHER.
I'M THE ONE KEEPING YOU ALIVE, AS USUAL.
SO SHUT THE *FUCK* UP AND STAY OUT OF IT.

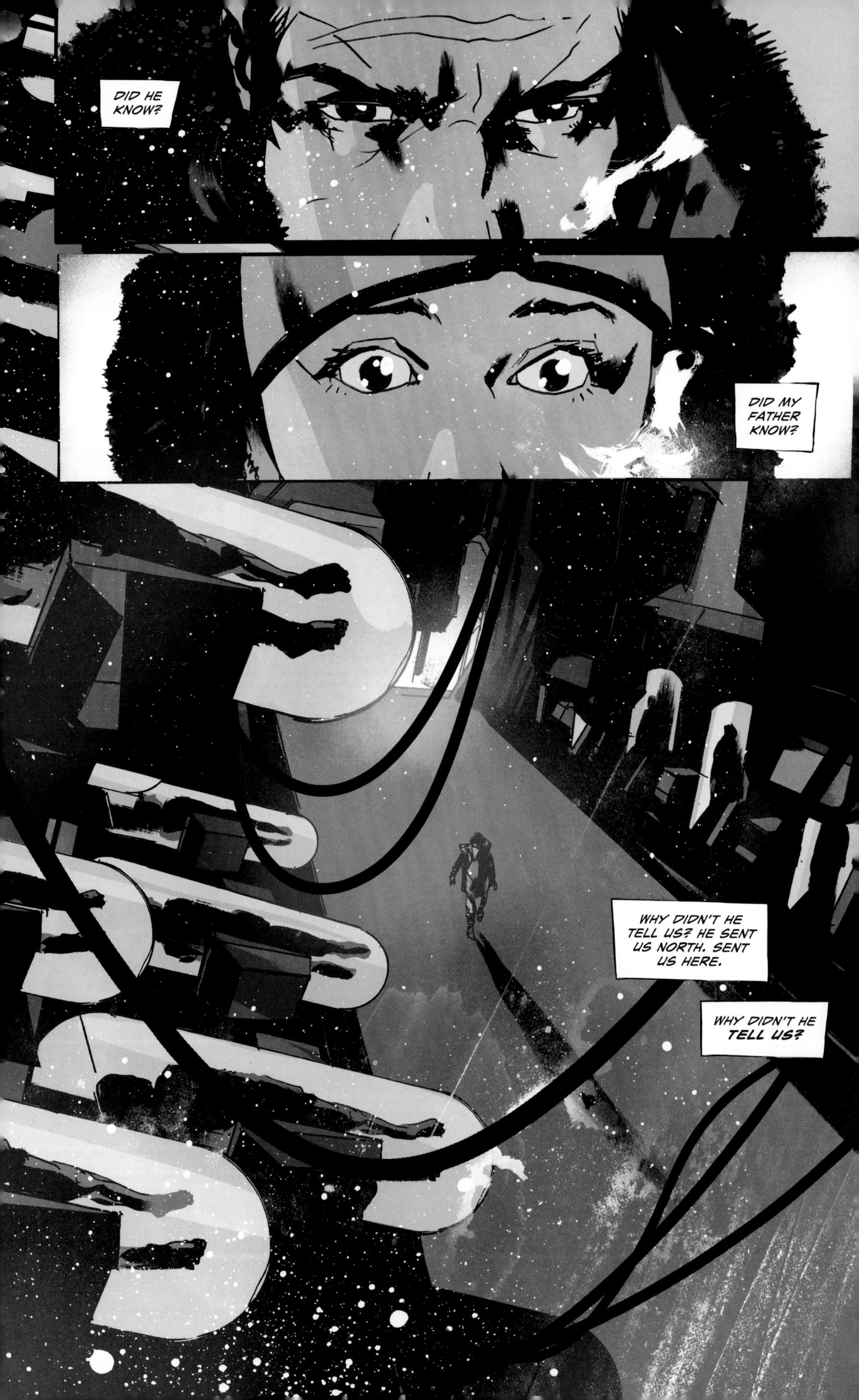
DID HE KNOW?
DID MY FATHER KNOW?
WHY DIDN'T HE TELL US? HE SENT US NORTH. SENT US HERE.
WHY DIDN'T HE TELL US?

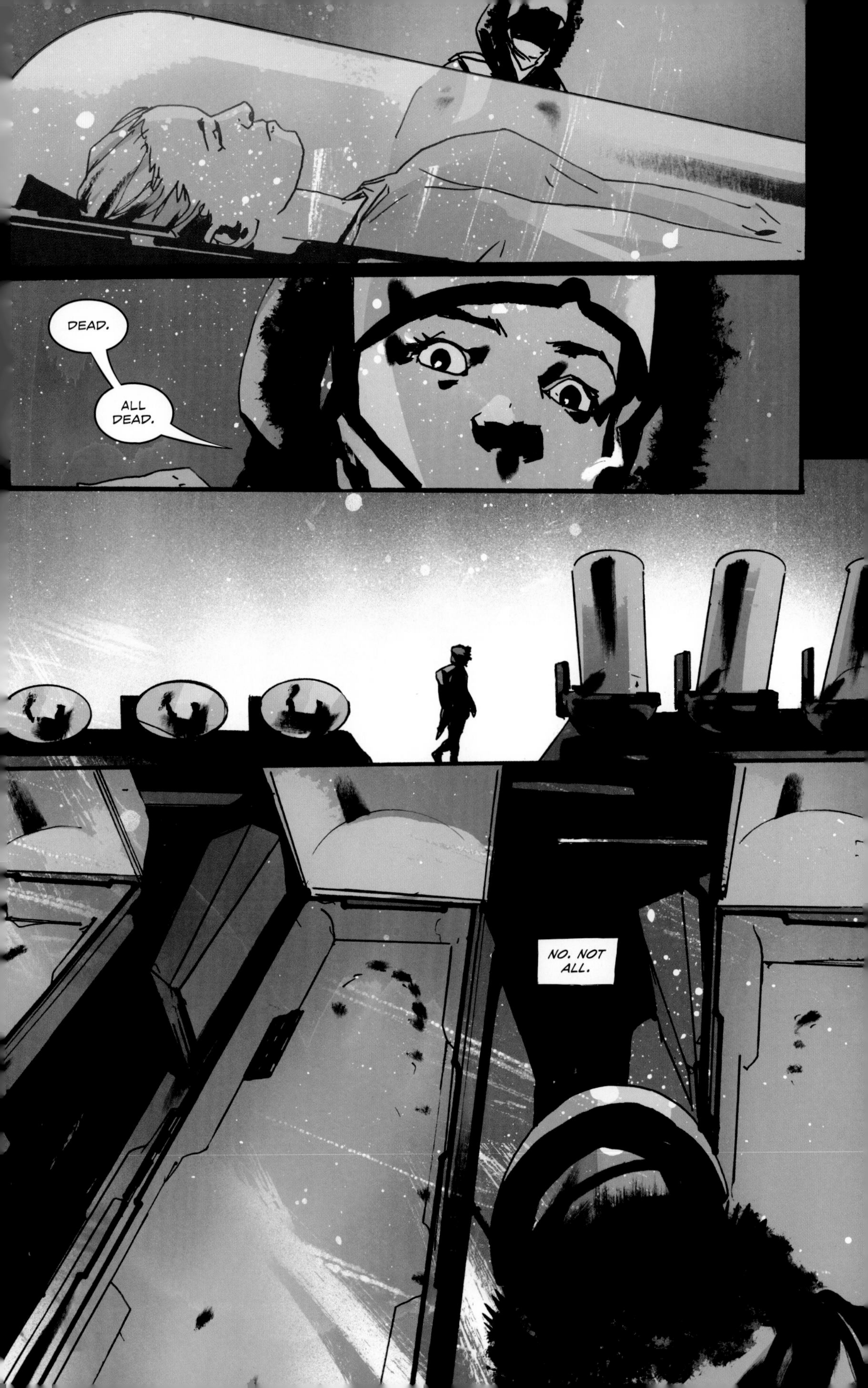
DEAD.
ALL DEAD.
NO. NOT ALL.

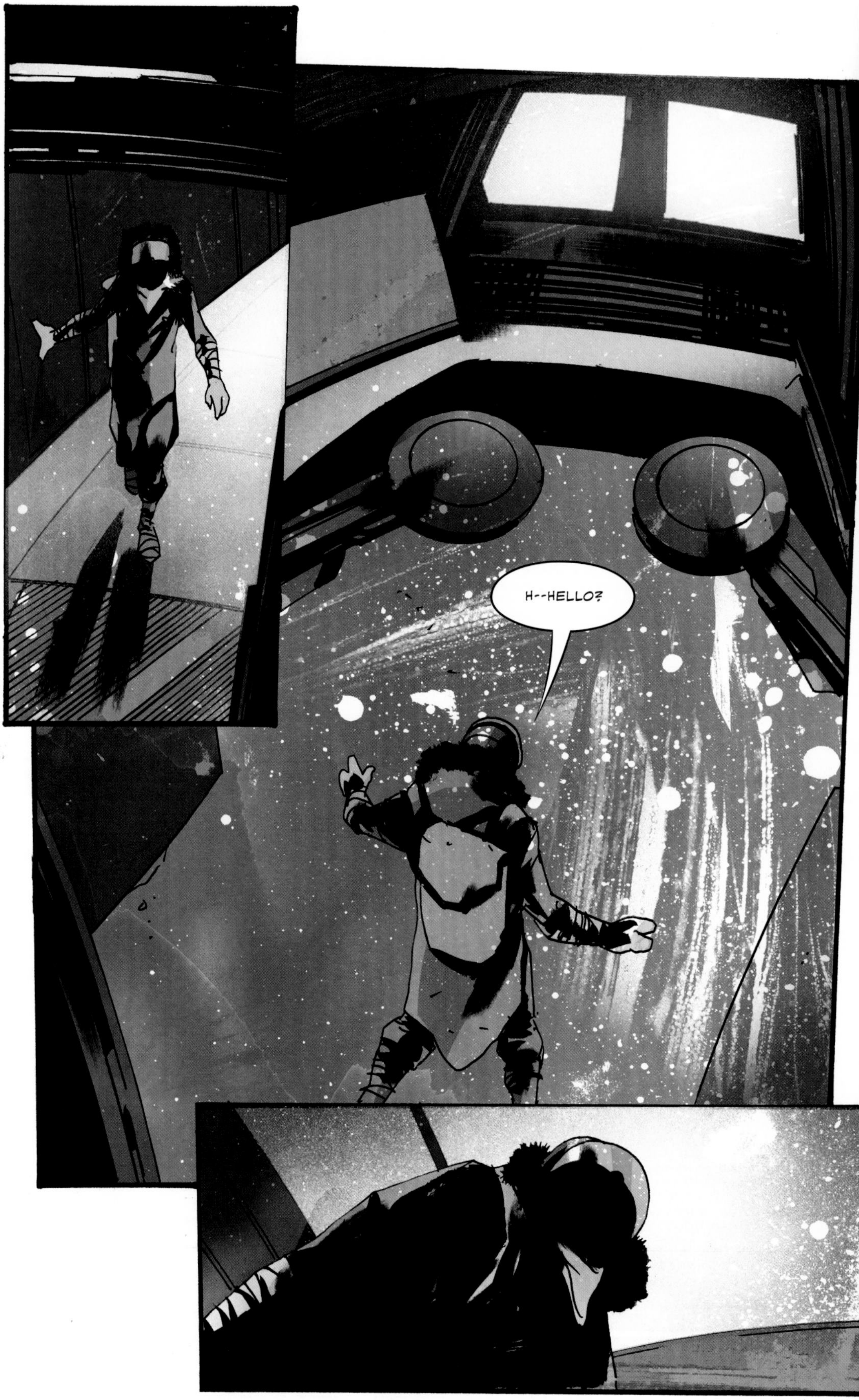
H--HELLO?

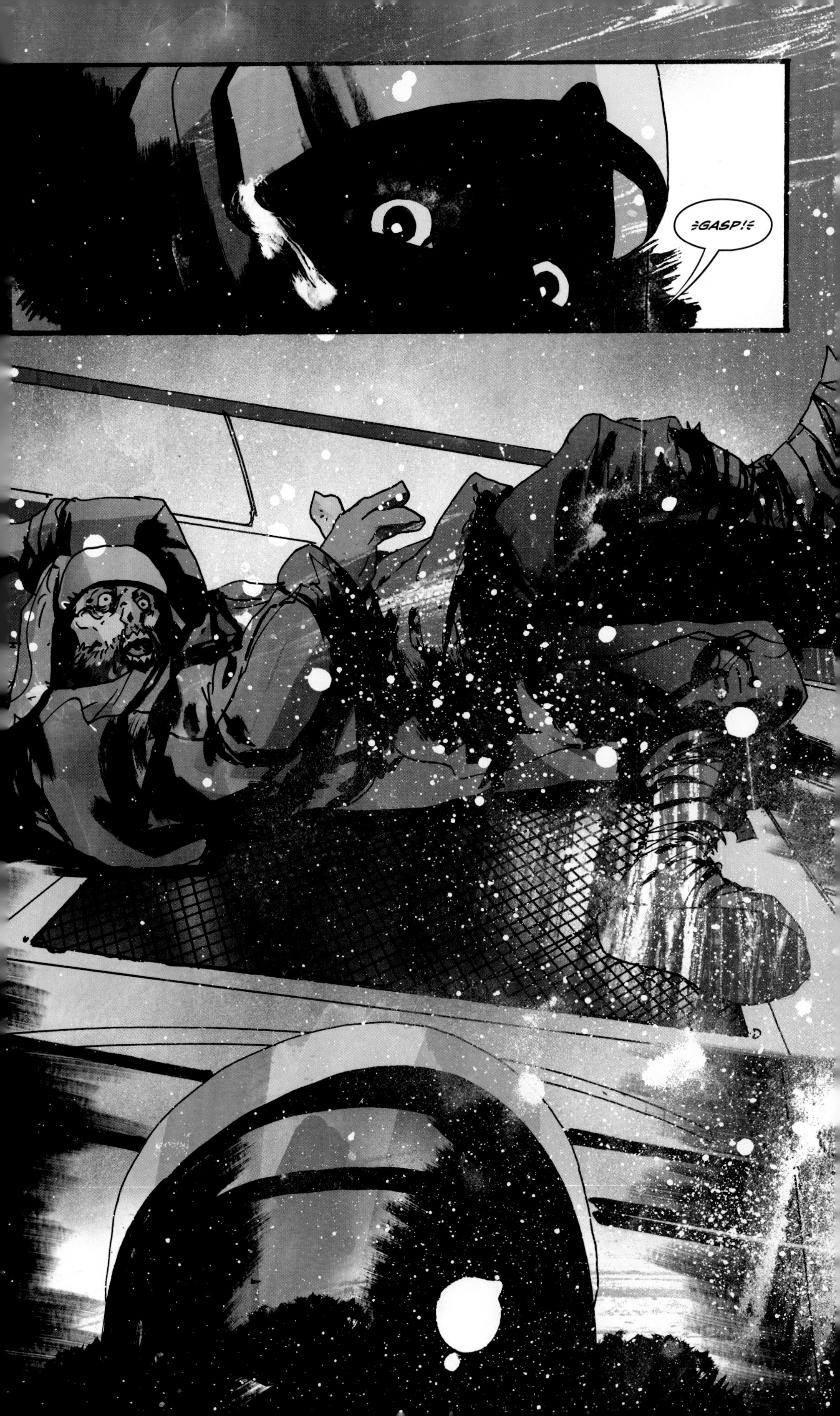
GASP!

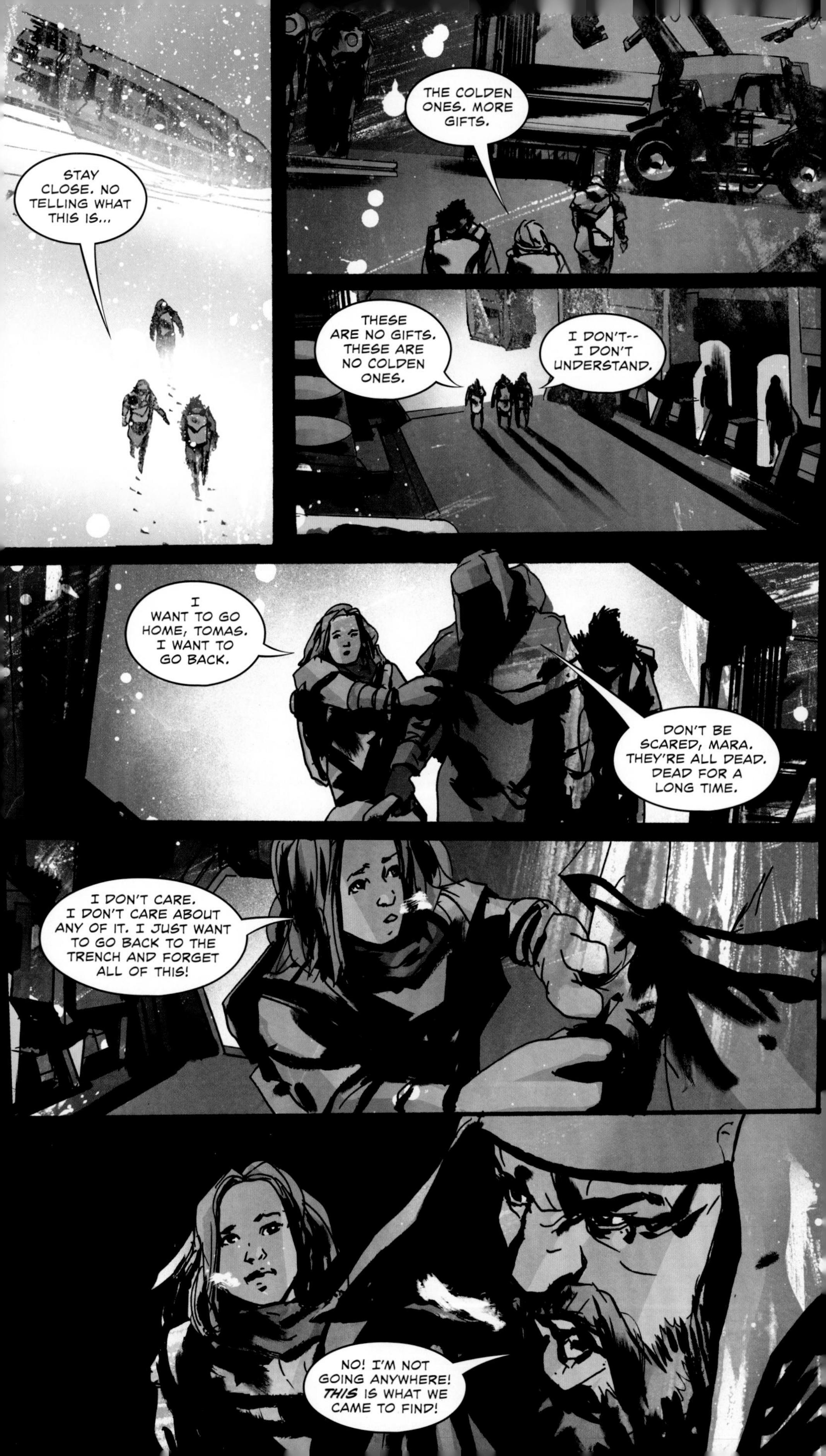
STAY CLOSE. NO TELLING WHAT THIS IS...
THE COLDEN ONES. MORE GIFTS.
THESE ARE NO GIFTS. THESE ARE NO COLDEN ONES.
I DON'T-- I DON'T UNDERSTAND.
I WANT TO GO HOME, TOMAS. I WANT TO GO BACK.
DON'T BE SCARED, MARA. THEY'RE ALL DEAD. DEAD FOR A LONG TIME.
I DON'T CARE. I DON'T CARE ABOUT ANY OF IT. I JUST WANT TO GO BACK TO THE TRENCH AND FORGET ALL OF THIS!
NO! I'M NOT GOING ANYWHERE! *THIS* IS WHAT WE CAME TO FIND!

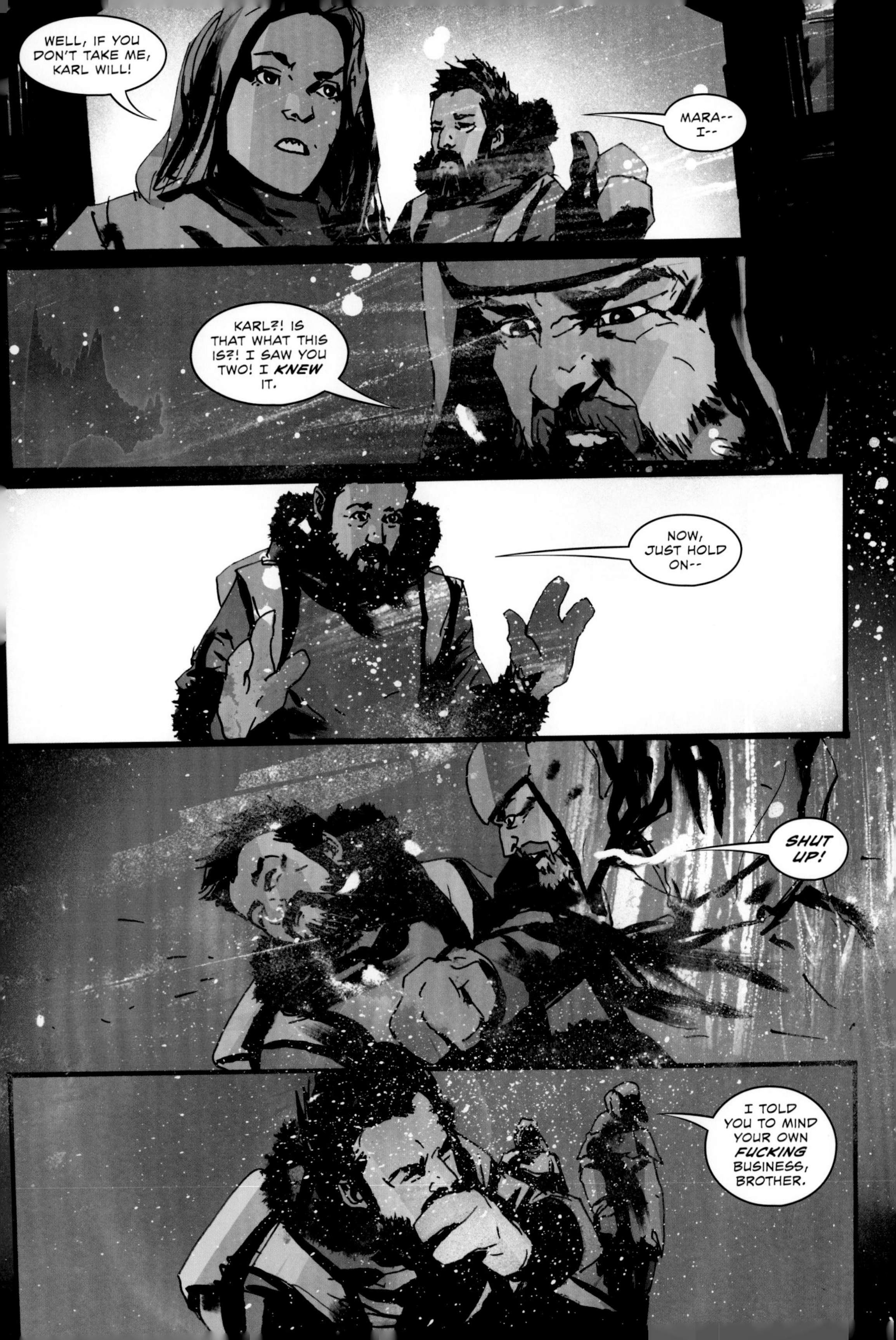
WELL, IF YOU DON'T TAKE ME, KARL WILL!
MARA-- I--
KARL?! IS THAT WHAT THIS IS?! I SAW YOU TWO! I *KNEW* IT.
NOW, JUST HOLD ON--
SHUT UP!
I TOLD YOU TO MIND YOUR OWN *FUCKING* BUSINESS, BROTHER.

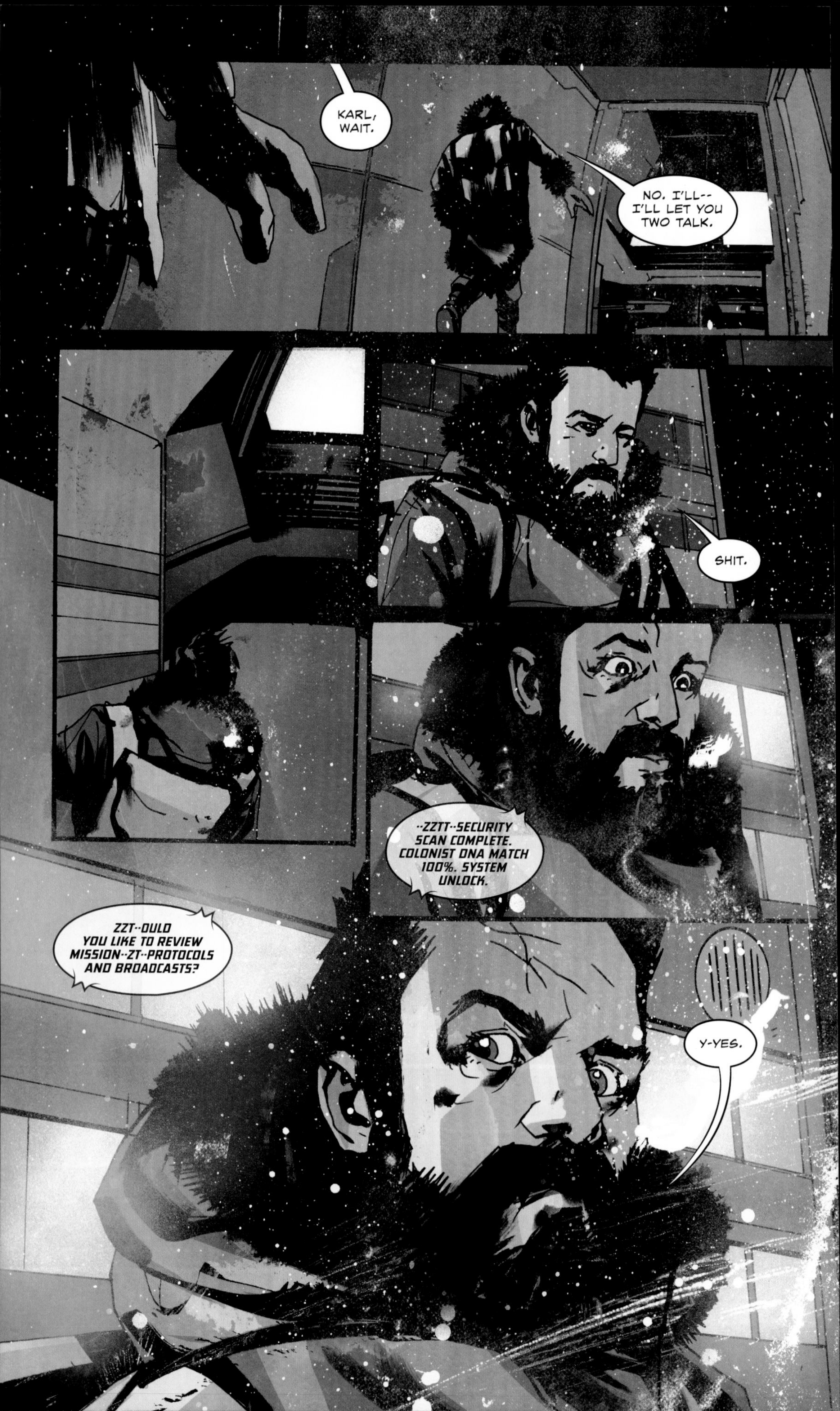
KARL, WAIT.
NO. I'LL-- I'LL LET YOU TWO TALK.
SHIT.
--ZZTT--SECURITY SCAN COMPLETE. COLONIST DNA MATCH 100%. SYSTEM UNLOCK.
ZZT--OULD YOU LIKE TO REVIEW MISSION--ZT--PROTOCOLS AND BROADCASTS?
Y-YES.

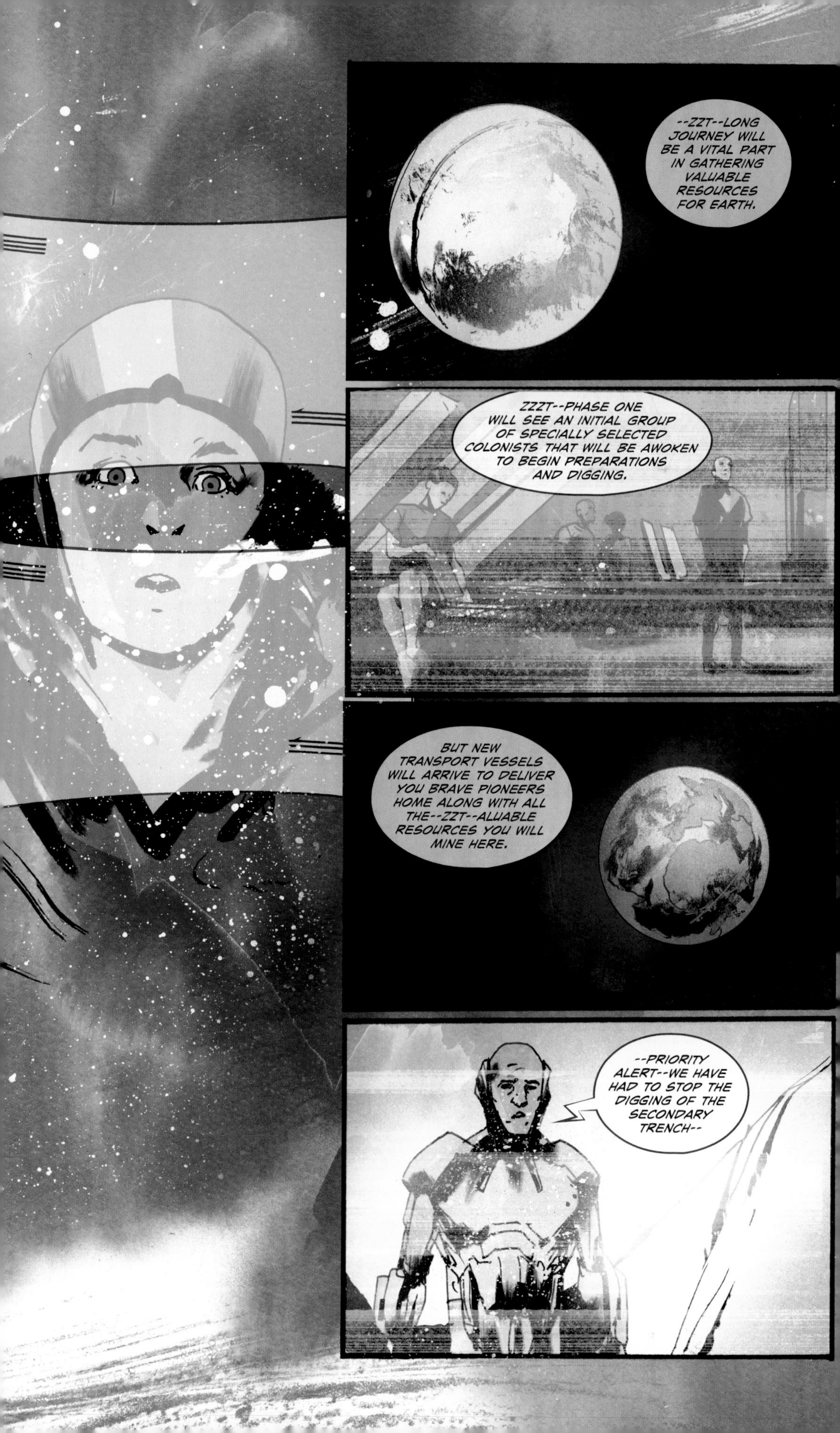
--ZZT--LONG JOURNEY WILL BE A VITAL PART IN GATHERING VALUABLE RESOURCES FOR EARTH.
ZZZT--PHASE ONE WILL SEE AN INITIAL GROUP OF SPECIALLY SELECTED COLONISTS THAT WILL BE AWOKEN TO BEGIN PREPARATIONS AND DIGGING.
BUT NEW TRANSPORT VESSELS WILL ARRIVE TO DELIVER YOU BRAVE PIONEERS HOME ALONG WITH ALL THE--ZZT--ALUABLE RESOURCES YOU WILL MINE HERE.
--PRIORITY ALERT--WE HAVE HAD TO STOP THE DIGGING OF THE SECONDARY TRENCH--

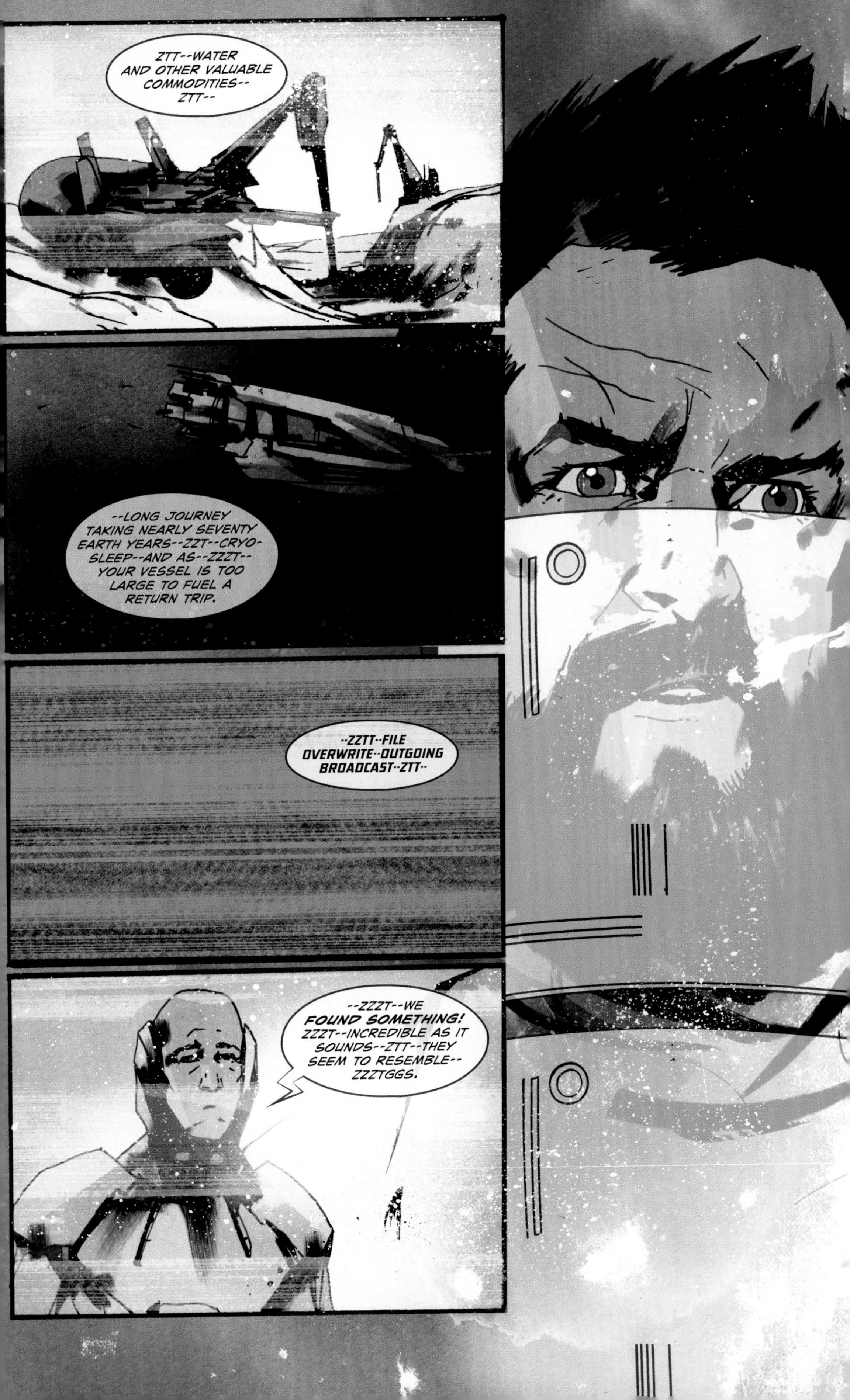
ZTT--WATER AND OTHER VALUABLE COMMODITIES-- ZTT--
--LONG JOURNEY TAKING NEARLY SEVENTY EARTH YEARS--ZZT--CRYO-SLEEP--AND AS--ZZZT-- YOUR VESSEL IS TOO LARGE TO FUEL A RETURN TRIP.
--ZZTT--FILE OVERWRITE--OUTGOING BROADCAST--ZTT--
--ZZZT--WE **FOUND SOMETHING!** ZZZT--INCREDIBLE AS IT SOUNDS--ZTT--THEY SEEM TO RESEMBLE-- ZZZTGGS.

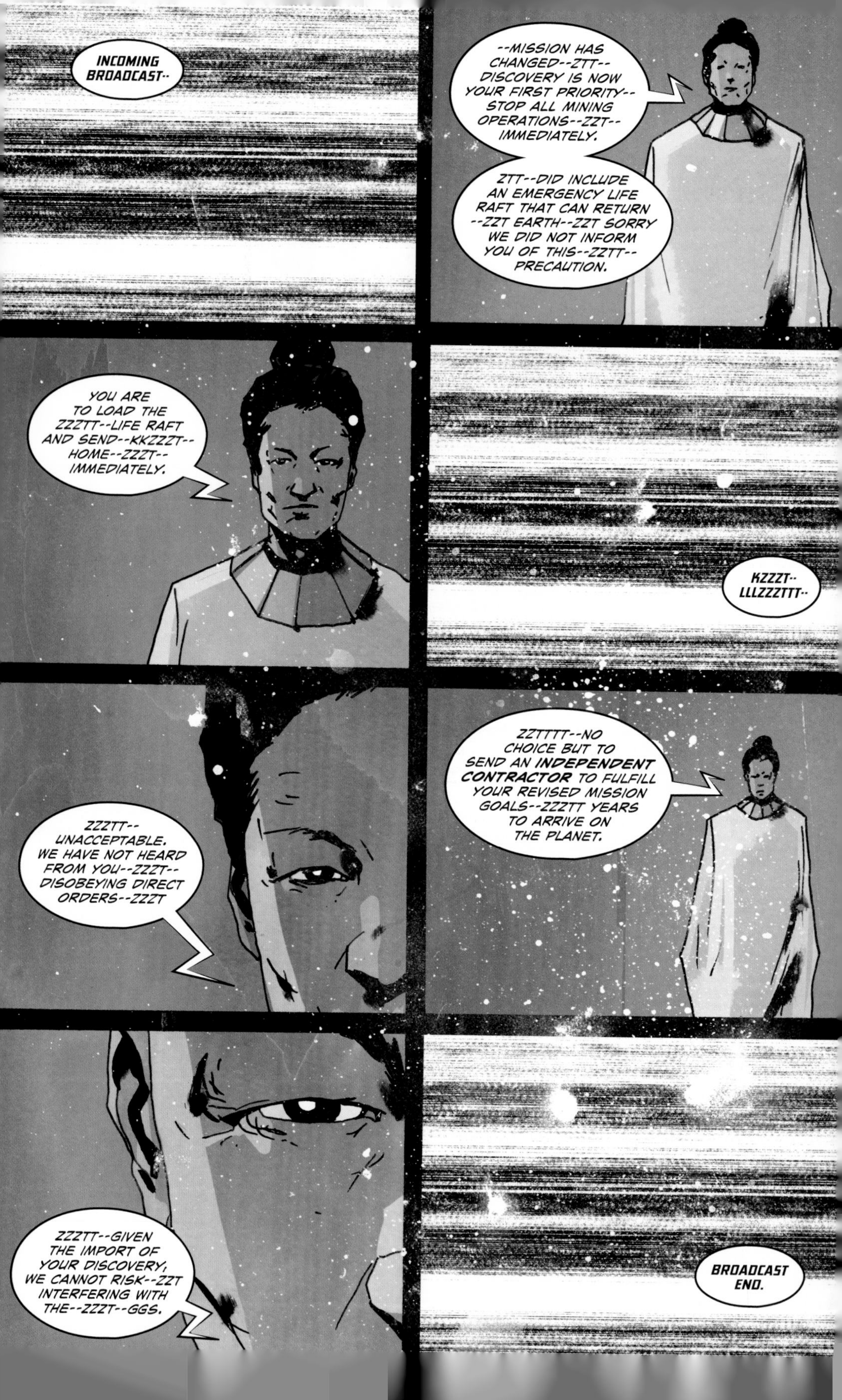
INCOMING BROADCAST--
--MISSION HAS CHANGED--ZTT-- DISCOVERY IS NOW YOUR FIRST PRIORITY-- STOP ALL MINING OPERATIONS--ZZT-- IMMEDIATELY.
ZTT--DID INCLUDE AN EMERGENCY LIFE RAFT THAT CAN RETURN --ZZT EARTH--ZZT SORRY WE DID NOT INFORM YOU OF THIS--ZZTT-- PRECAUTION.
YOU ARE TO LOAD THE ZZZTT--LIFE RAFT AND SEND--KKZZZT-- HOME--ZZZT-- IMMEDIATELY.
KZZZT-- LLLZZZTTT--
ZZZTT-- UNACCEPTABLE. WE HAVE NOT HEARD FROM YOU--ZZZT-- DISOBEYING DIRECT ORDERS--ZZZT
ZZTTTT--NO CHOICE BUT TO SEND AN INDEPENDENT CONTRACTOR TO FULFILL YOUR REVISED MISSION GOALS--ZZZTT YEARS TO ARRIVE ON THE PLANET.
ZZZTT--GIVEN THE IMPORT OF YOUR DISCOVERY, WE CANNOT RISK--ZZT INTERFERING WITH THE--ZZZT--GGS.
BROADCAST END.

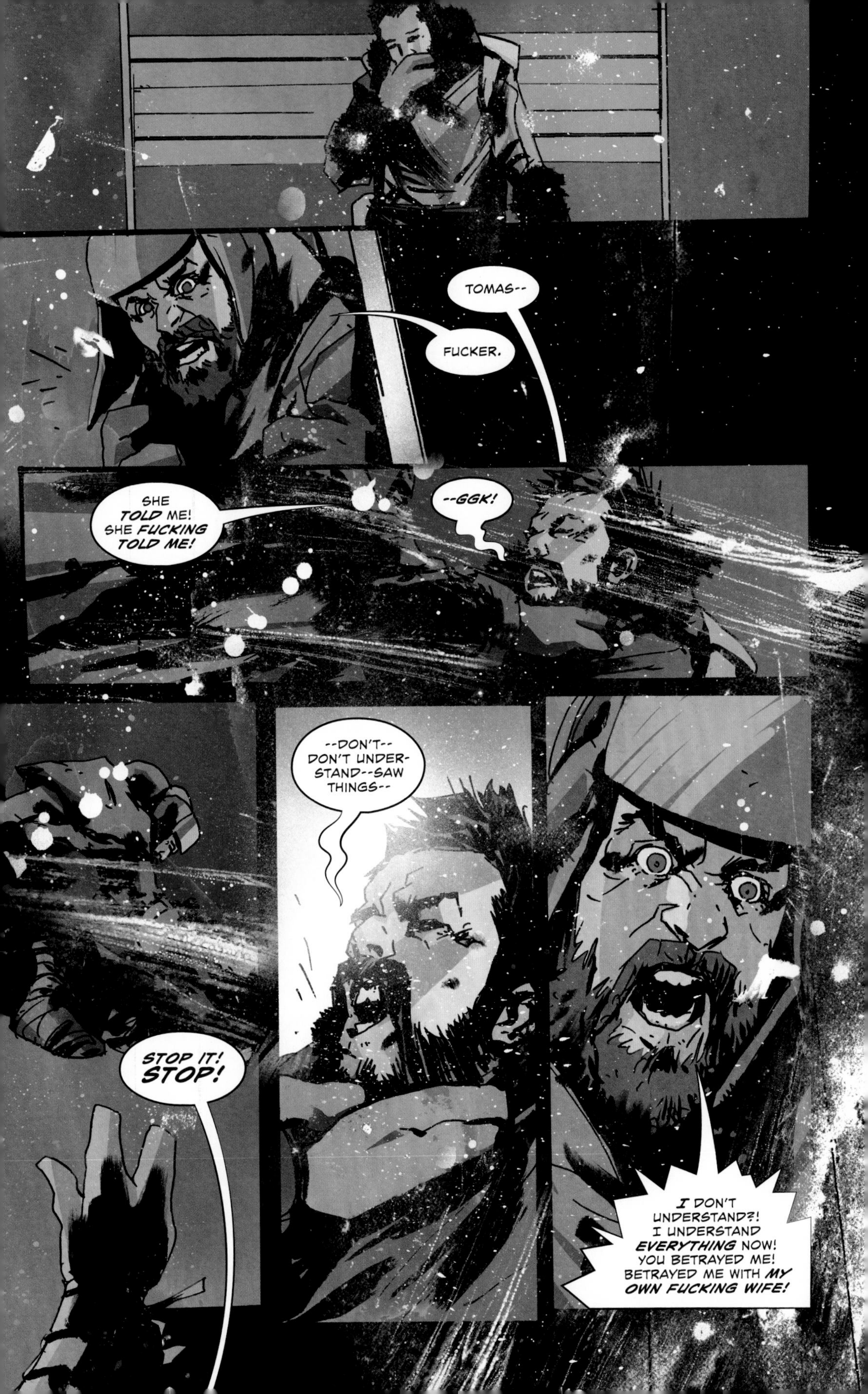
TOMAS--
FUCKER.
SHE TOLD ME! SHE FUCKING TOLD ME!
--GGK!
--DON'T-- DON'T UNDERSTAND--SAW THINGS--
STOP IT! STOP!
I DON'T UNDERSTAND?! I UNDERSTAND EVERYTHING NOW! YOU BETRAYED ME! BETRAYED ME WITH MY OWN FUCKING WIFE!

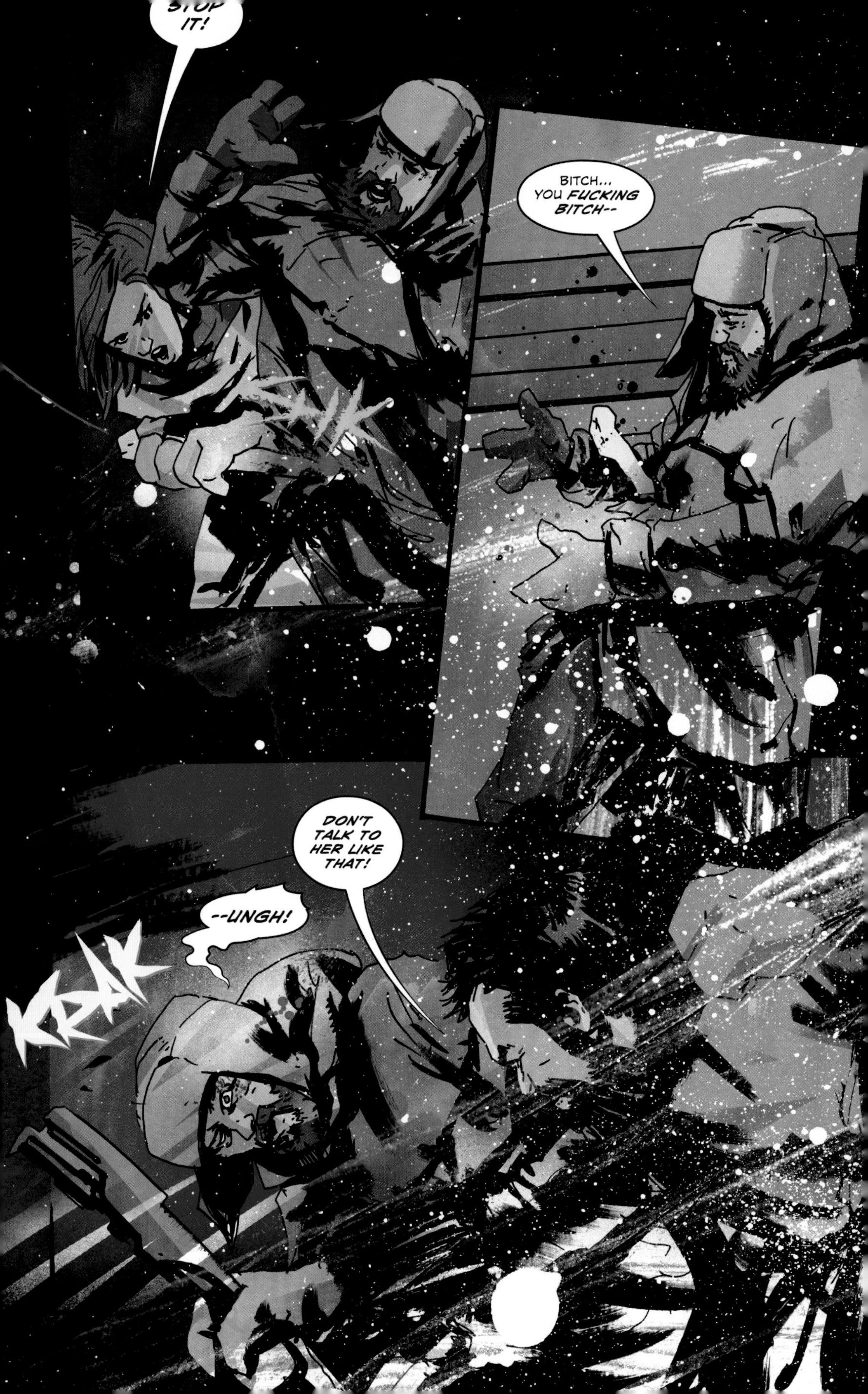
STOP IT!
BITCH... YOU FUCKING BITCH--
DON'T TALK TO HER LIKE THAT!
--UNGH!
KRAK

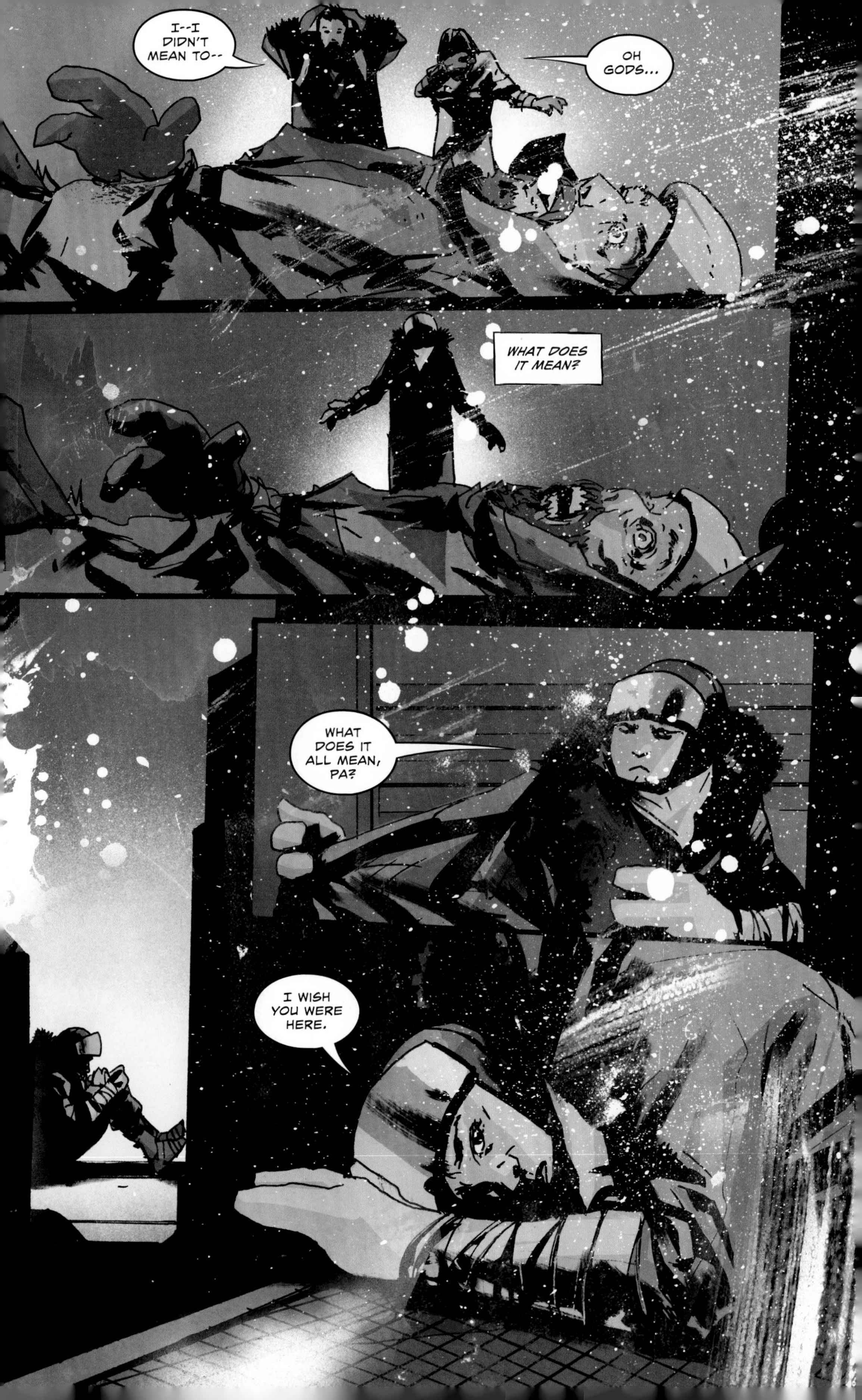
I--I DIDN'T MEAN TO--
OH GODS...
WHAT DOES IT MEAN?
WHAT DOES IT ALL MEAN, PA?
I WISH YOU WERE HERE.

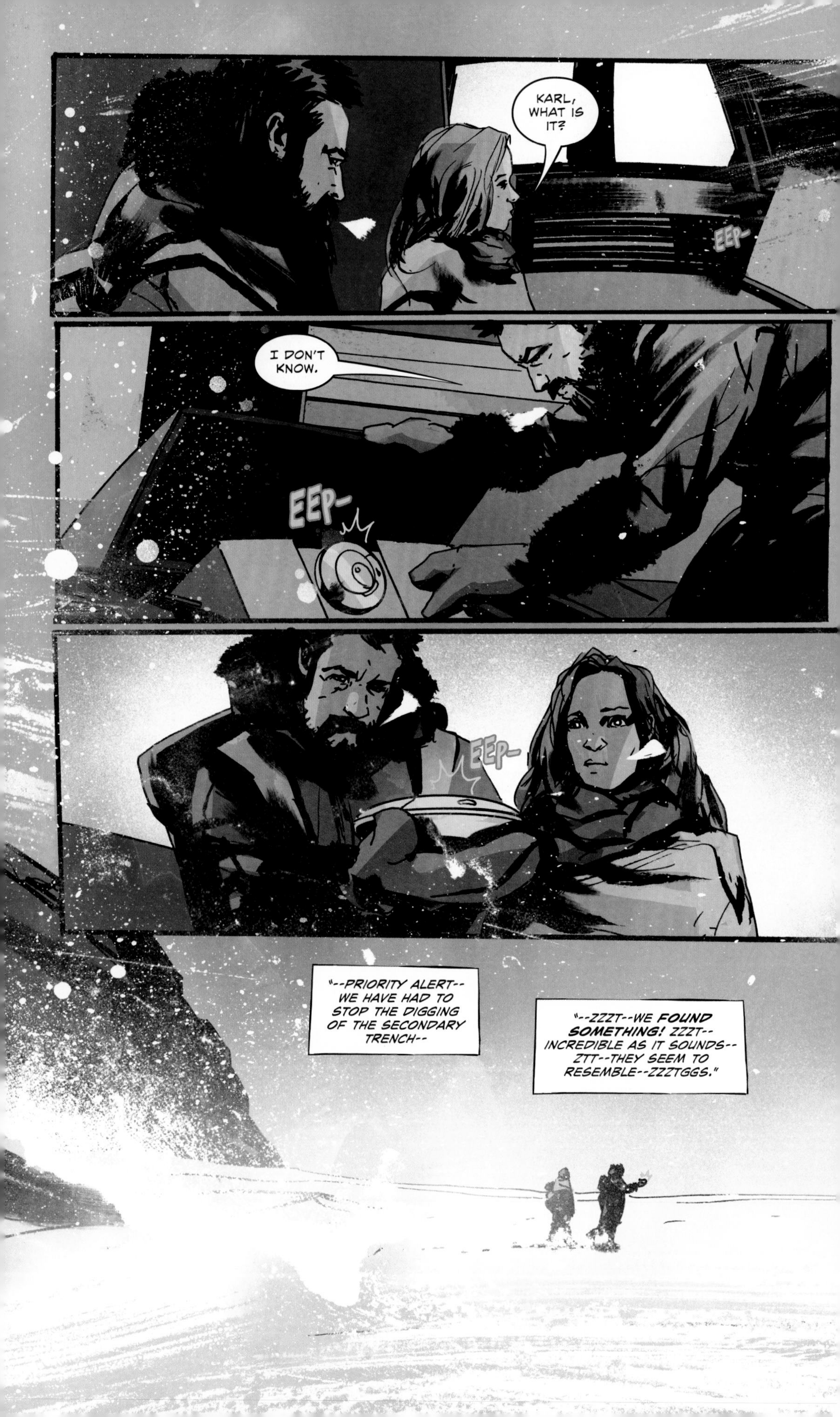
KARL, WHAT IS IT?
EEP-
I DON'T KNOW.
EEP-
EEP-
"--PRIORITY ALERT-- WE HAVE HAD TO STOP THE DIGGING OF THE SECONDARY TRENCH--
"--ZZZT--WE FOUND SOMETHING! ZZZT-- INCREDIBLE AS IT SOUNDS-- ZTT--THEY SEEM TO RESEMBLE--ZZZTGGS."

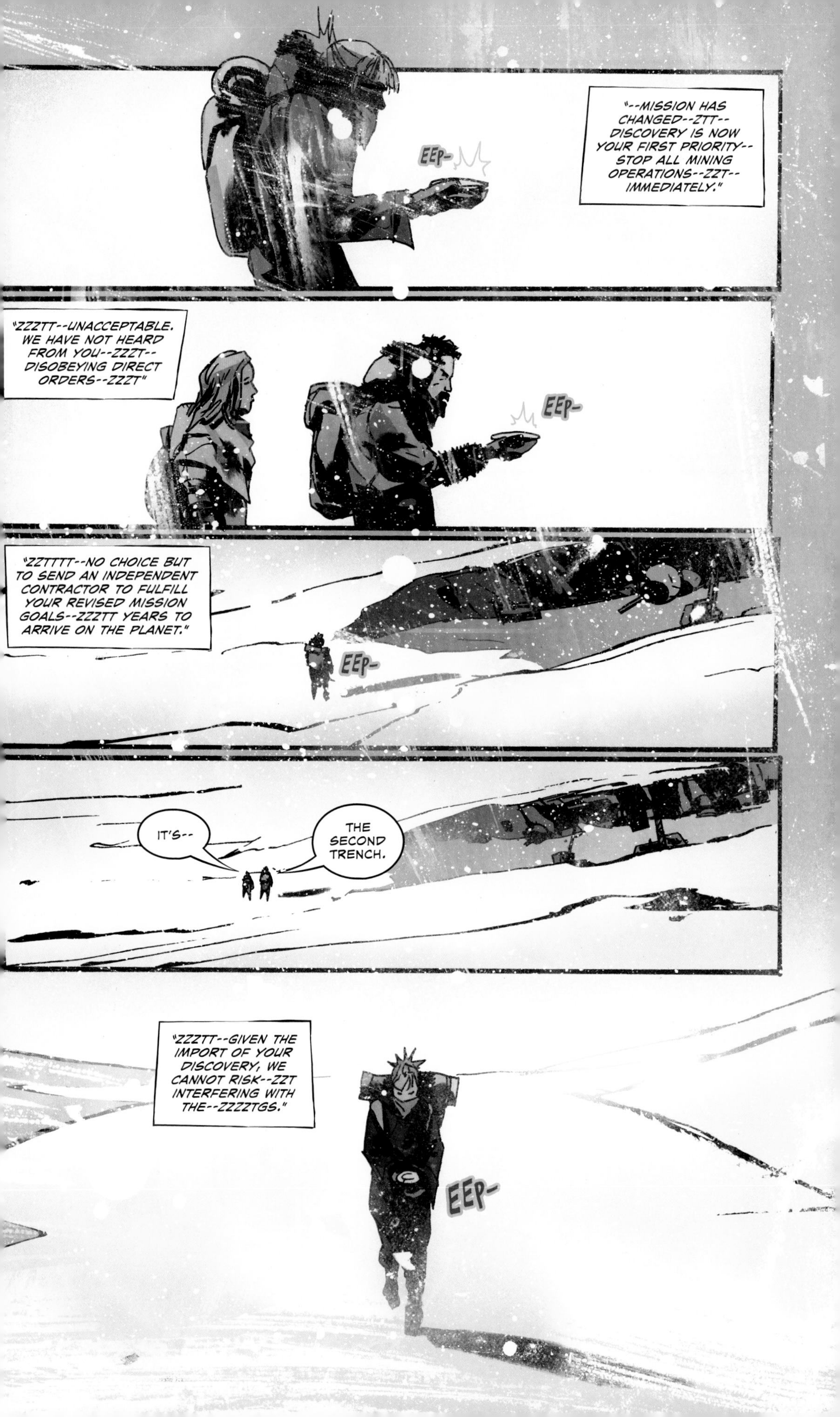
"--MISSION HAS CHANGED--ZTT--DISCOVERY IS NOW YOUR FIRST PRIORITY--STOP ALL MINING OPERATIONS--ZZT--IMMEDIATELY."
EEP-
"ZZZTT--UNACCEPTABLE. WE HAVE NOT HEARD FROM YOU--ZZZT--DISOBEYING DIRECT ORDERS--ZZZT"
EEP-
"ZZTTTT--NO CHOICE BUT TO SEND AN INDEPENDENT CONTRACTOR TO FULFILL YOUR REVISED MISSION GOALS--ZZZTT YEARS TO ARRIVE ON THE PLANET."
EEP-
IT'S--
THE SECOND TRENCH.
"ZZZTT--GIVEN THE IMPORT OF YOUR DISCOVERY, WE CANNOT RISK--ZZT INTERFERING WITH THE--ZZZZTGS."
EEP-

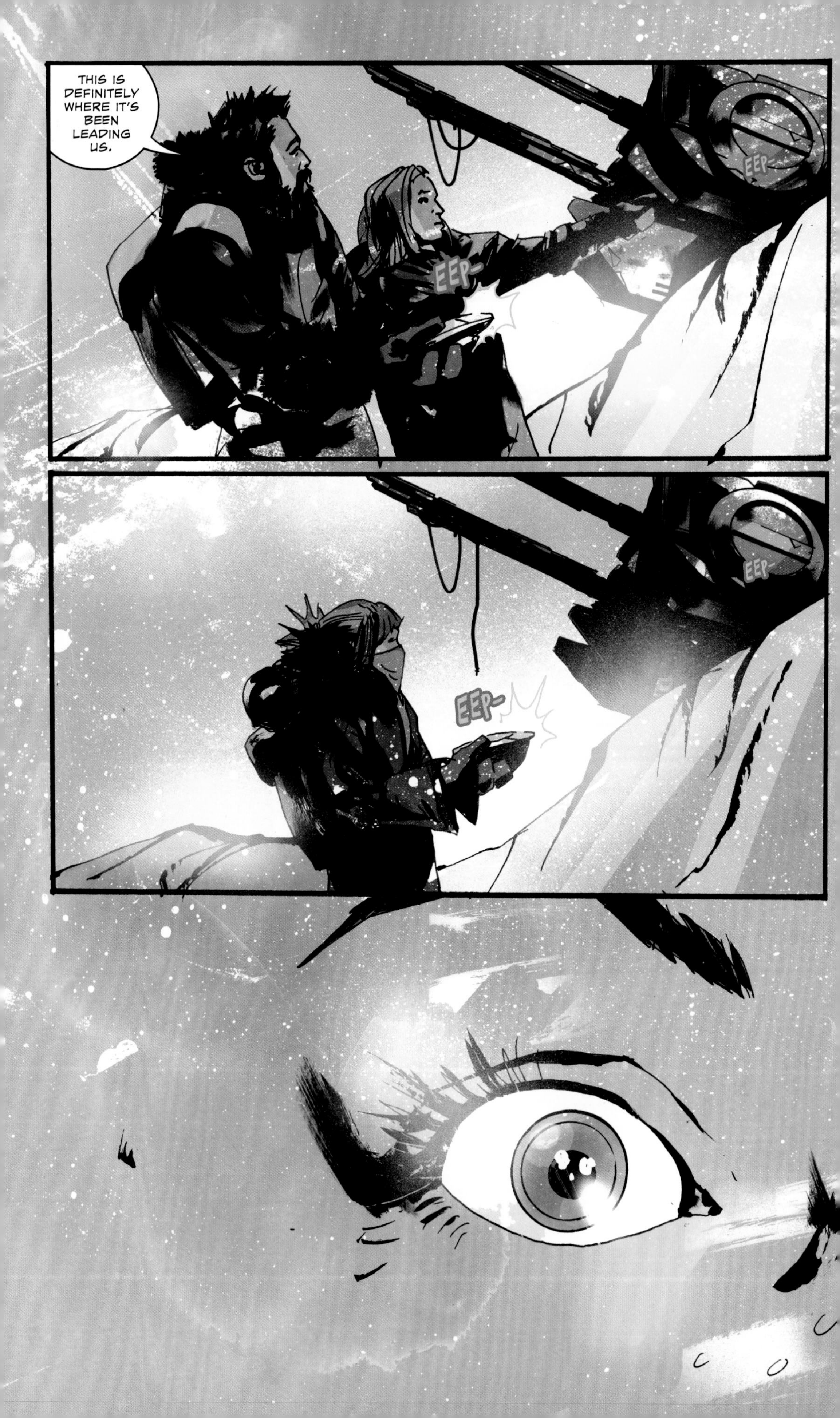
THIS IS DEFINITELY WHERE IT'S BEEN LEADING US.
EEP-
EEP-
EEP-
EEP-

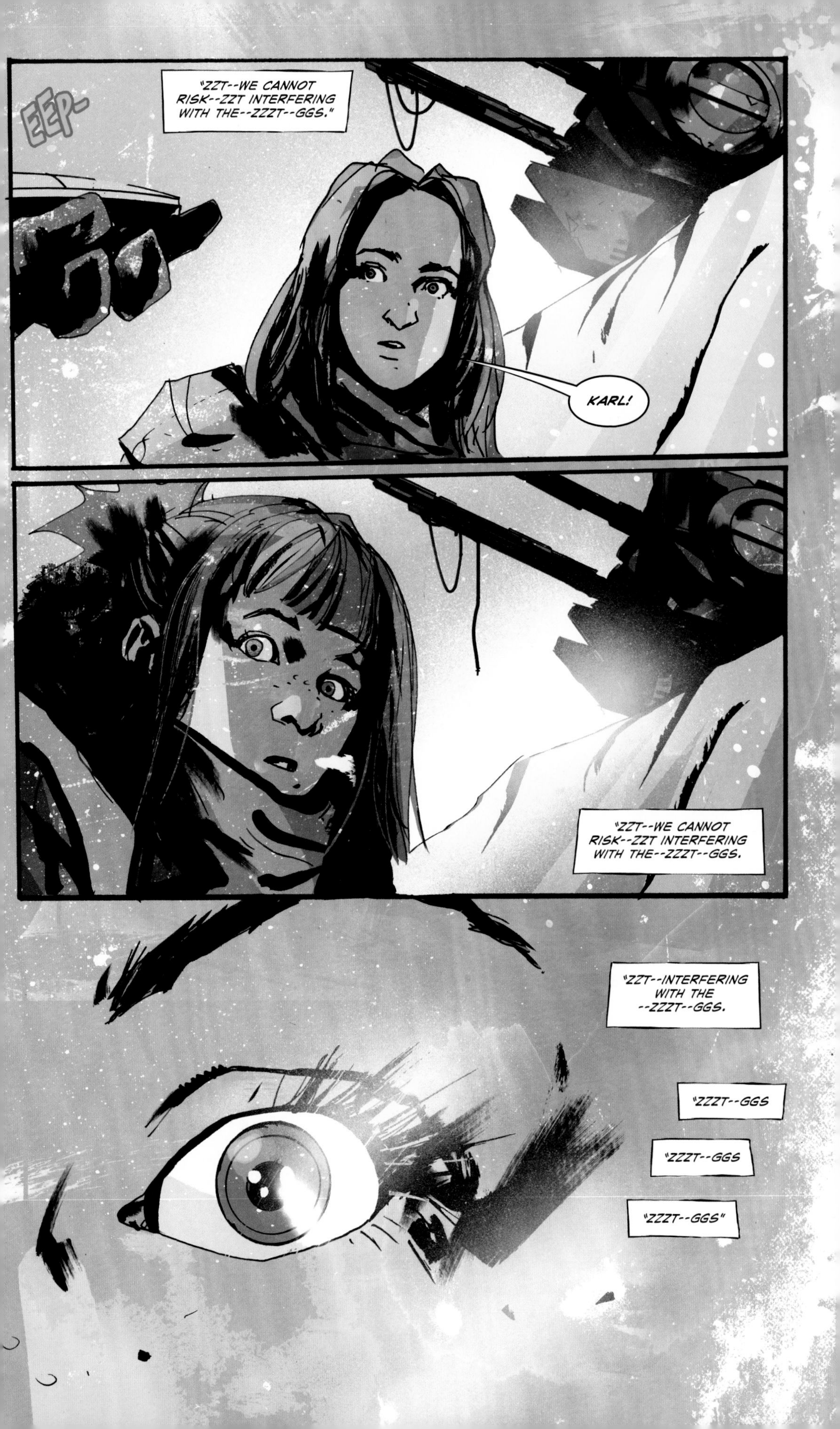
EEP-
"ZZT--WE CANNOT RISK--ZZT INTERFERING WITH THE--ZZZT--GGS."
KARL!
"ZZT--WE CANNOT RISK--ZZT INTERFERING WITH THE--ZZZT--GGS.
"ZZT--INTERFERING WITH THE --ZZZT--GGS.
"ZZZT--GGS
"ZZZT--GGS
"ZZZT--GGS"

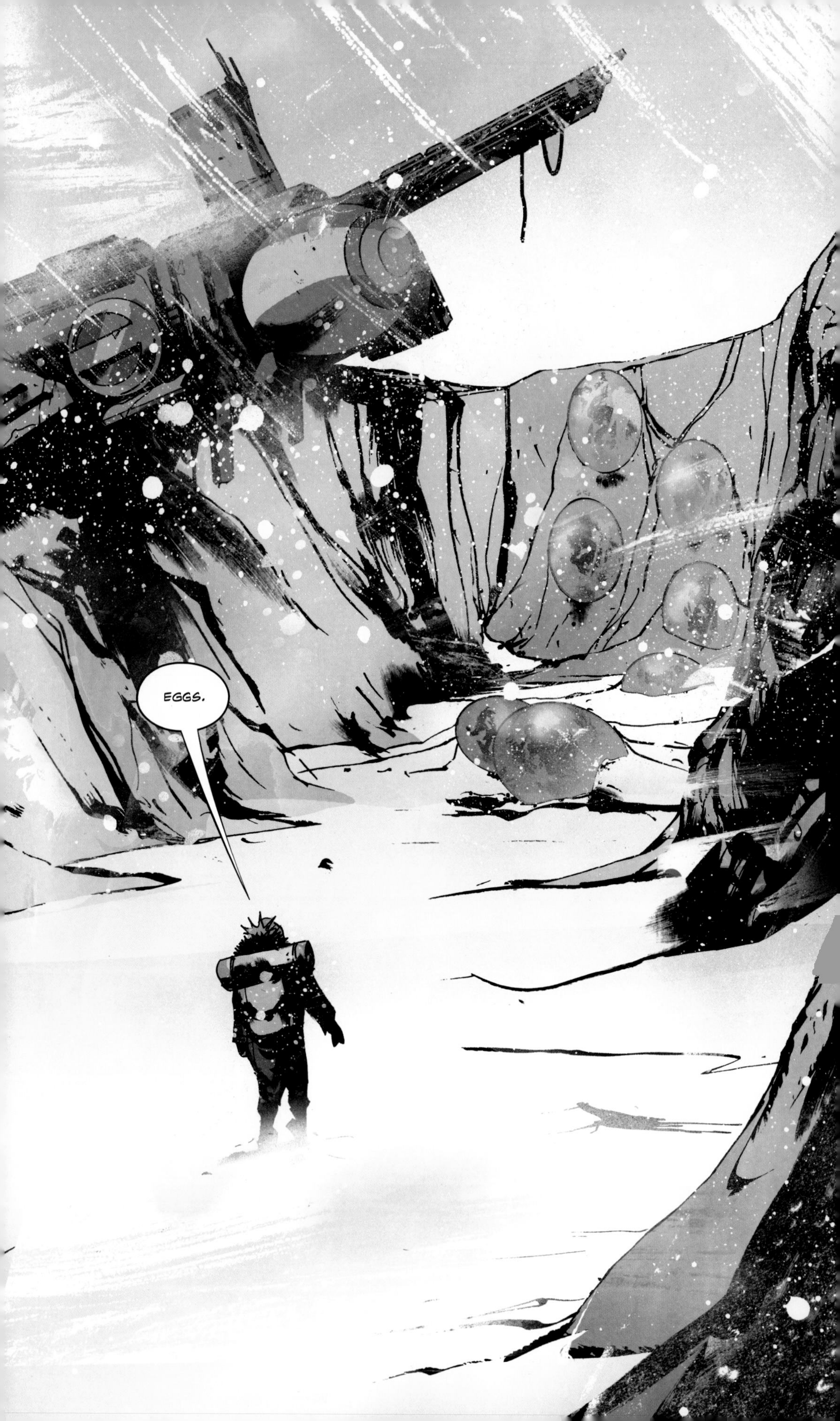
EGGS.

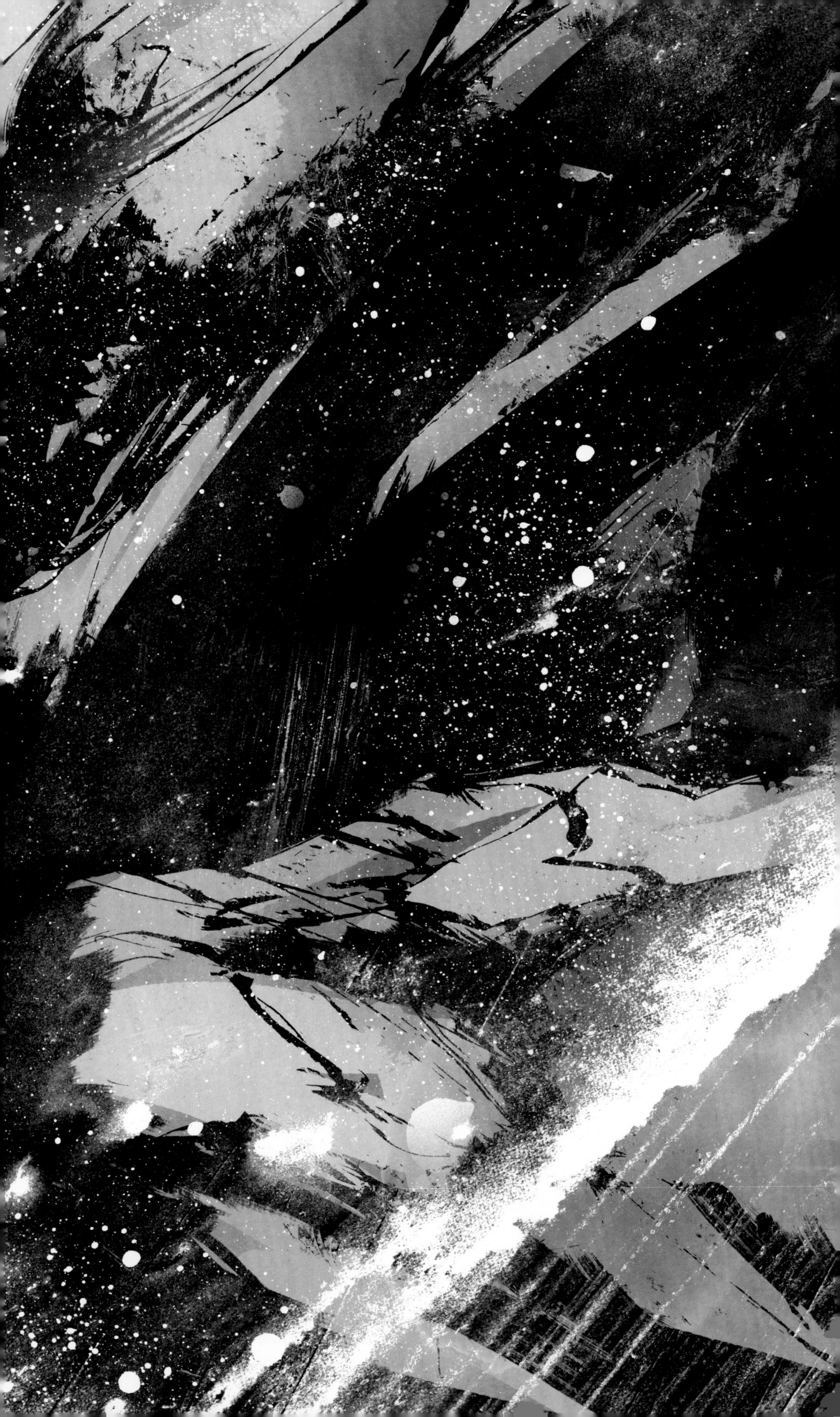

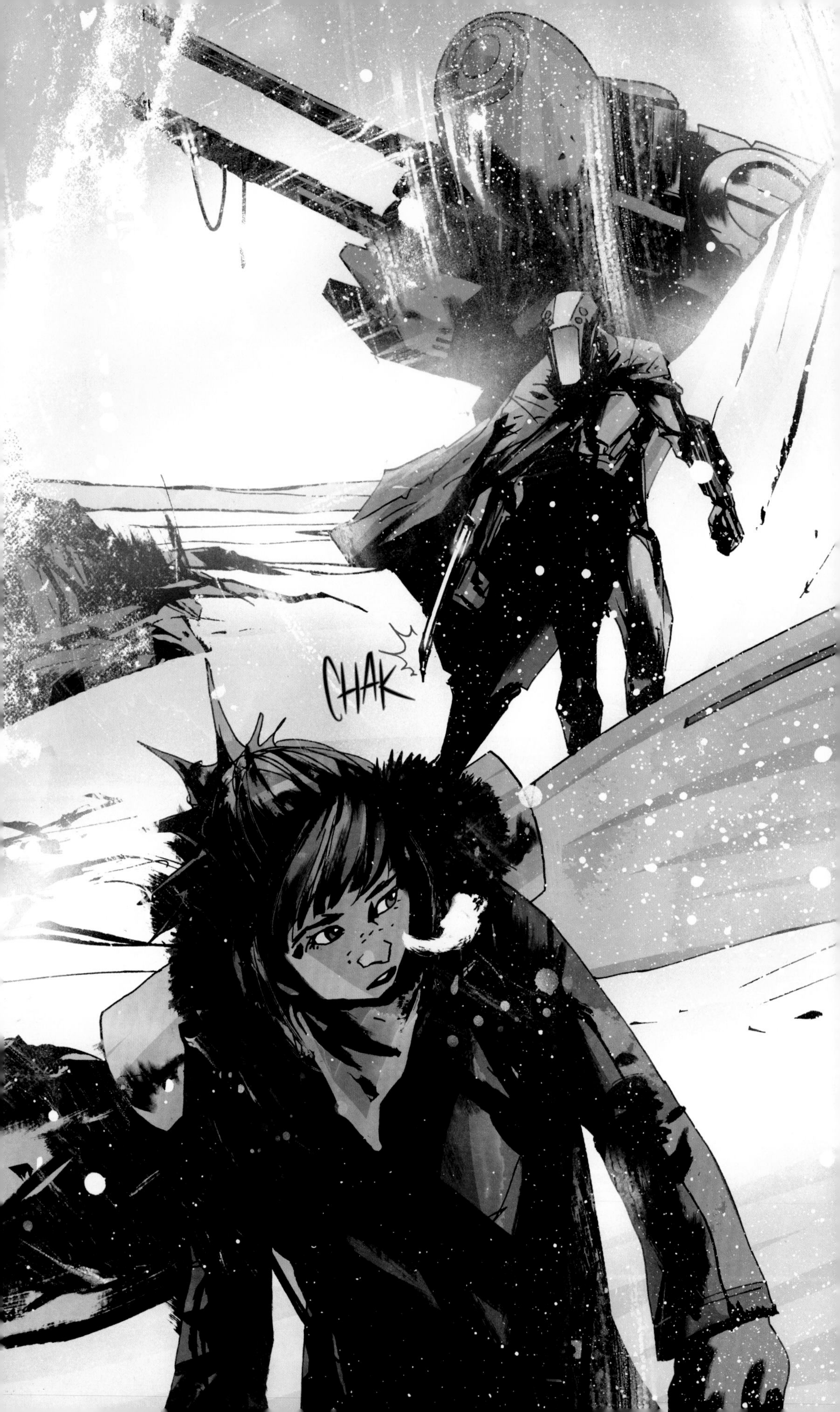
CHAK

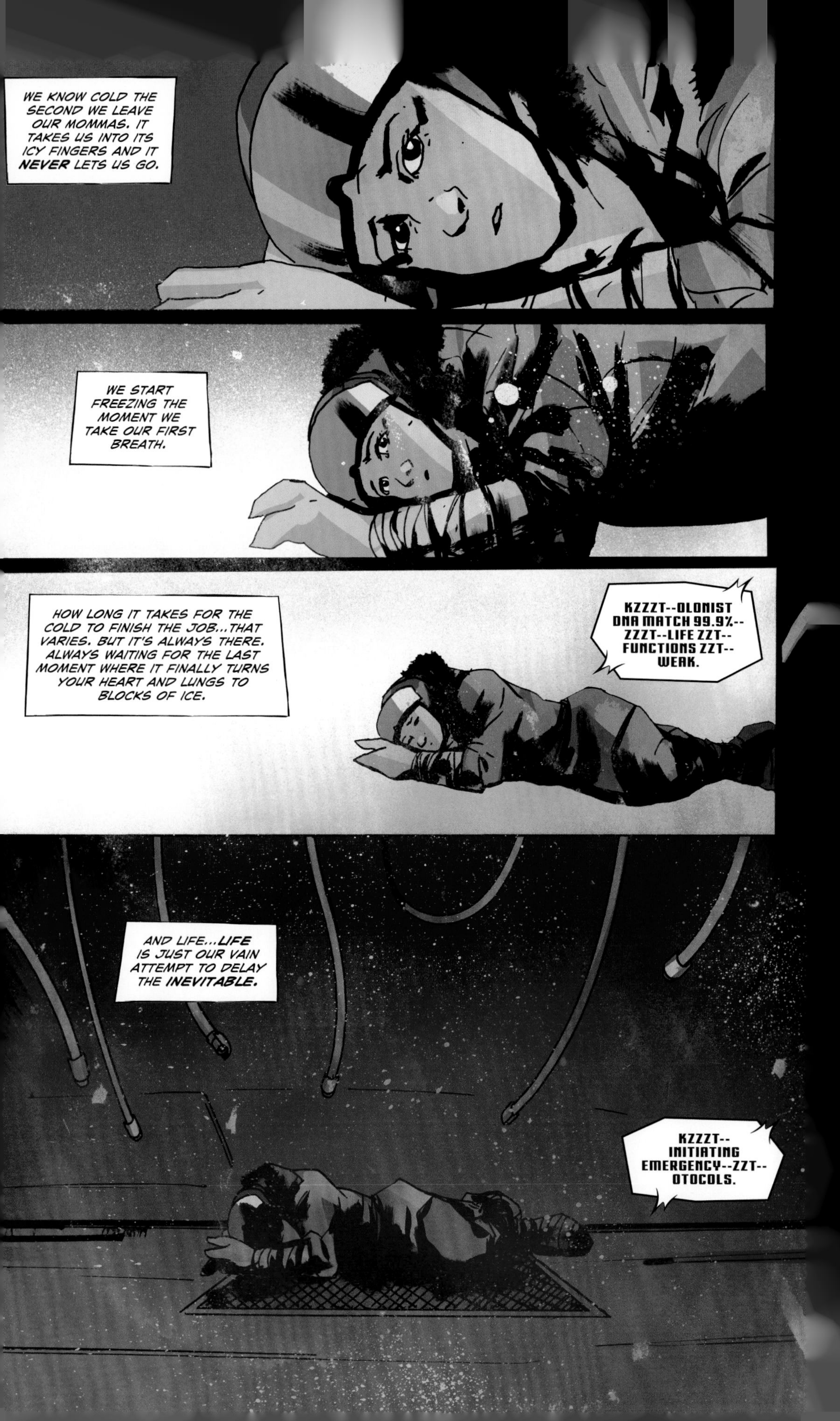
WE KNOW COLD THE SECOND WE LEAVE OUR MOMMAS. IT TAKES US INTO ITS ICY FINGERS AND IT **NEVER** LETS US GO.
WE START FREEZING THE MOMENT WE TAKE OUR FIRST BREATH.
HOW LONG IT TAKES FOR THE COLD TO FINISH THE JOB...THAT VARIES. BUT IT'S ALWAYS THERE. ALWAYS WAITING FOR THE LAST MOMENT WHERE IT FINALLY TURNS YOUR HEART AND LUNGS TO BLOCKS OF ICE.
KZZZT--OLONIST DNA MATCH 99.9%--ZZZT--LIFE ZZT--FUNCTIONS ZZT--WEAK.
AND LIFE...**LIFE** IS JUST OUR VAIN ATTEMPT TO DELAY THE **INEVITABLE.**
KZZZT--INITIATING EMERGENCY--ZZT--OTOCOLS.

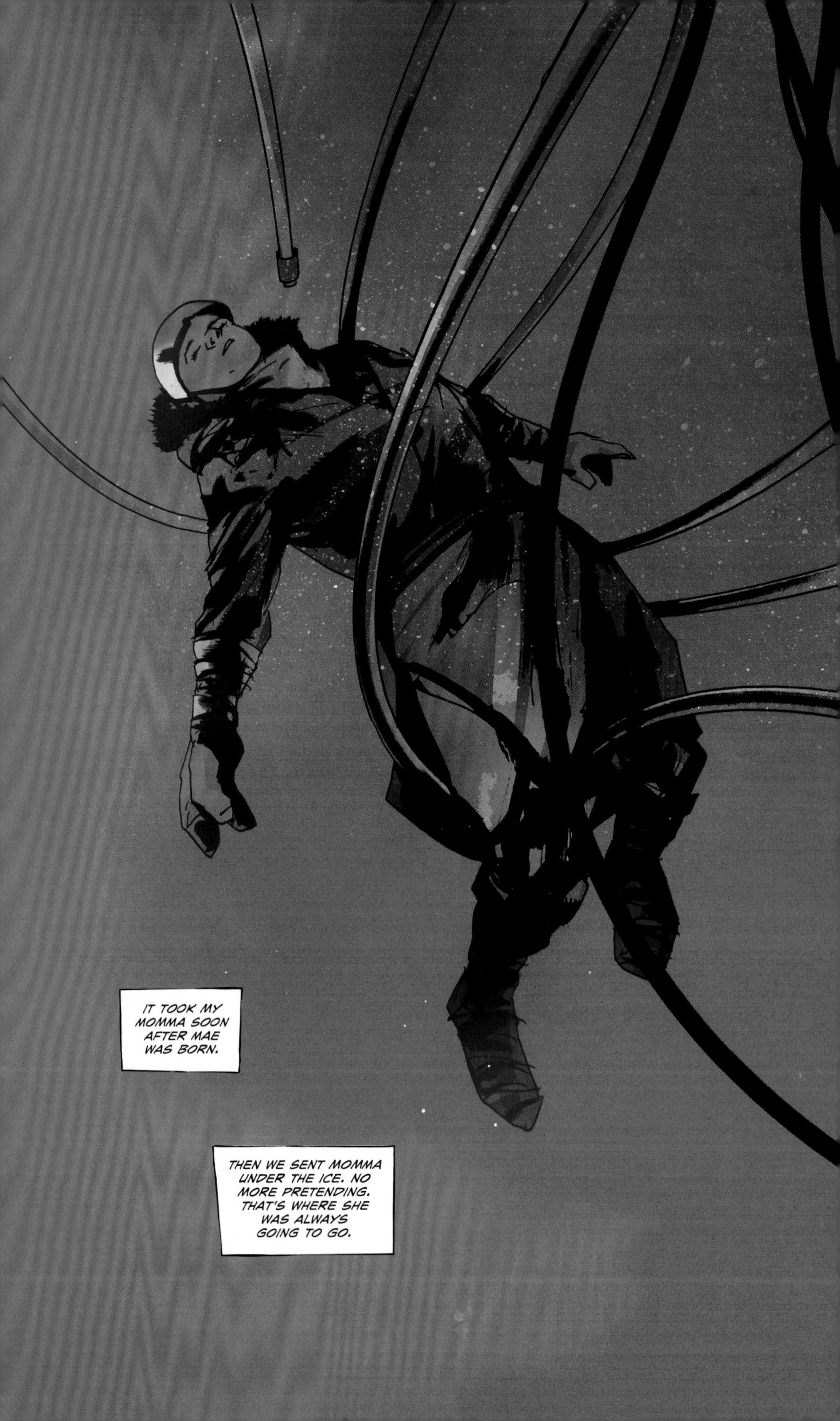
IT TOOK MY MOMMA SOON AFTER MAE WAS BORN.
THEN WE SENT MOMMA UNDER THE ICE. NO MORE PRETENDING. THAT'S WHERE SHE WAS ALWAYS GOING TO GO.

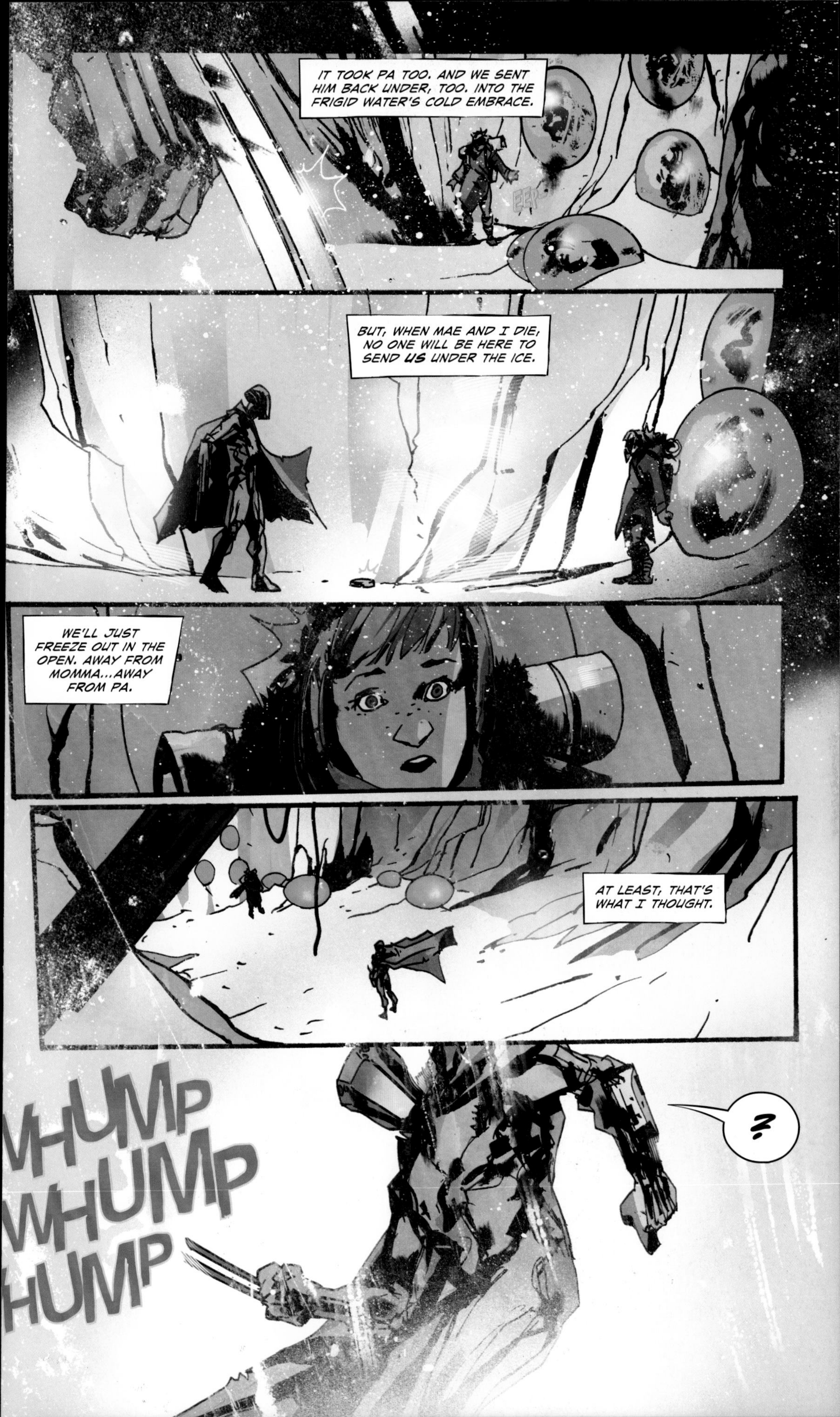
IT TOOK PA TOO. AND WE SENT HIM BACK UNDER, TOO. INTO THE FRIGID WATER'S COLD EMBRACE.
EEP
BUT, WHEN MAE AND I DIE, NO ONE WILL BE HERE TO SEND US UNDER THE ICE.
WE'LL JUST FREEZE OUT IN THE OPEN. AWAY FROM MOMMA...AWAY FROM PA.
AT LEAST, THAT'S WHAT I THOUGHT.
HUMP
WHUMP
HUMP
?

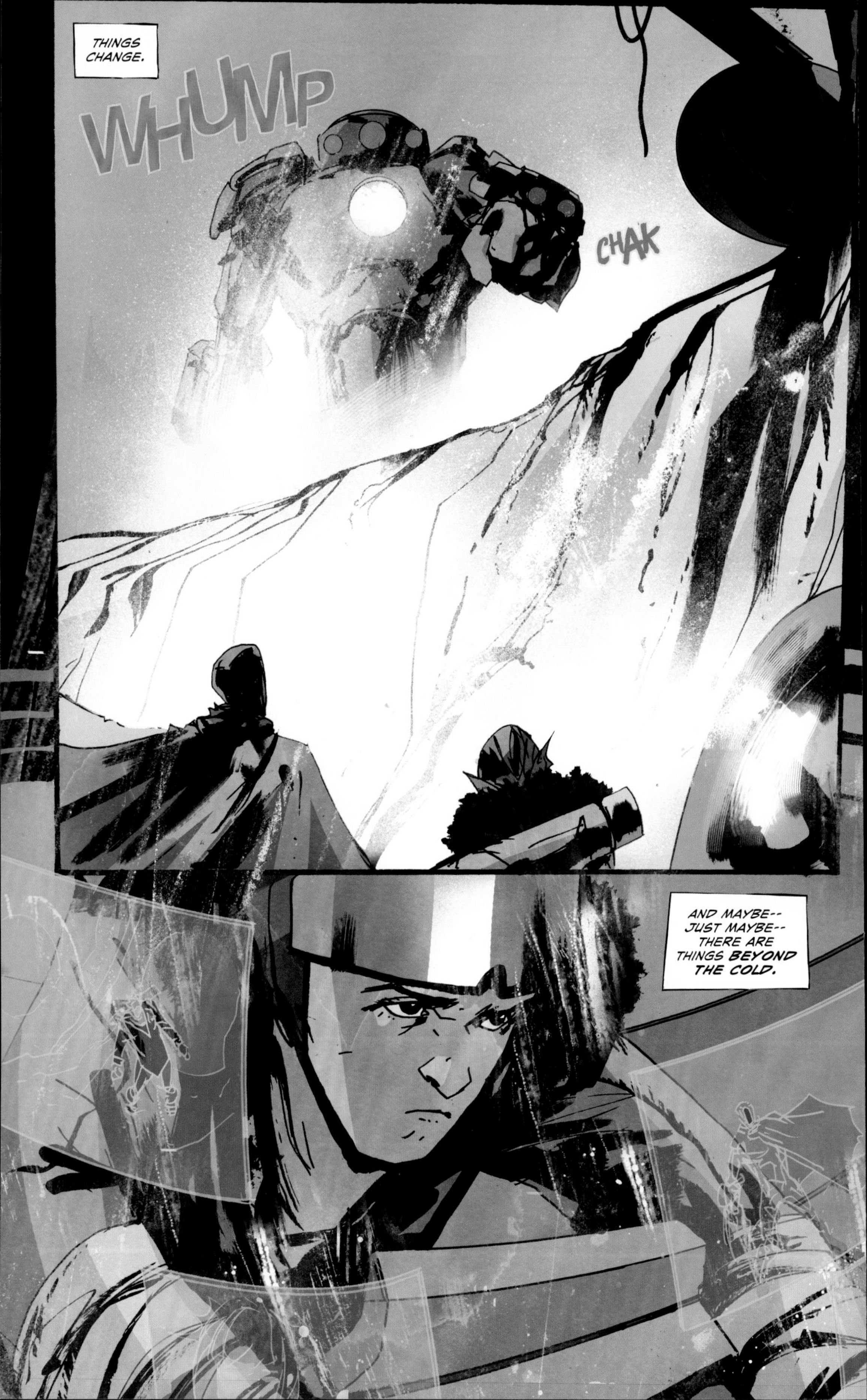
THINGS CHANGE.
WHUMP
CHAK
AND MAYBE-- JUST MAYBE-- THERE ARE THINGS **BEYOND THE COLD.**

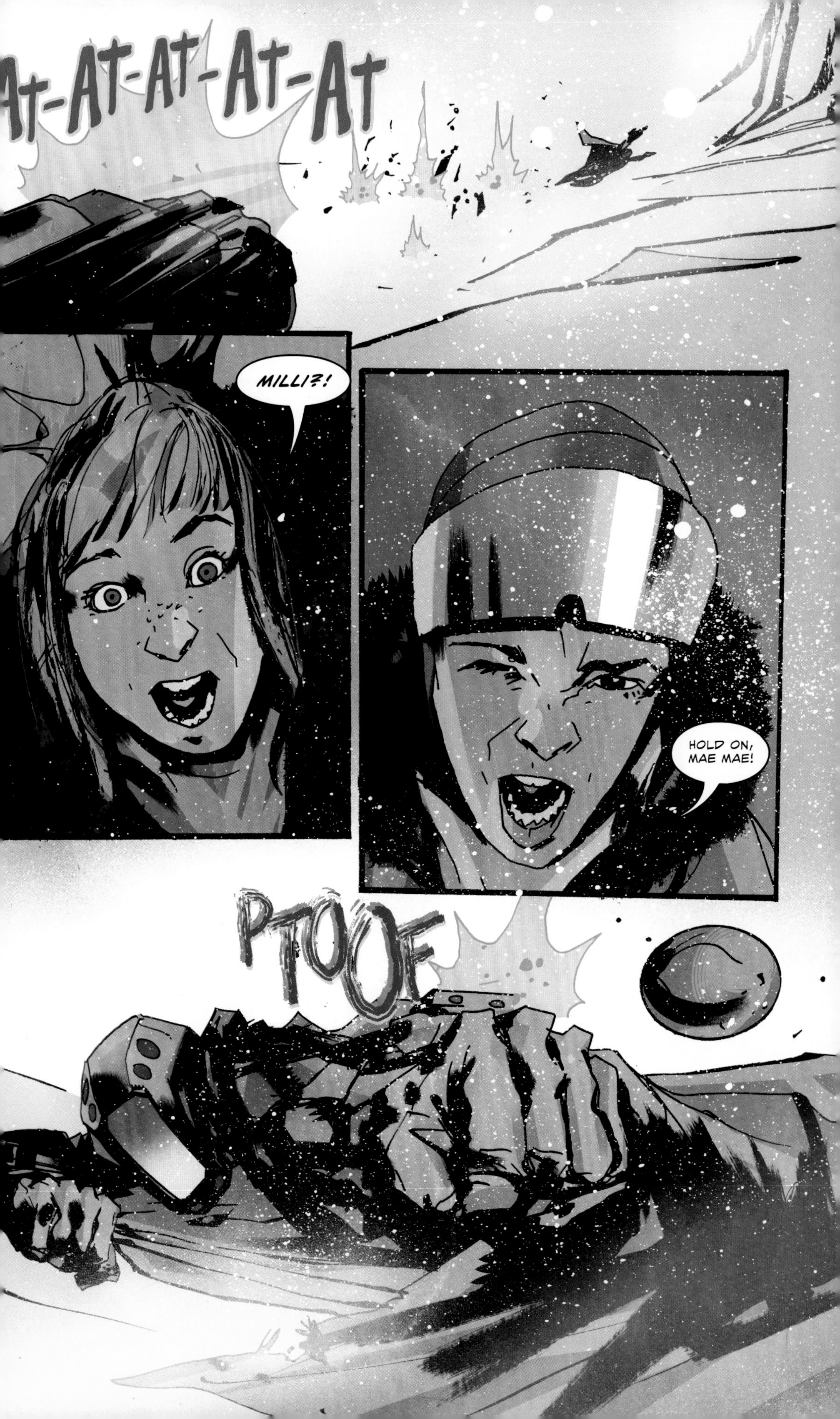
AT-AT-AT-AT-AT
MILLI?!
HOLD ON, MAE MAE!
PTOOF

THOOOM

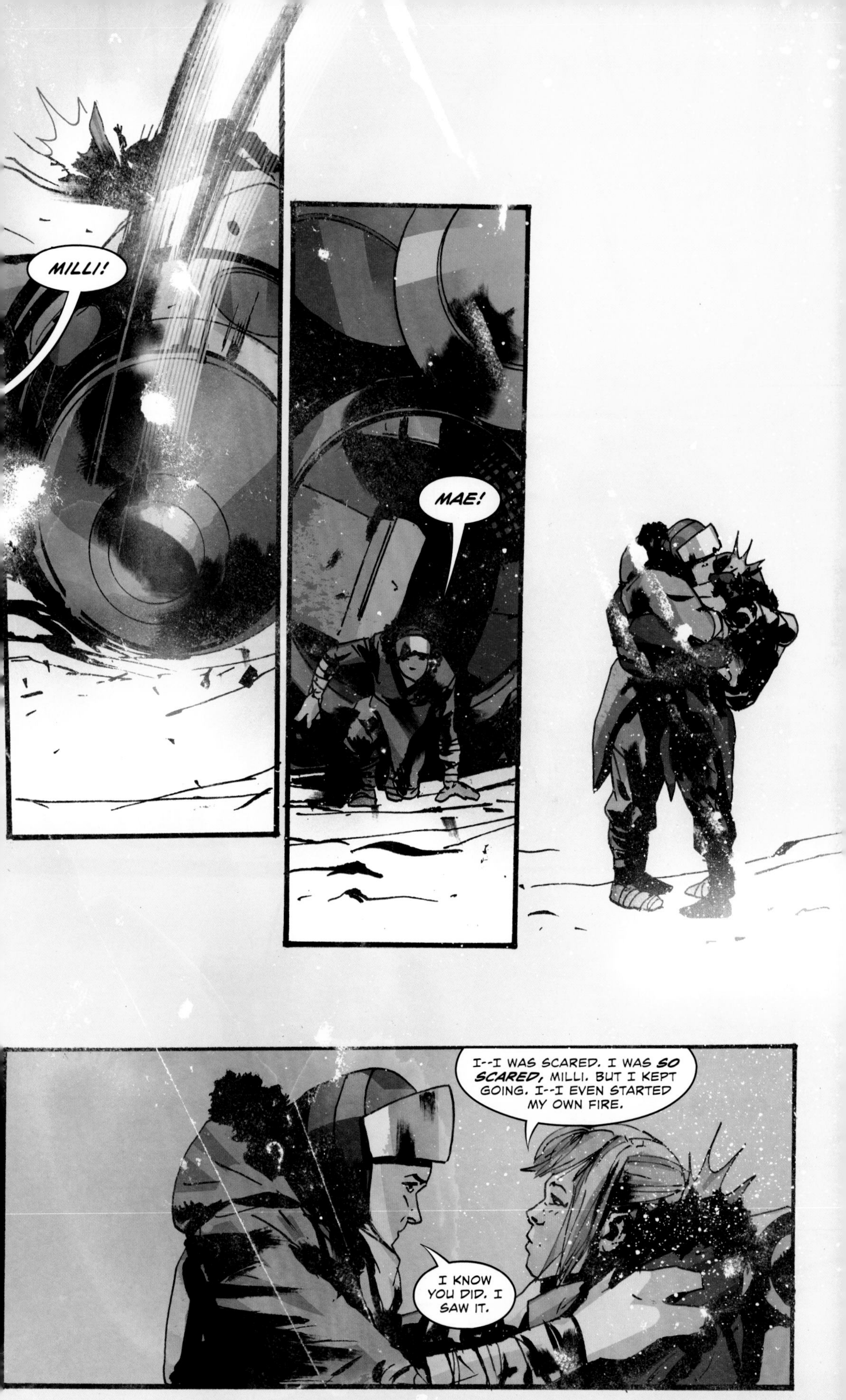
MILLI!
MAE!
I--I WAS SCARED. I WAS SO SCARED, MILLI. BUT I KEPT GOING. I--I EVEN STARTED MY OWN FIRE.
I KNOW YOU DID. I SAW IT.

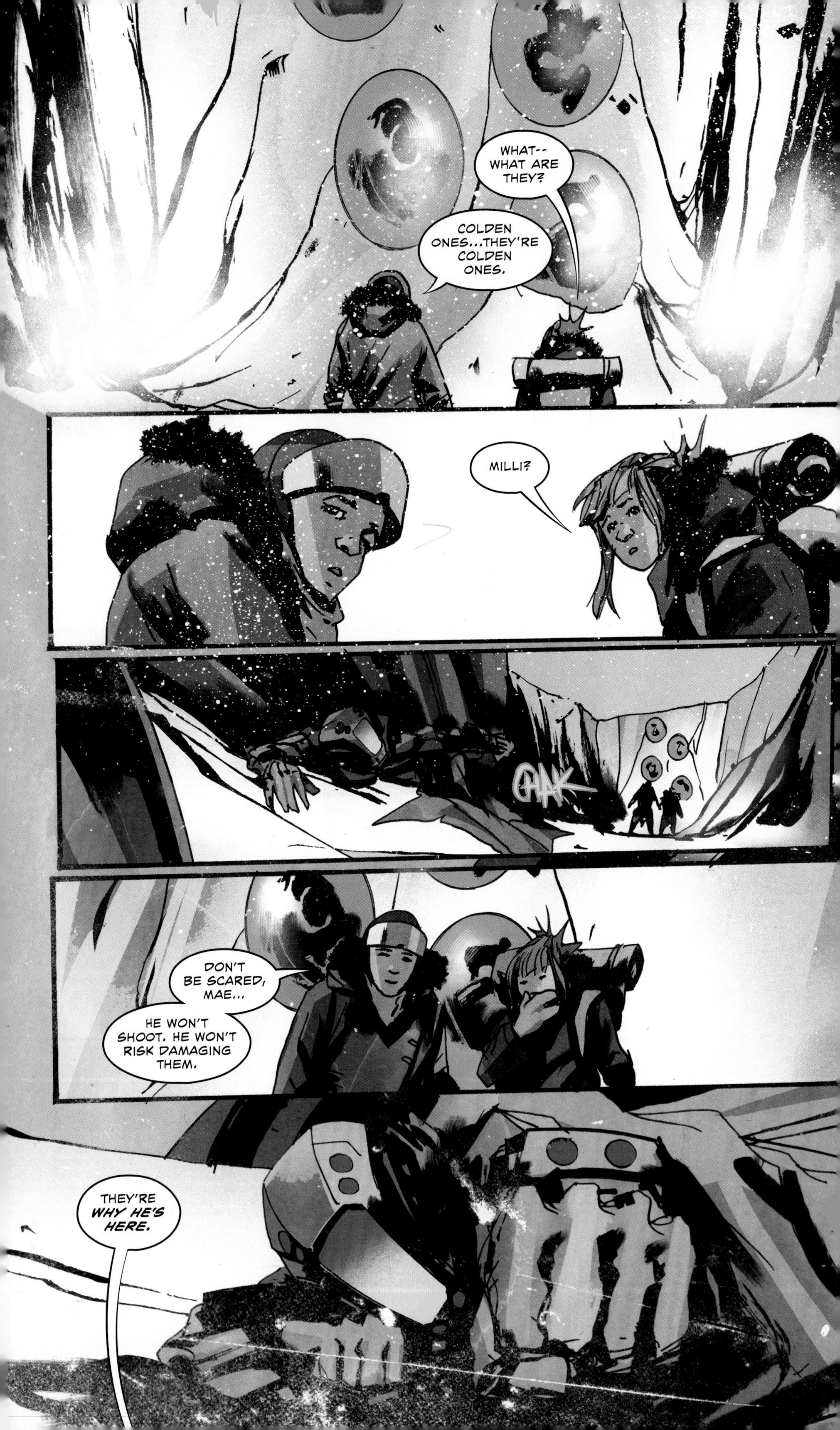
WHAT--
WHAT ARE THEY?
COLDEN ONES...THEY'RE COLDEN ONES.
MILLI?
CHAK
DON'T BE SCARED, MAE...
HE WON'T SHOOT. HE WON'T RISK DAMAGING THEM.
THEY'RE *WHY HE'S HERE.*

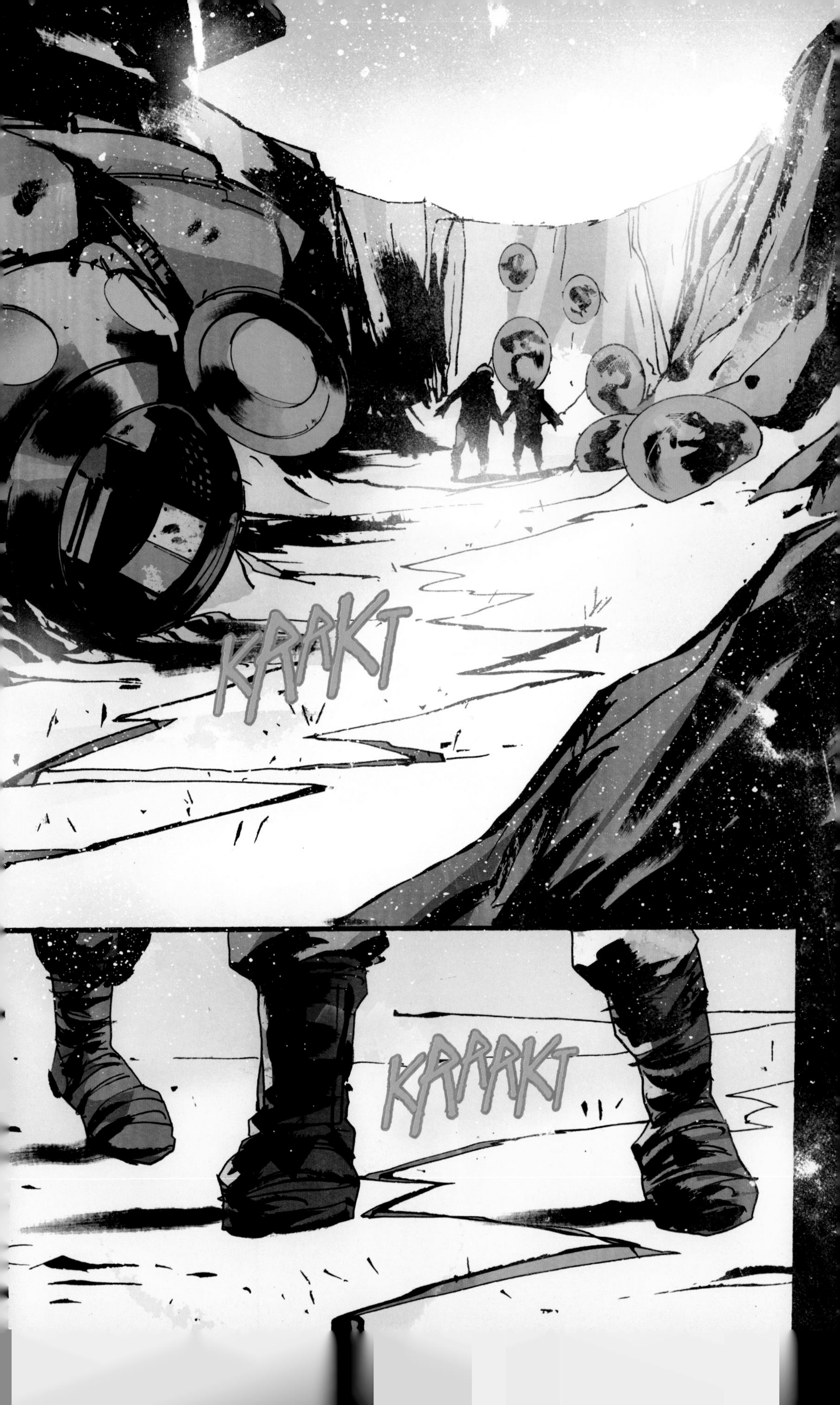
KRRKT
KRRRKT

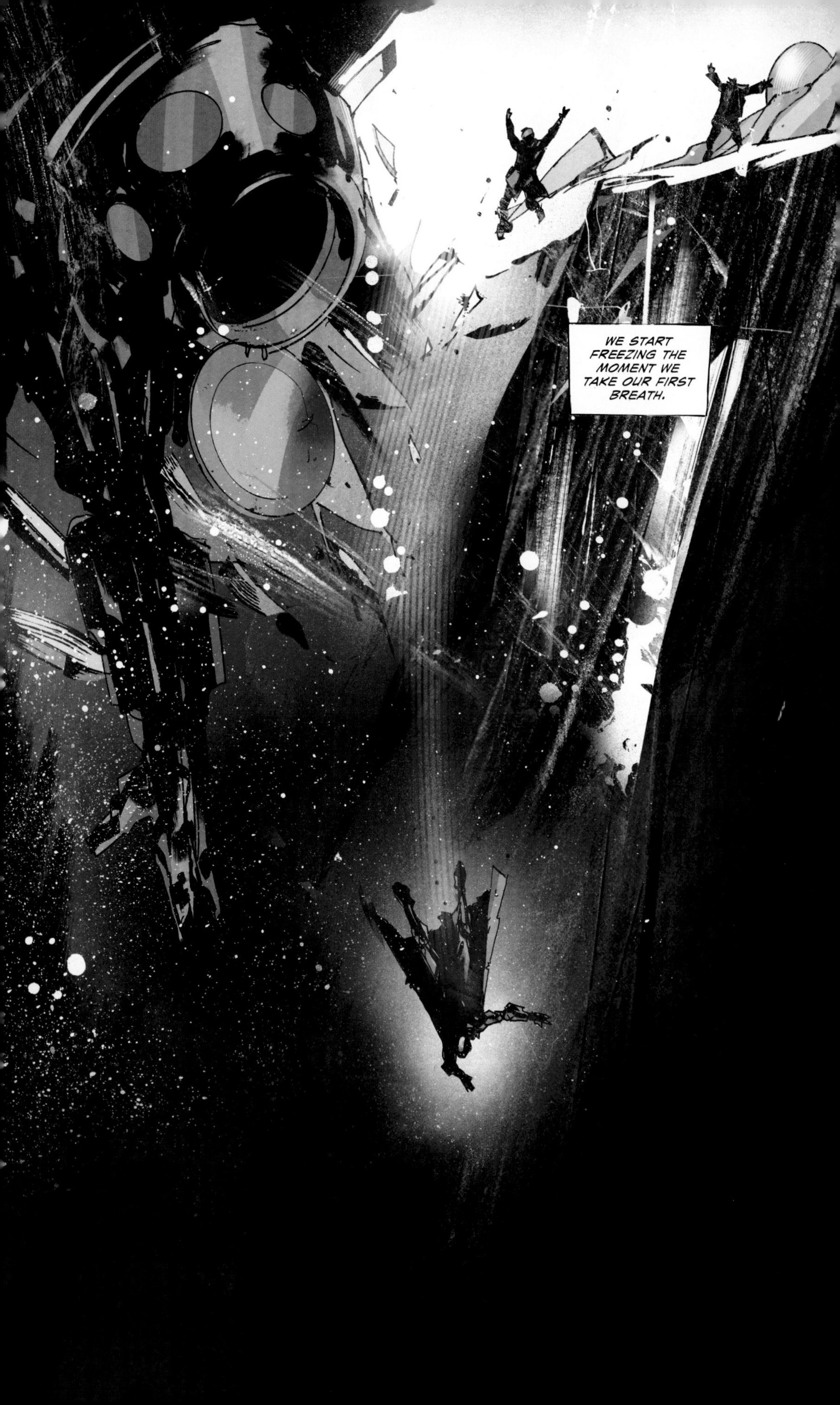
WE START FREEZING THE MOMENT WE TAKE OUR FIRST BREATH.

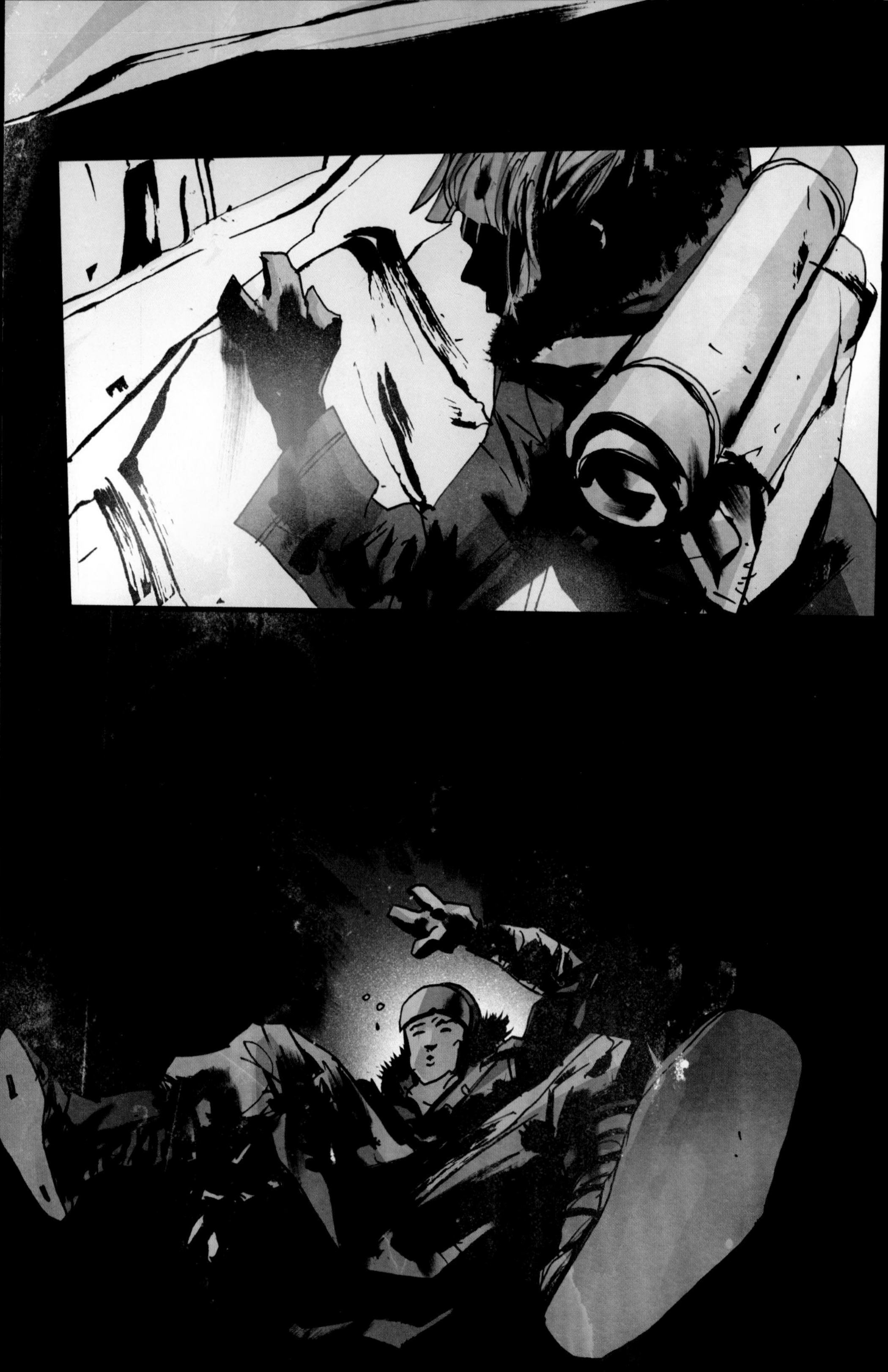

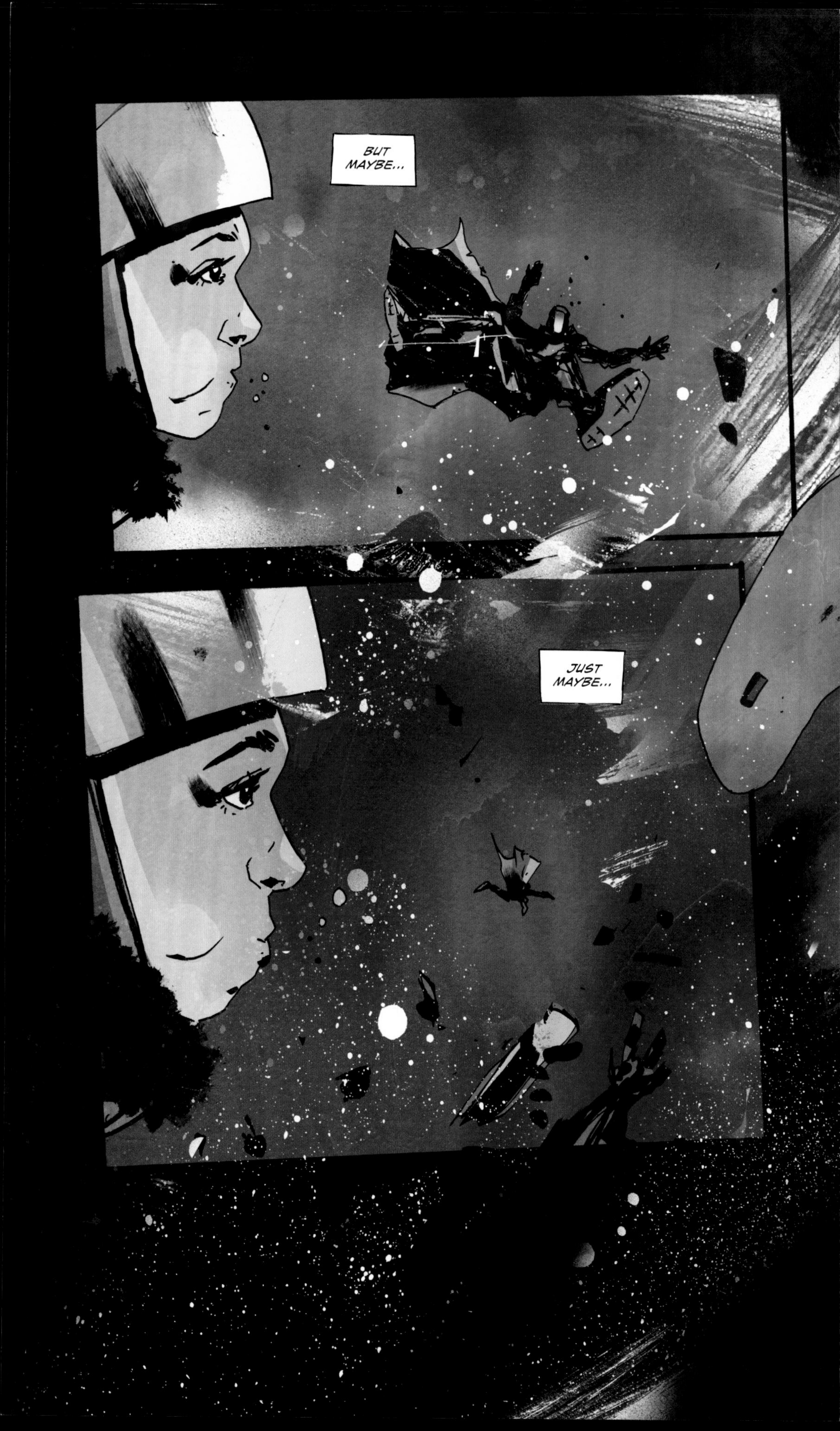
BUT MAYBE...
JUST MAYBE...

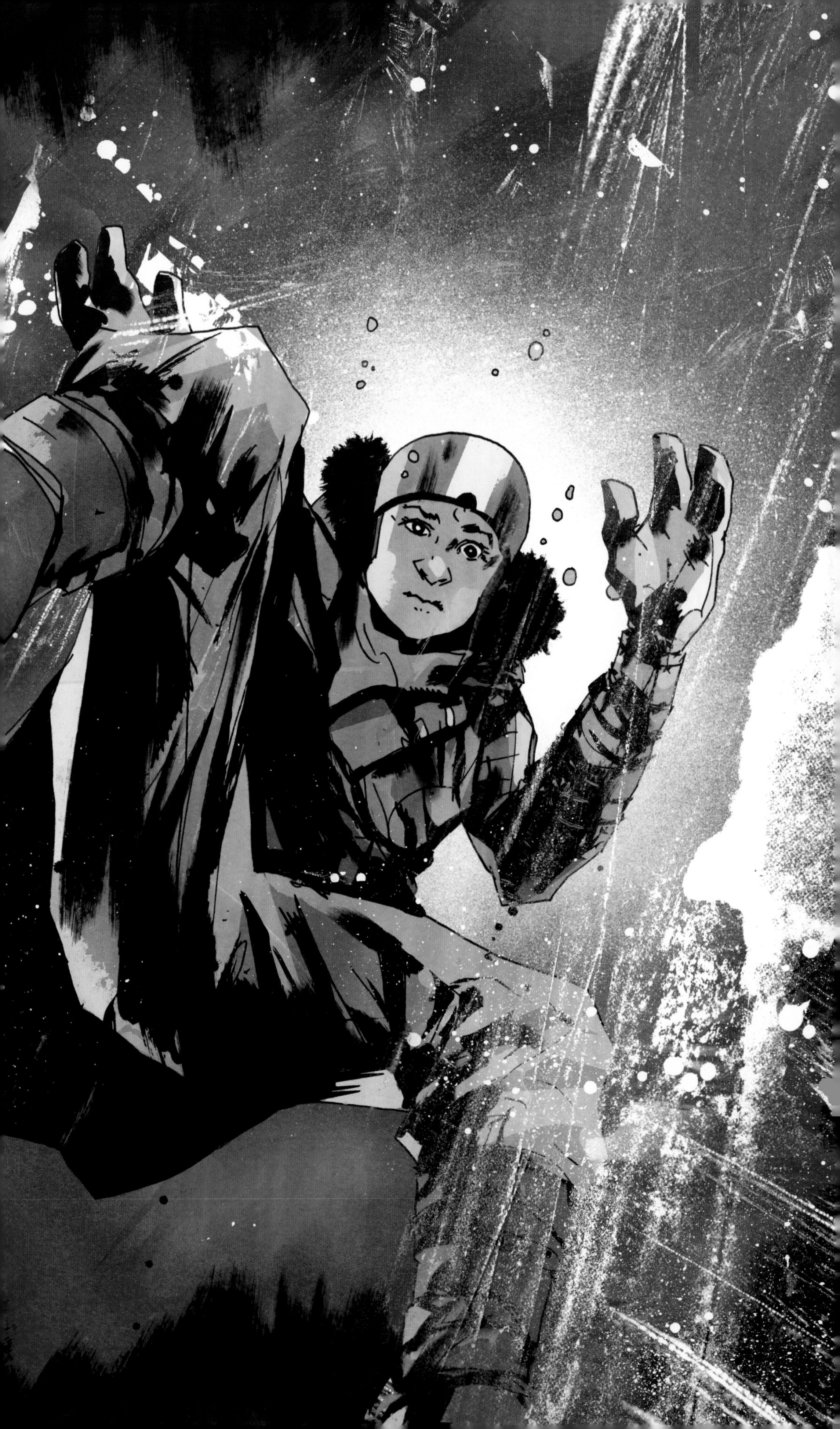

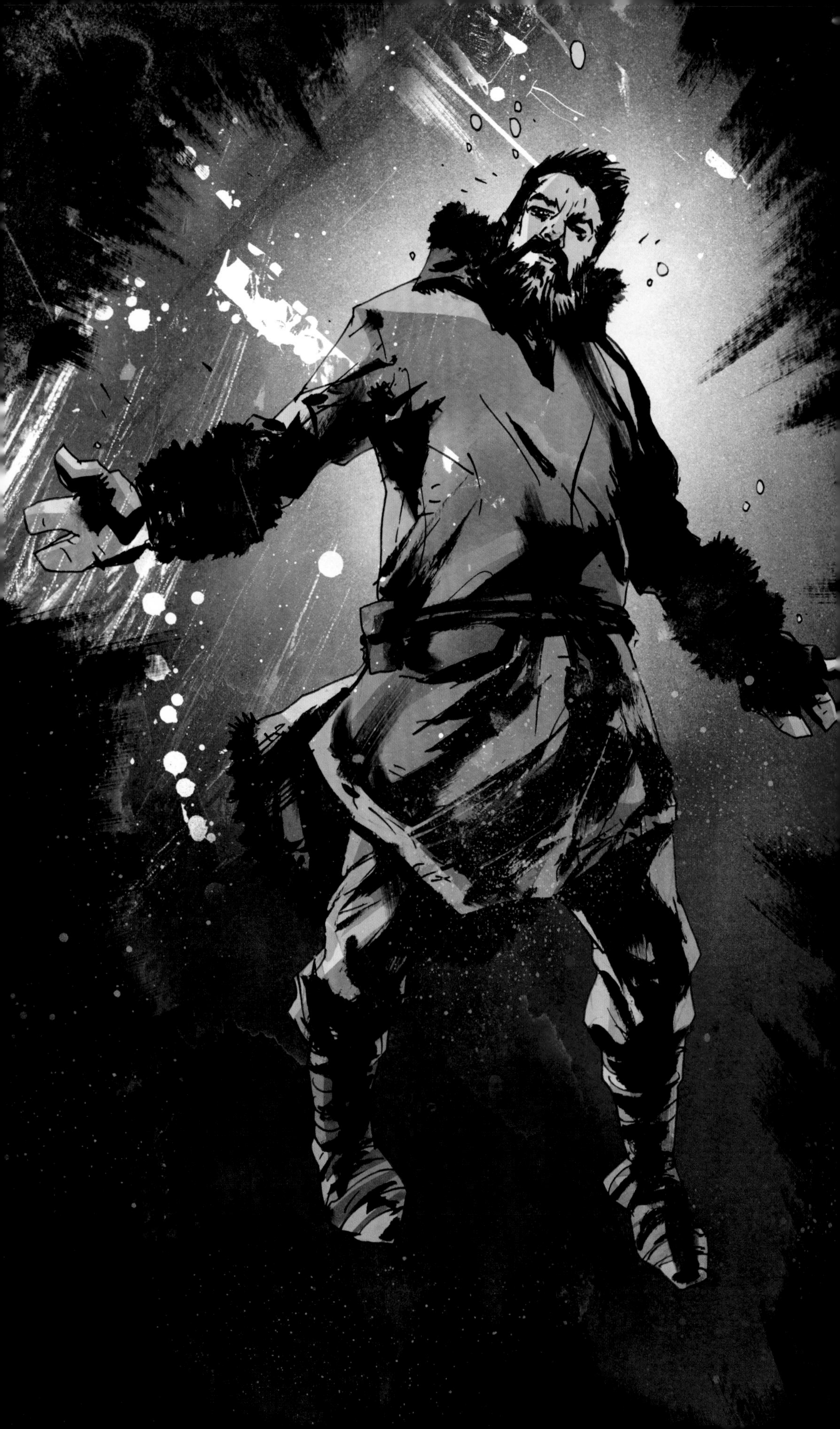

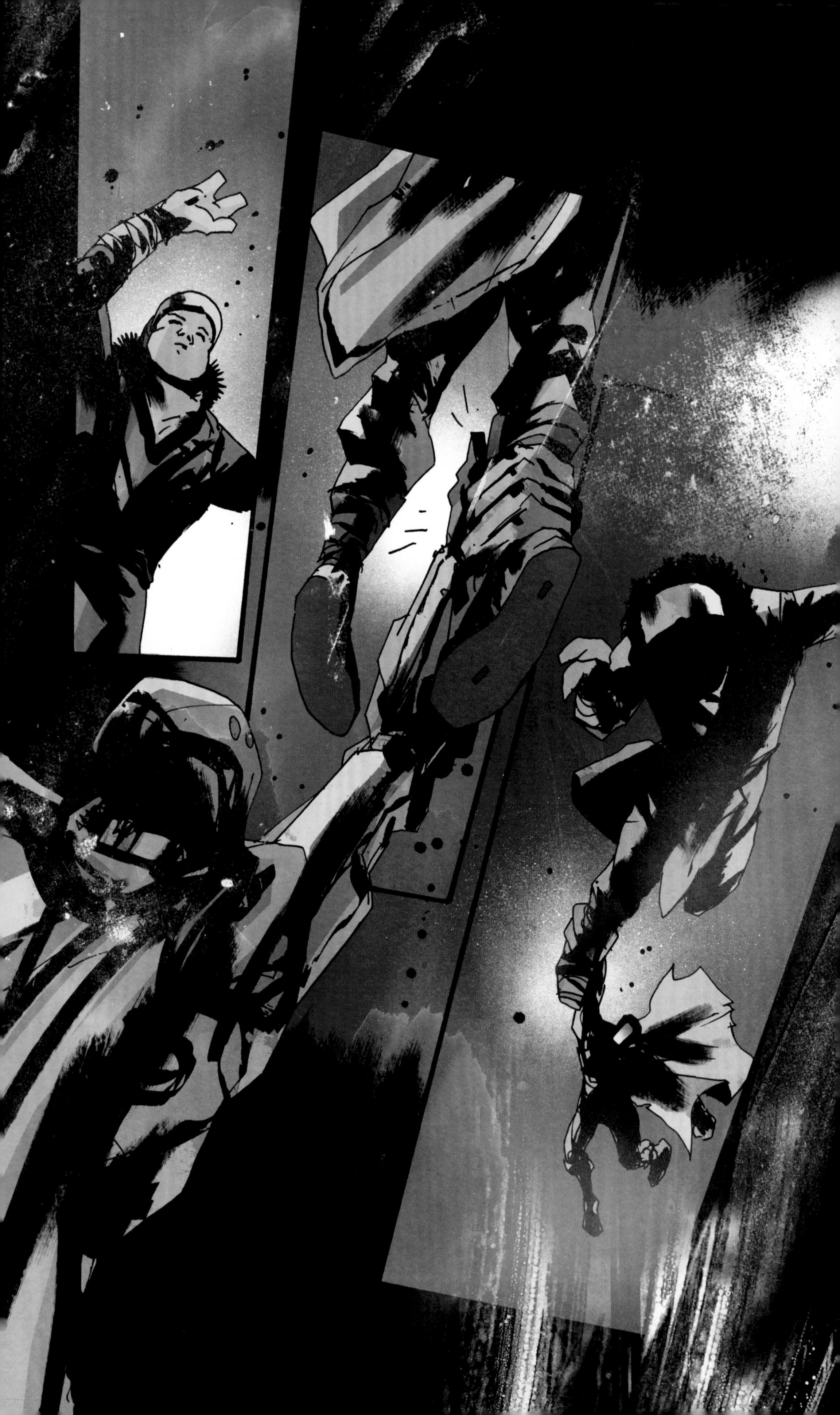

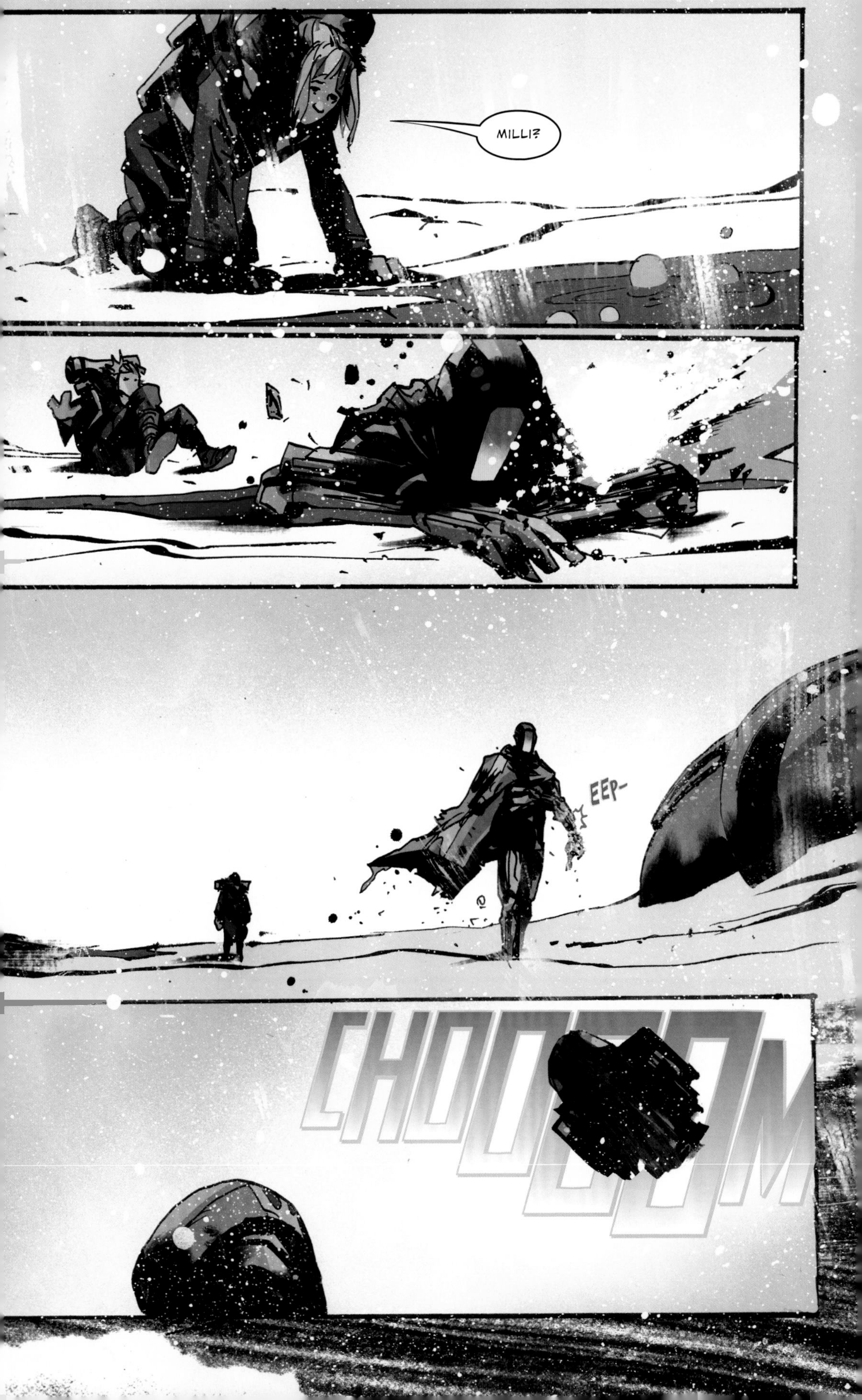
MILLI?
EEP-
CHOOOOM

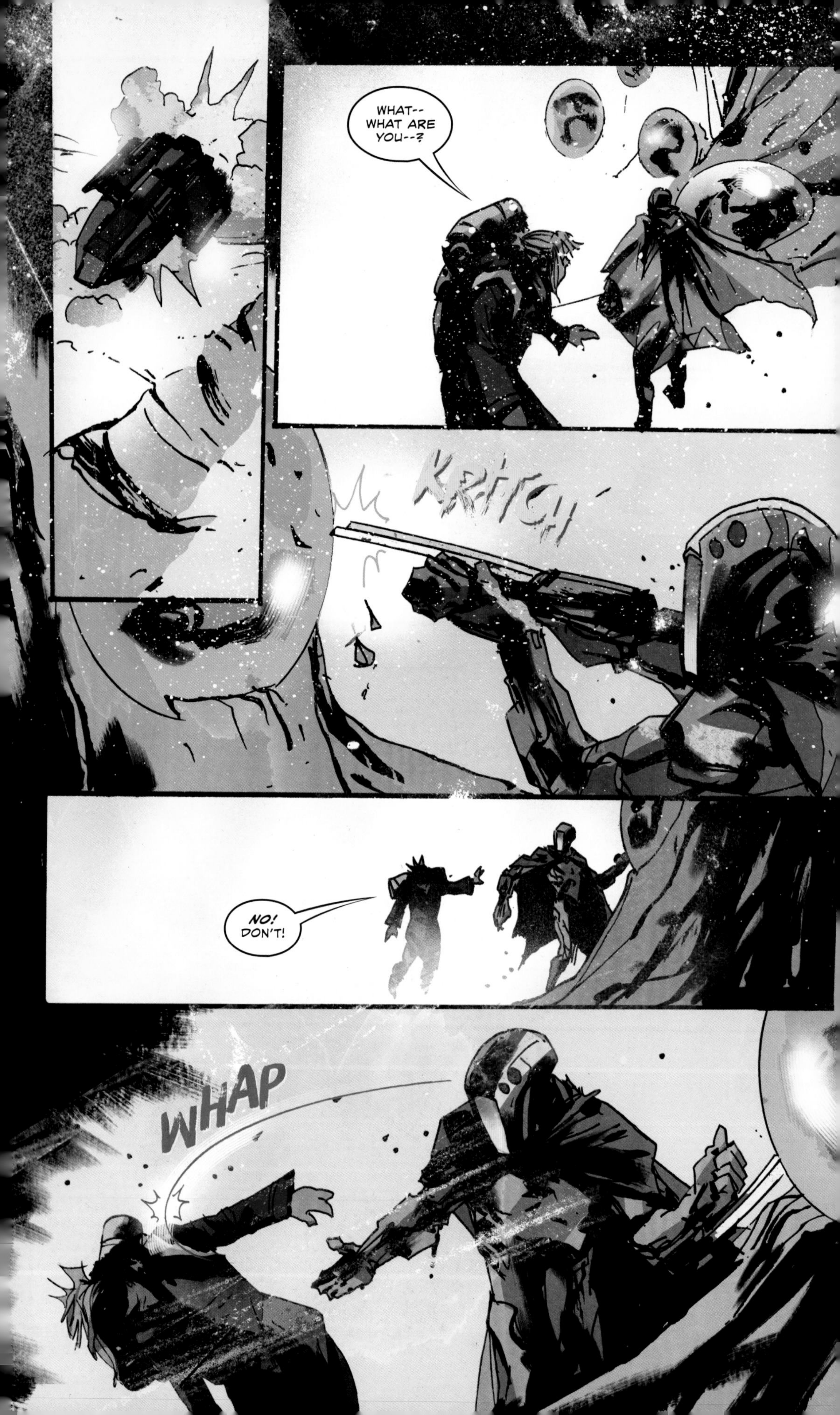
WHAT--
WHAT ARE
YOU--?
KRTCH
NO!
DON'T!
WHAP

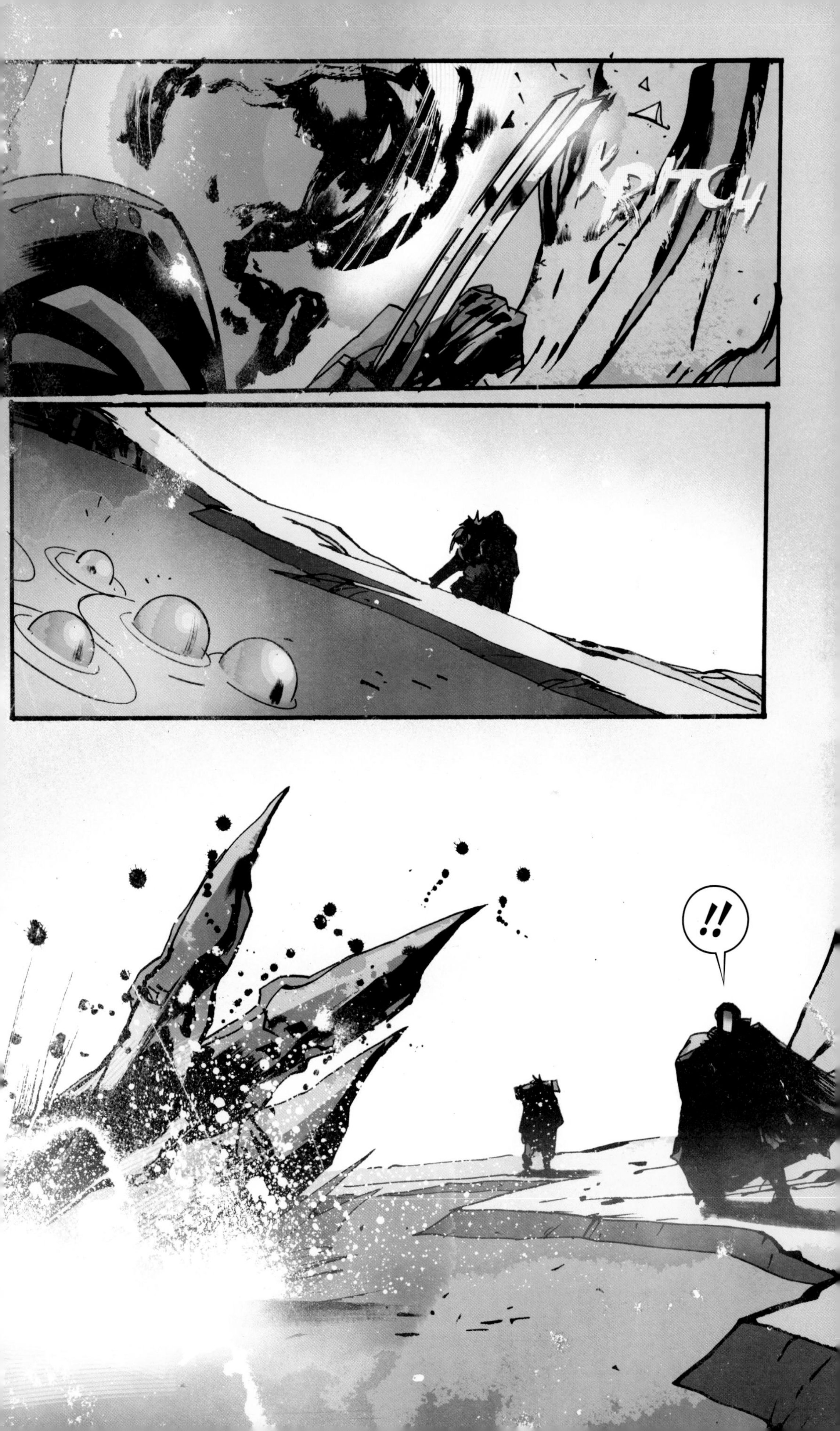
KRITCH
!!

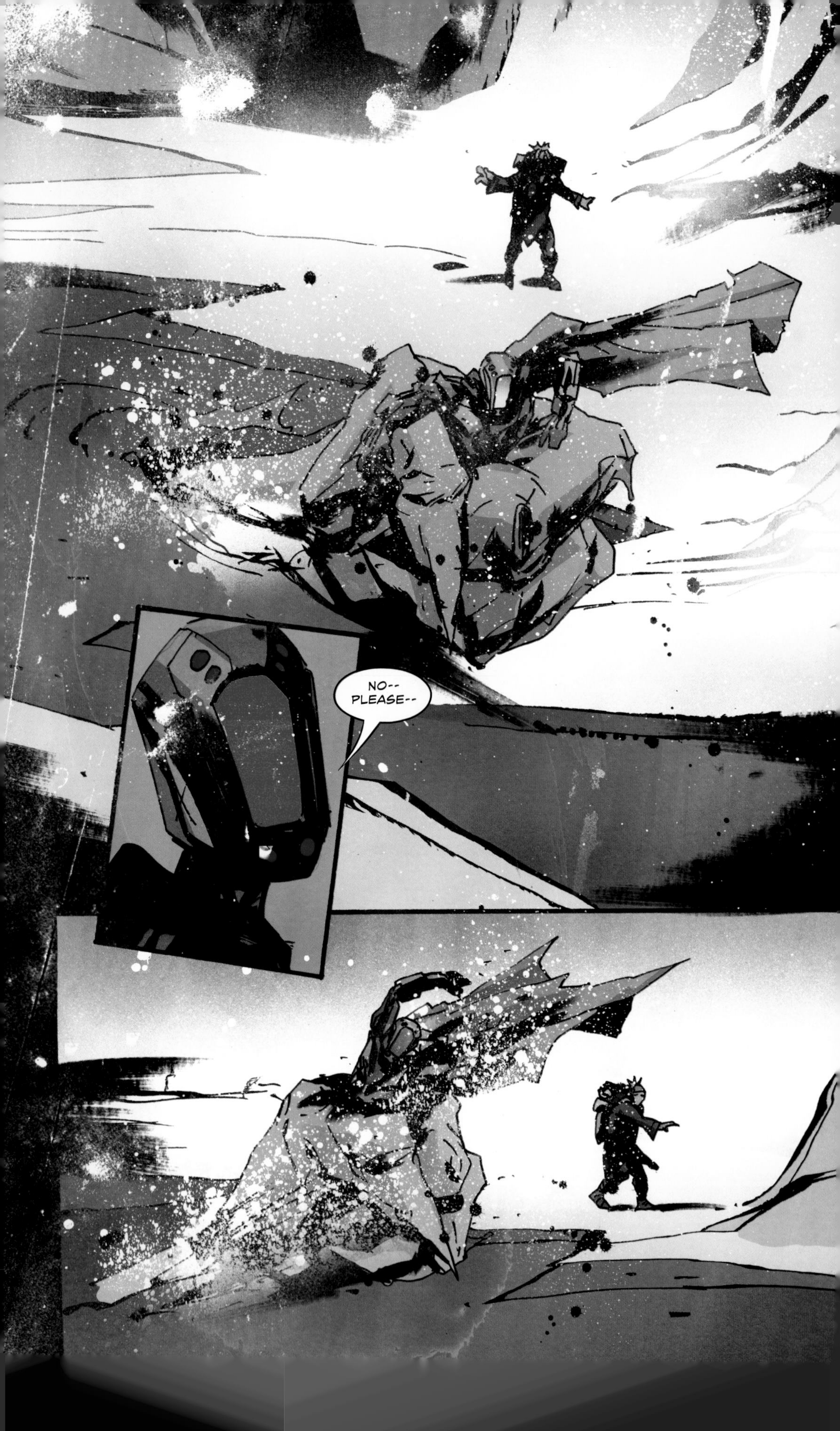
NO--
PLEASE--

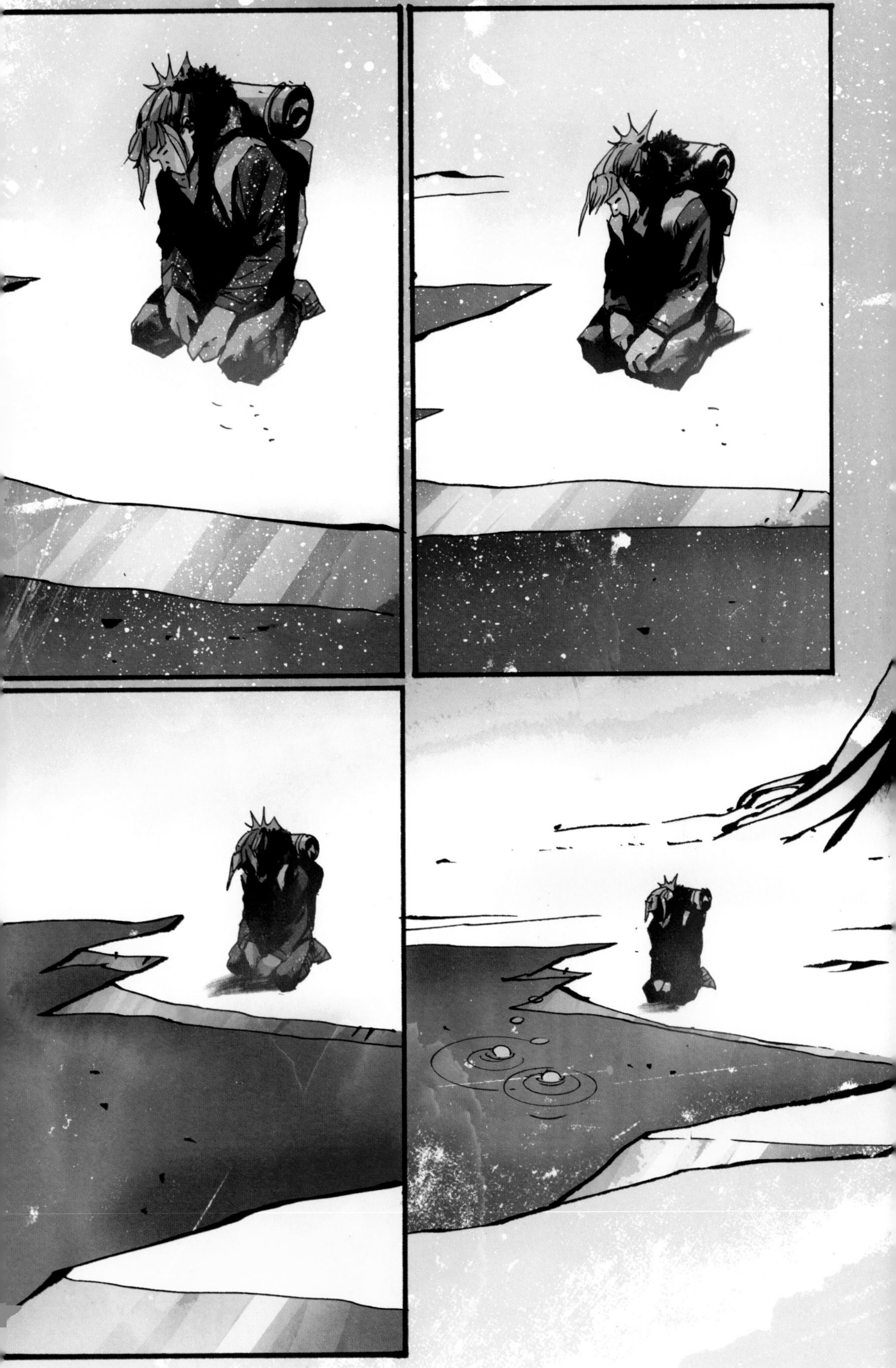

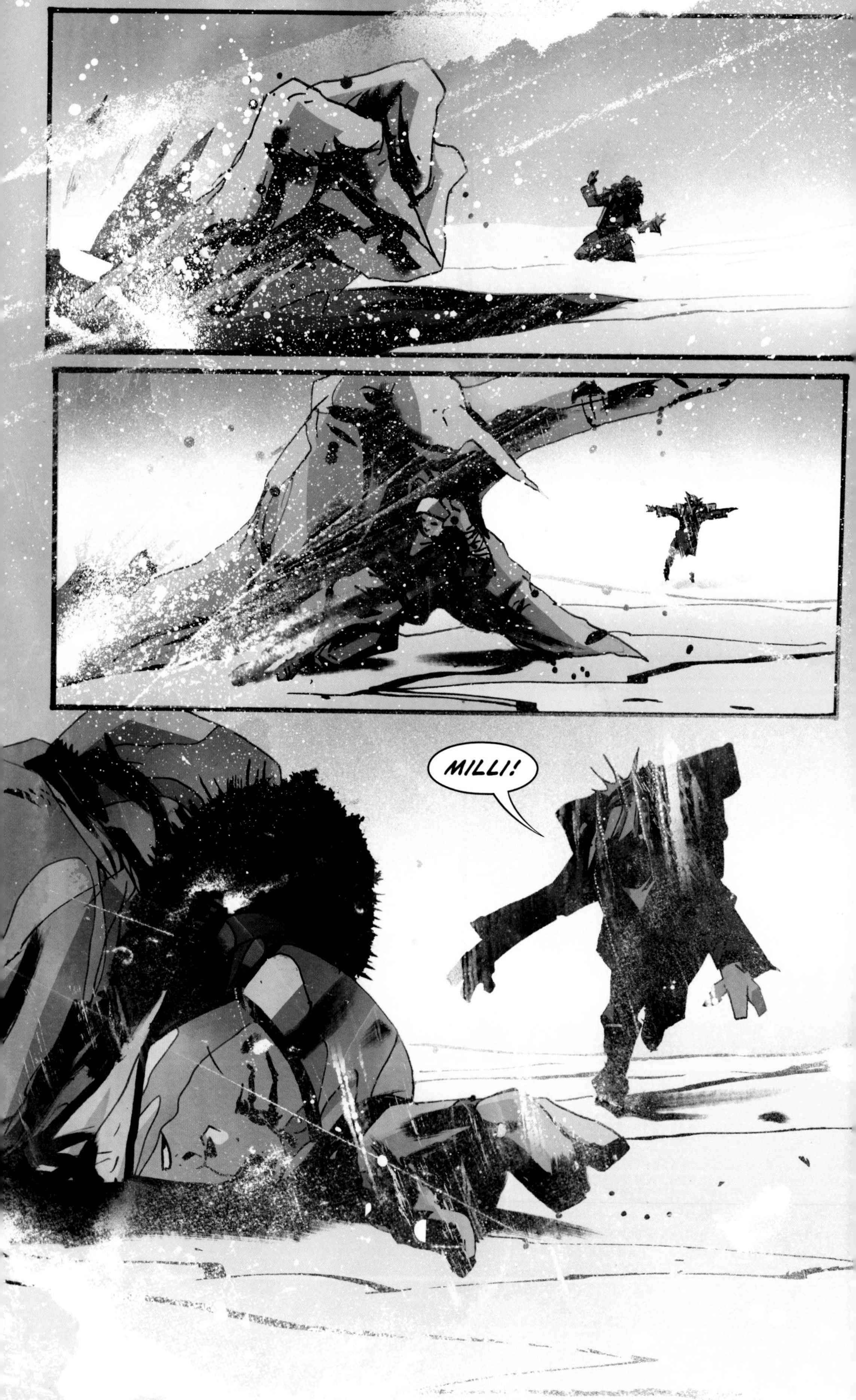
MILLI!

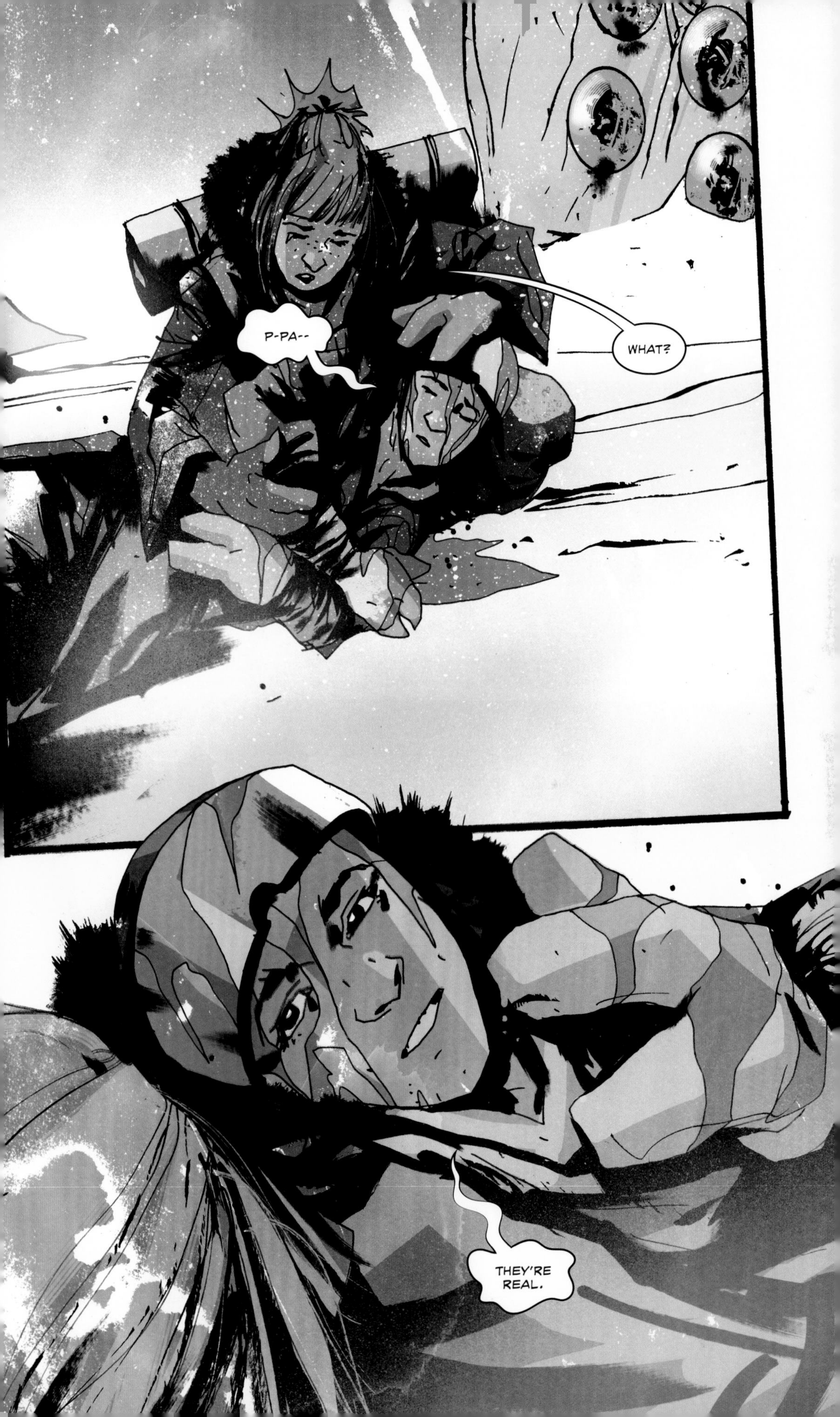
P-PA--
WHAT?
THEY'RE REAL.

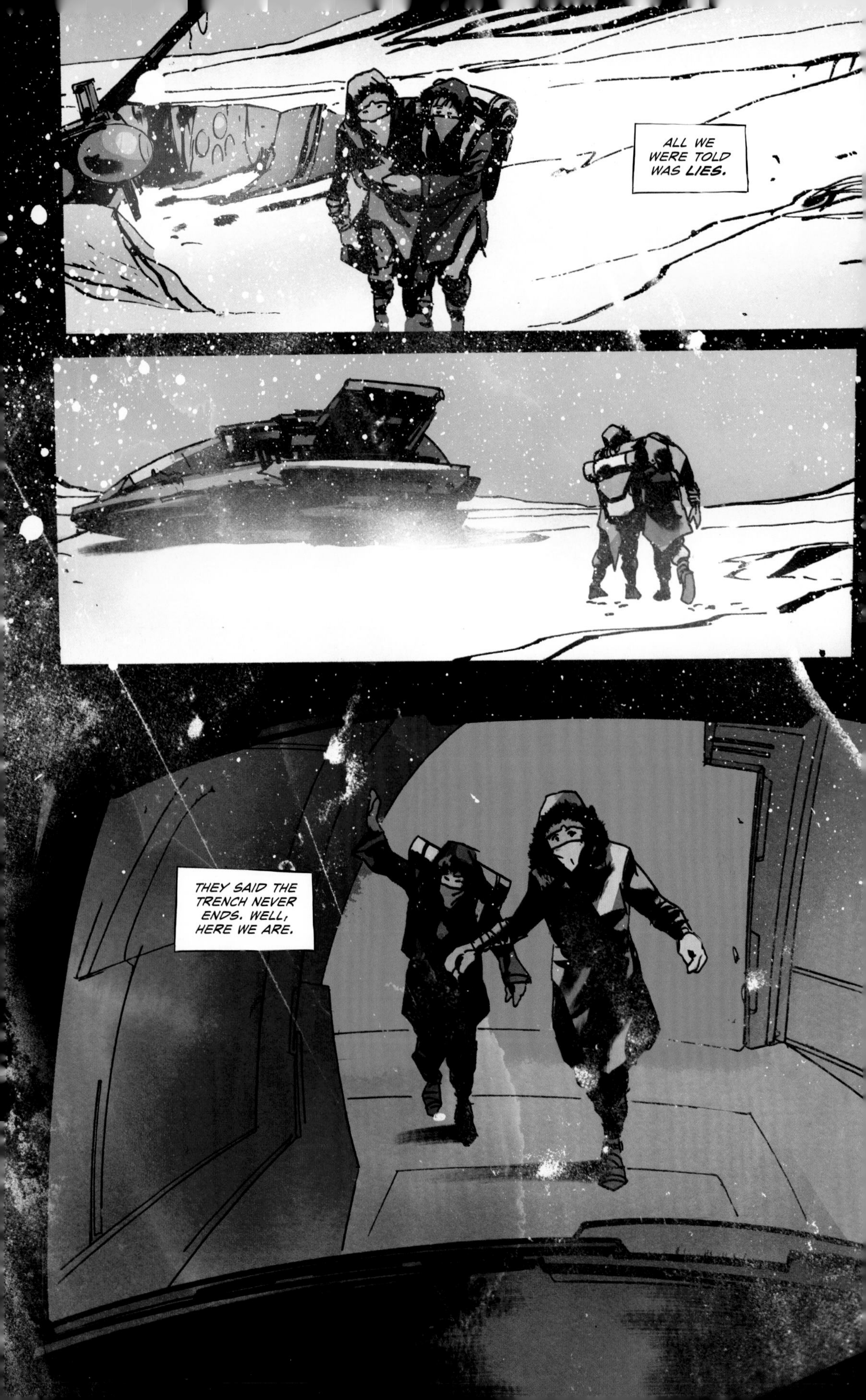
ALL WE WERE TOLD WAS LIES.
THEY SAID THE TRENCH NEVER ENDS. WELL, HERE WE ARE.

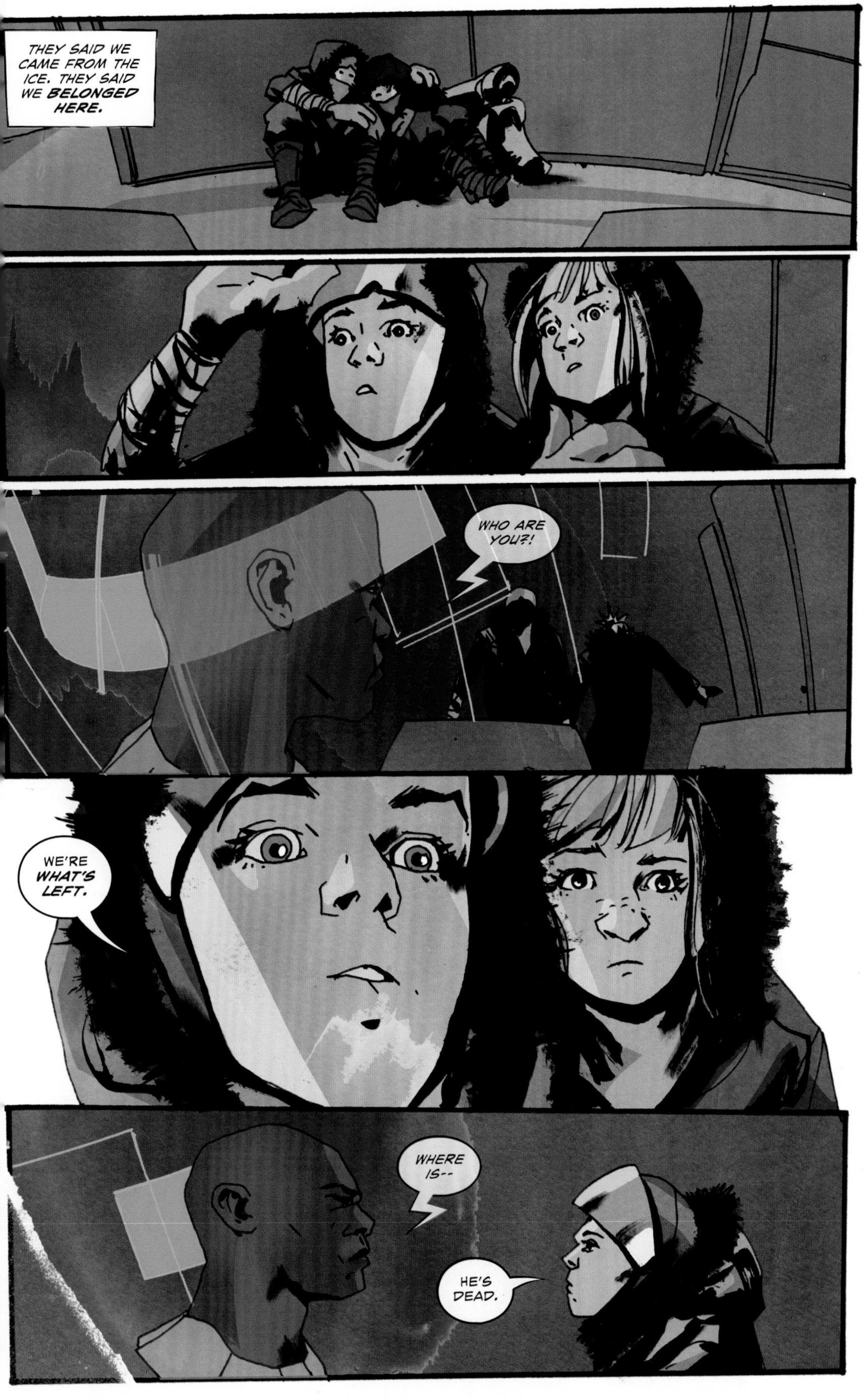
THEY SAID WE CAME FROM THE ICE. THEY SAID WE BELONGED HERE.
WHO ARE YOU?!
WE'RE WHAT'S LEFT.
WHERE IS--
HE'S DEAD.

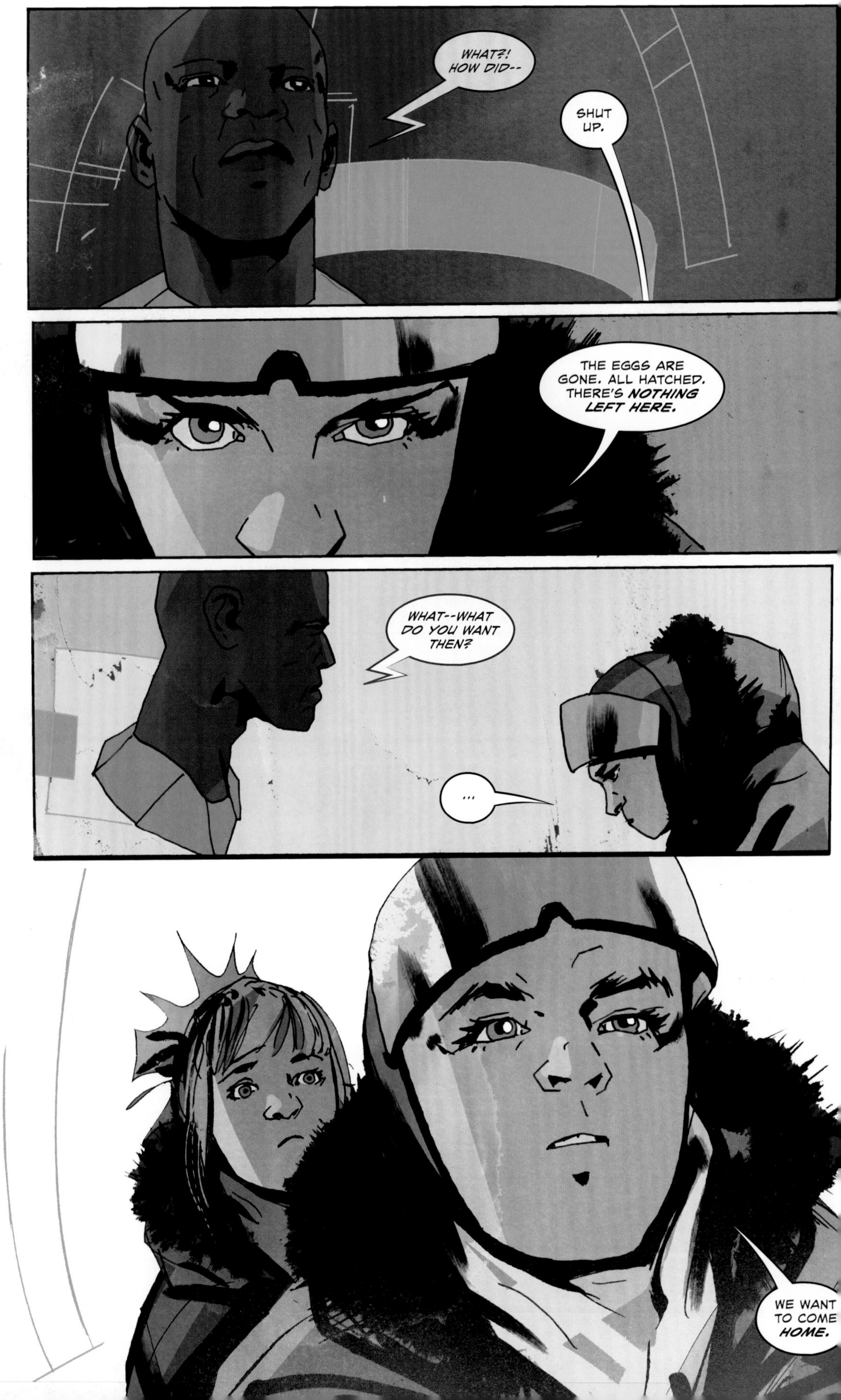
WHAT?! HOW DID--
SHUT UP.
THE EGGS ARE GONE. ALL HATCHED. THERE'S NOTHING LEFT HERE.
WHAT--WHAT DO YOU WANT THEN?
...
WE WANT TO COME HOME.

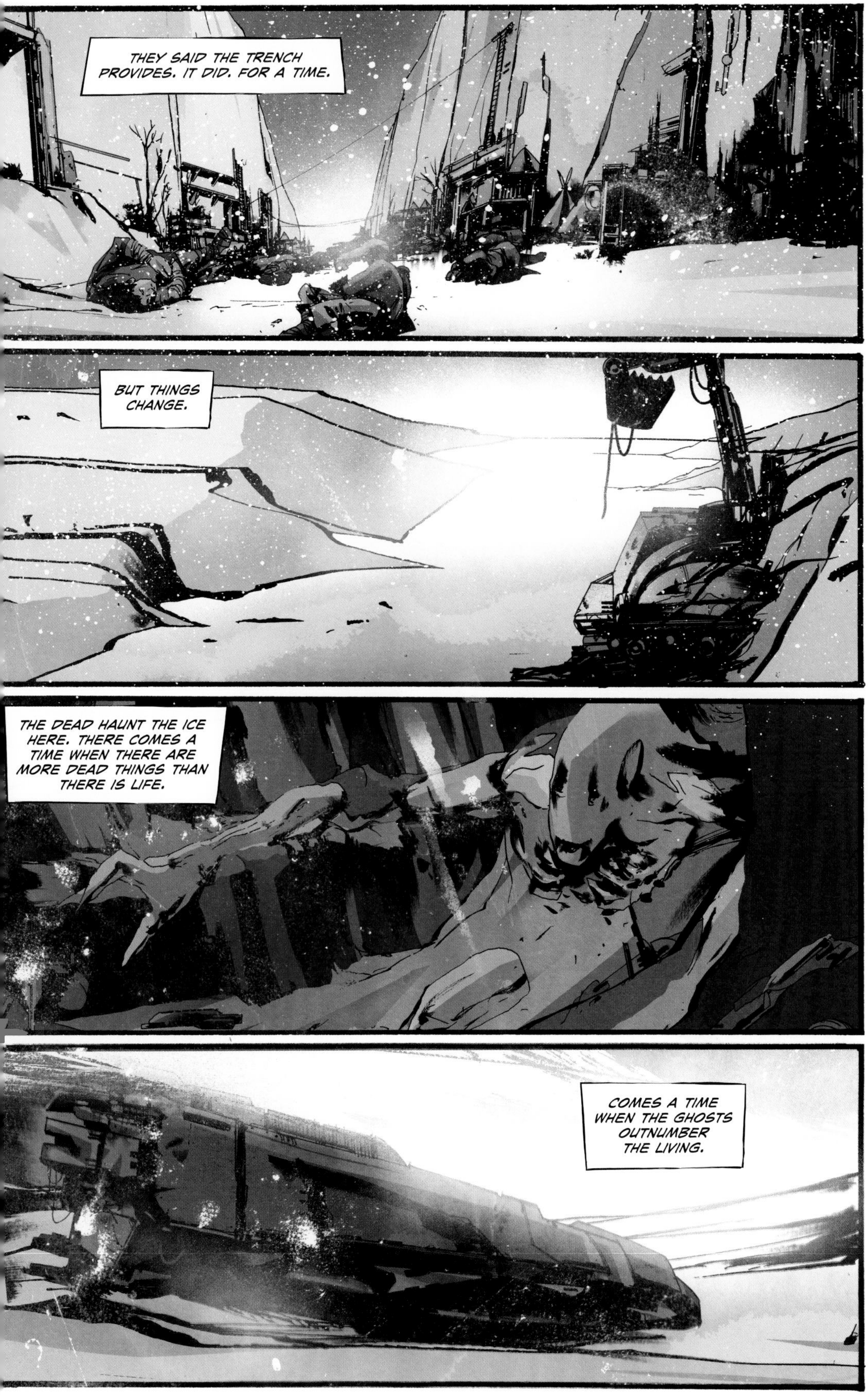
THEY SAID THE TRENCH PROVIDES. IT DID. FOR A TIME.
BUT THINGS CHANGE.
THE DEAD HAUNT THE ICE HERE. THERE COMES A TIME WHEN THERE ARE MORE DEAD THINGS THAN THERE IS LIFE.
COMES A TIME WHEN THE GHOSTS OUTNUMBER THE LIVING.

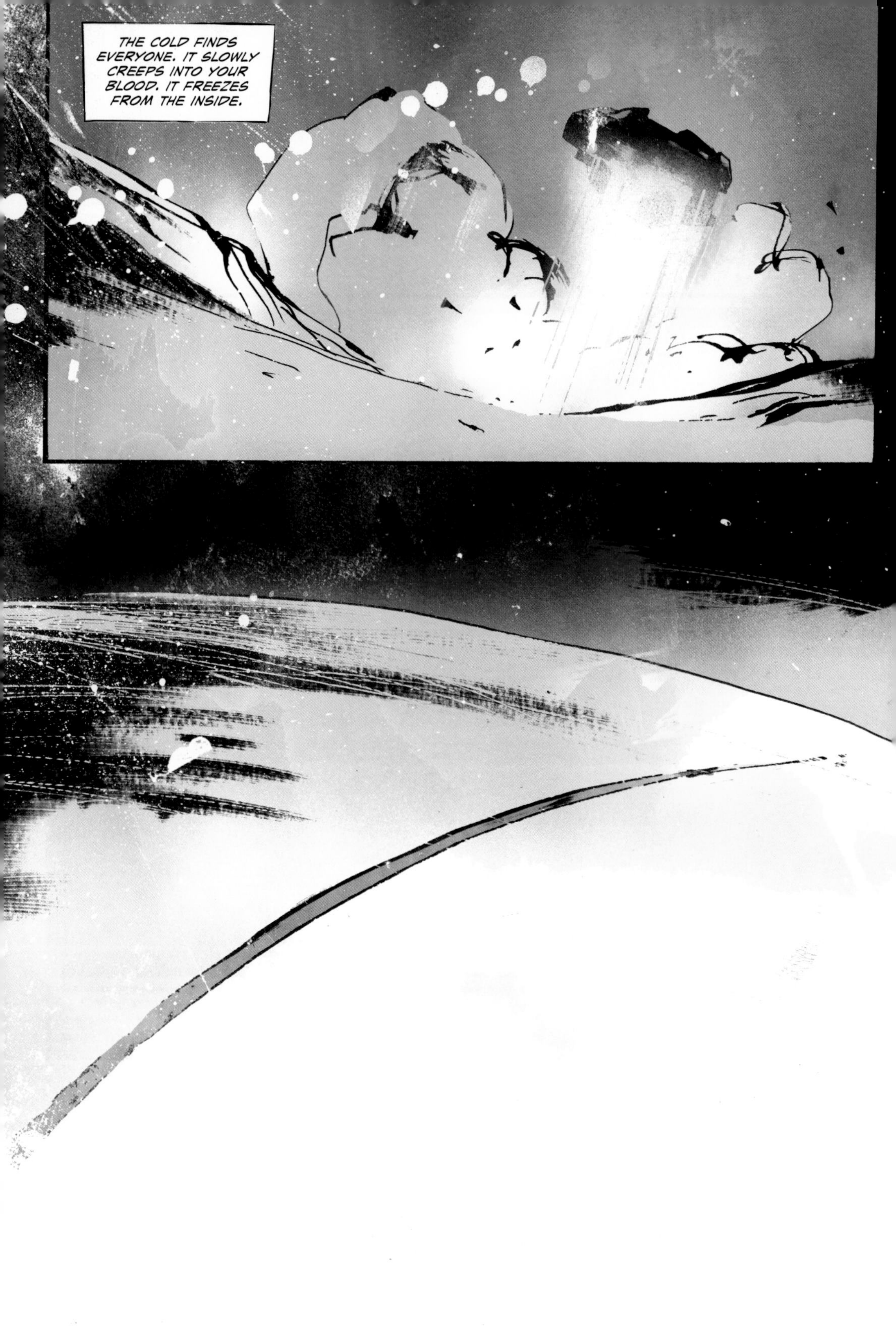
THE COLD FINDS EVERYONE. IT SLOWLY CREEPS INTO YOUR BLOOD. IT FREEZES FROM THE INSIDE.

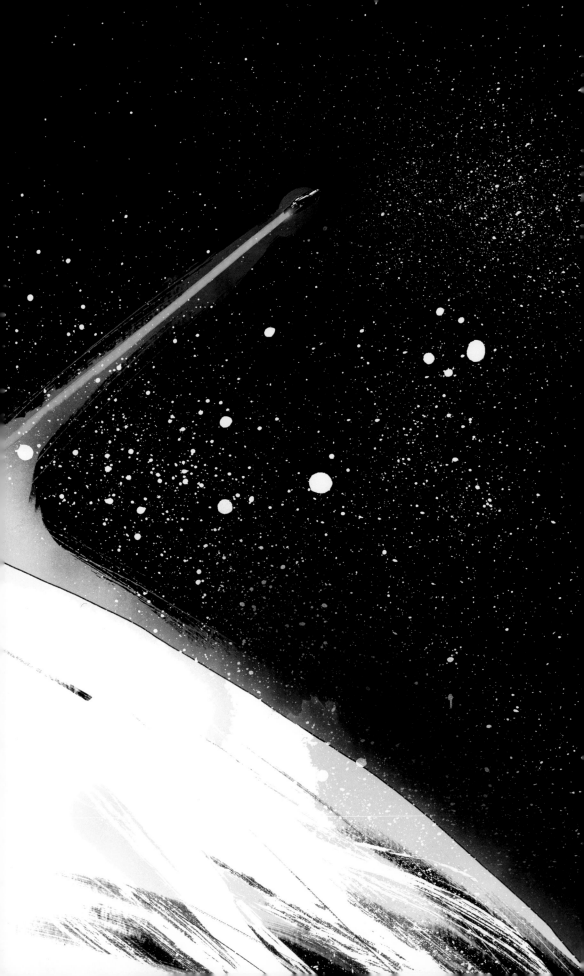

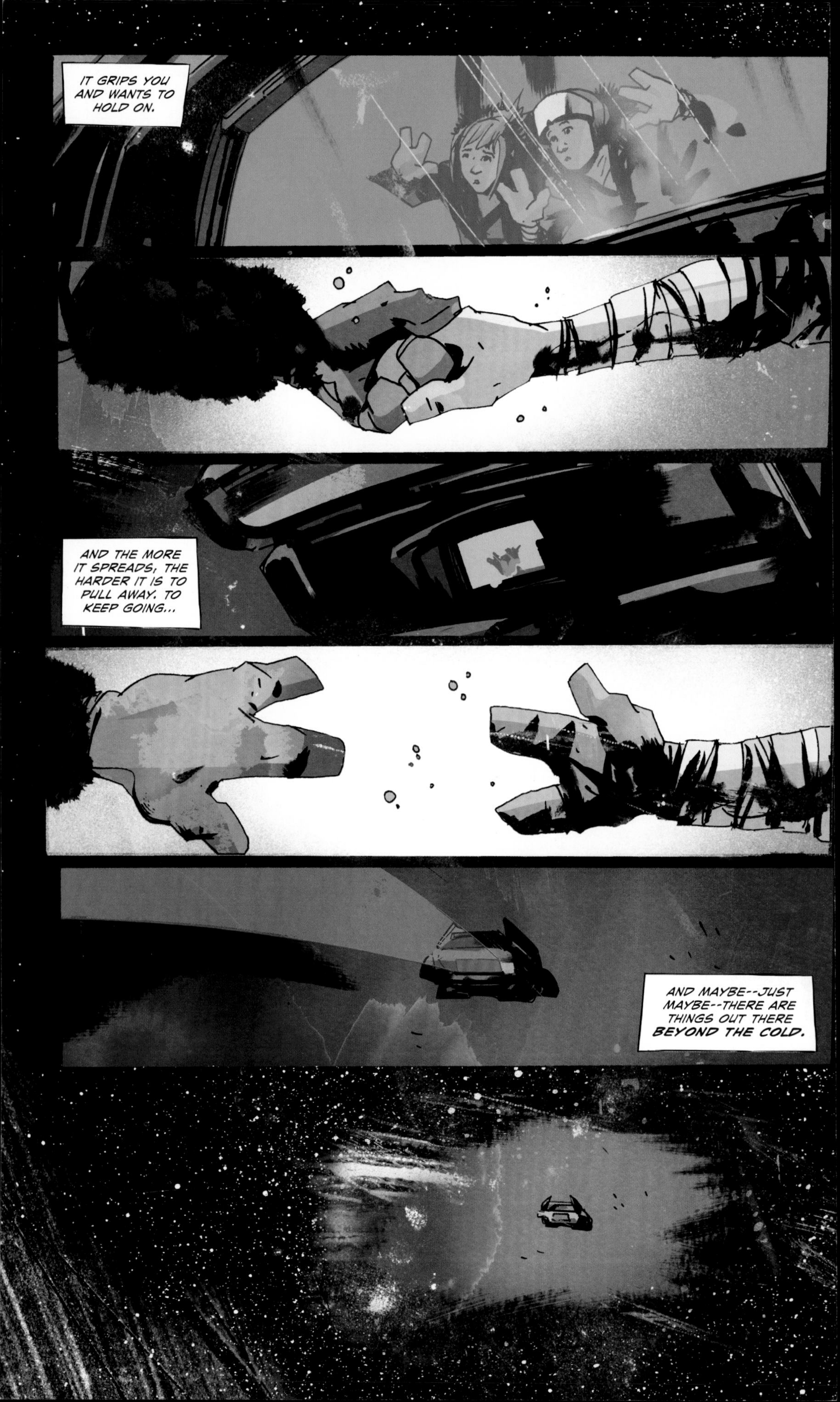
IT GRIPS YOU AND WANTS TO HOLD ON.
AND THE MORE IT SPREADS, THE HARDER IT IS TO PULL AWAY. TO KEEP GOING...
AND MAYBE--JUST MAYBE--THERE ARE THINGS OUT THERE BEYOND THE COLD.

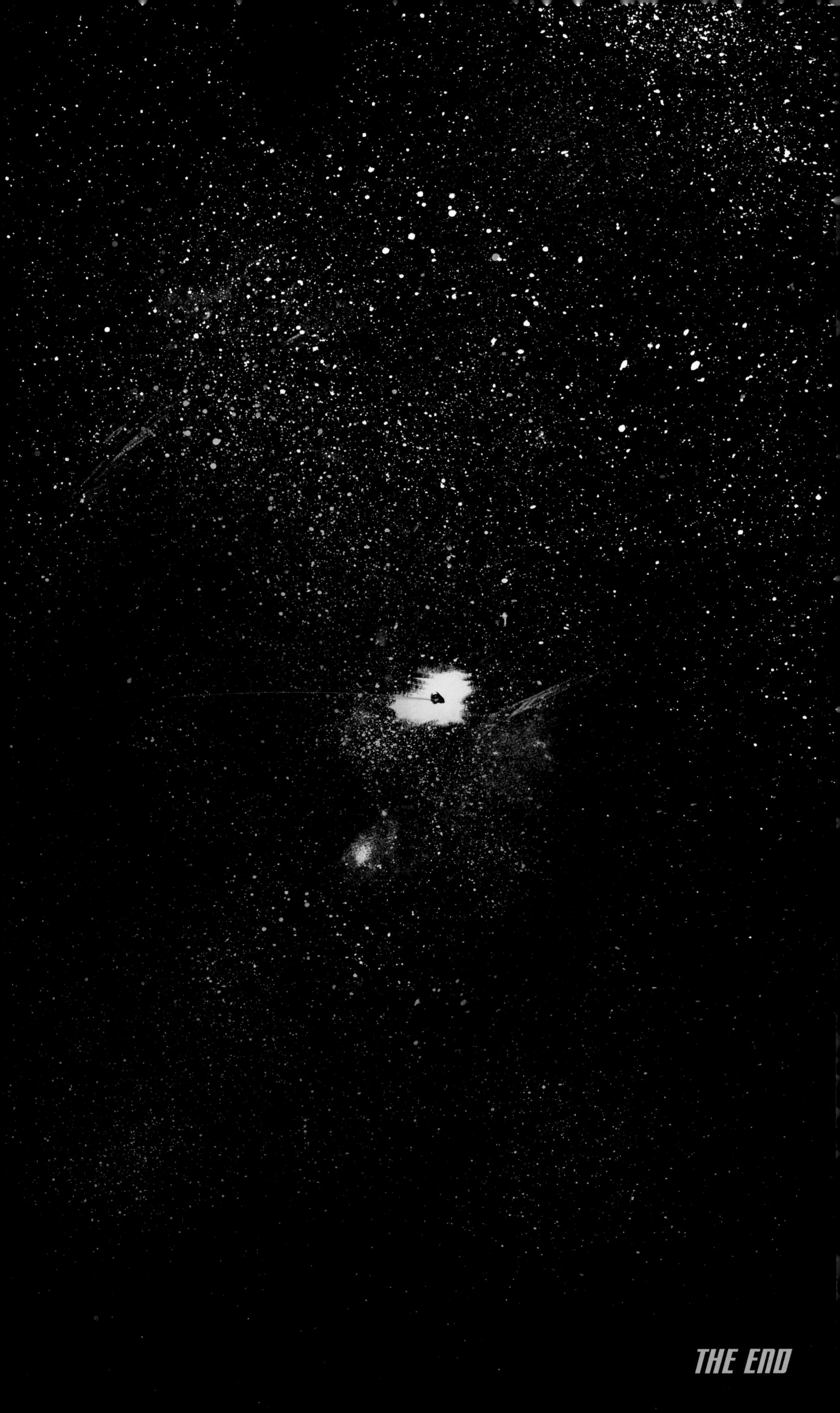
THE END

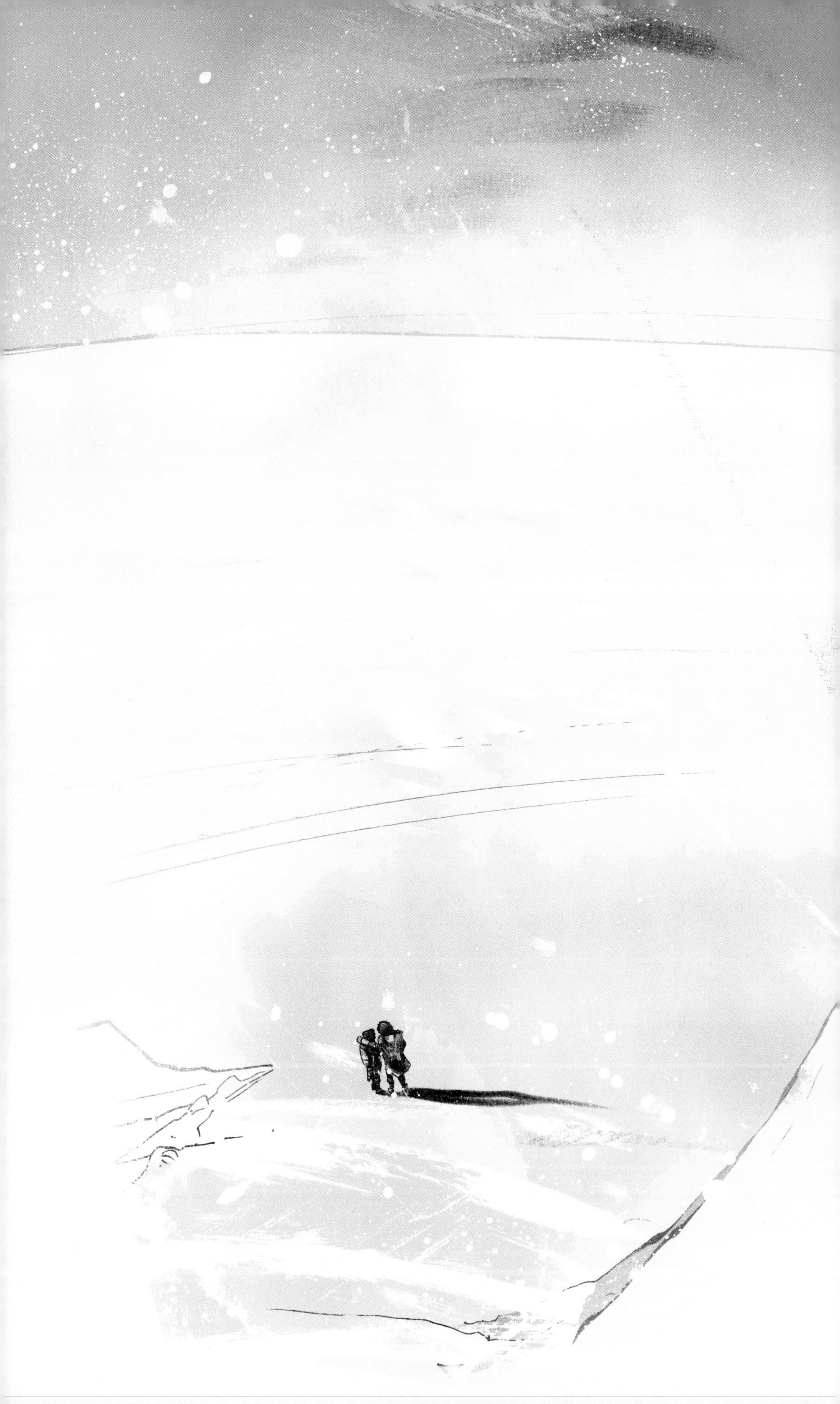

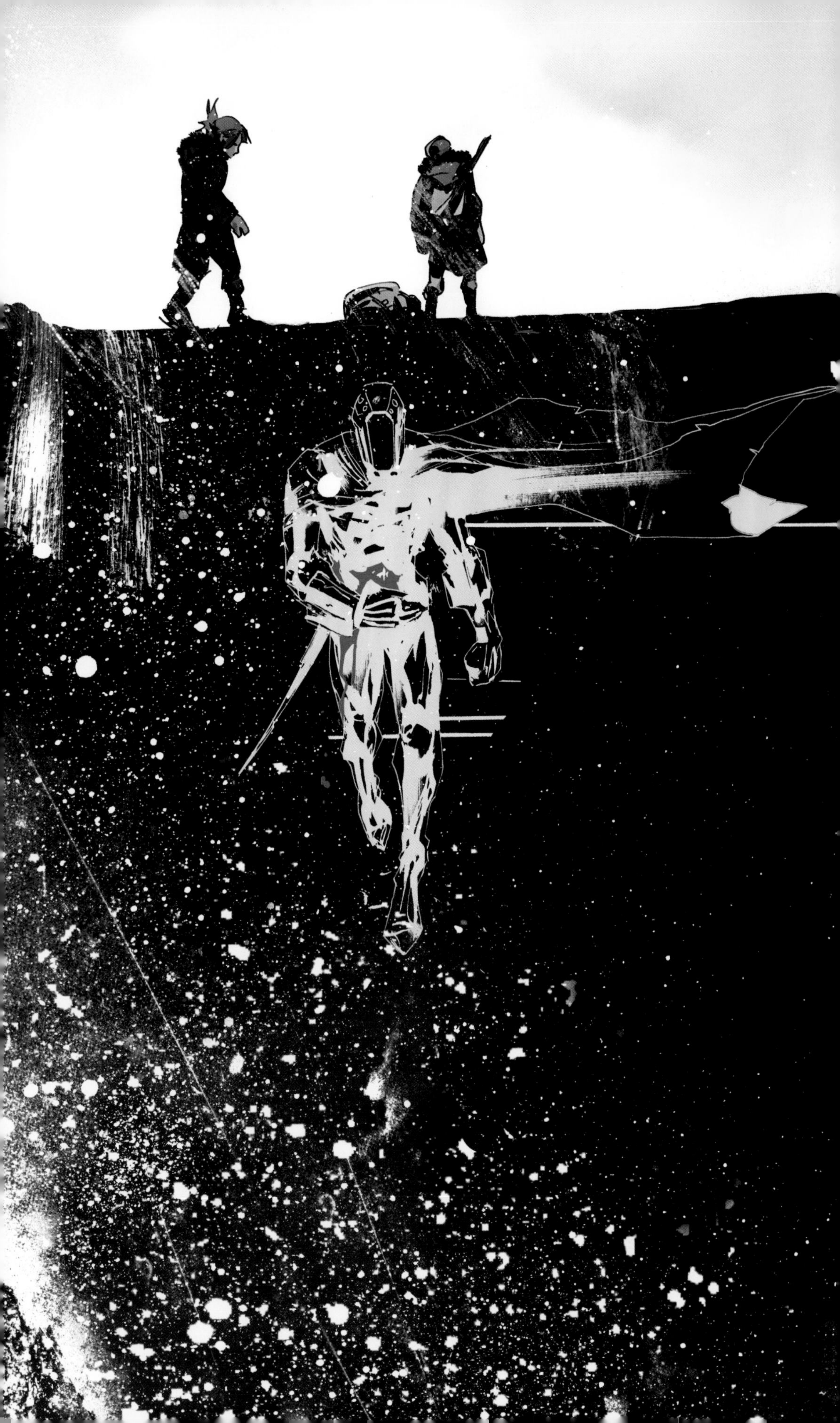

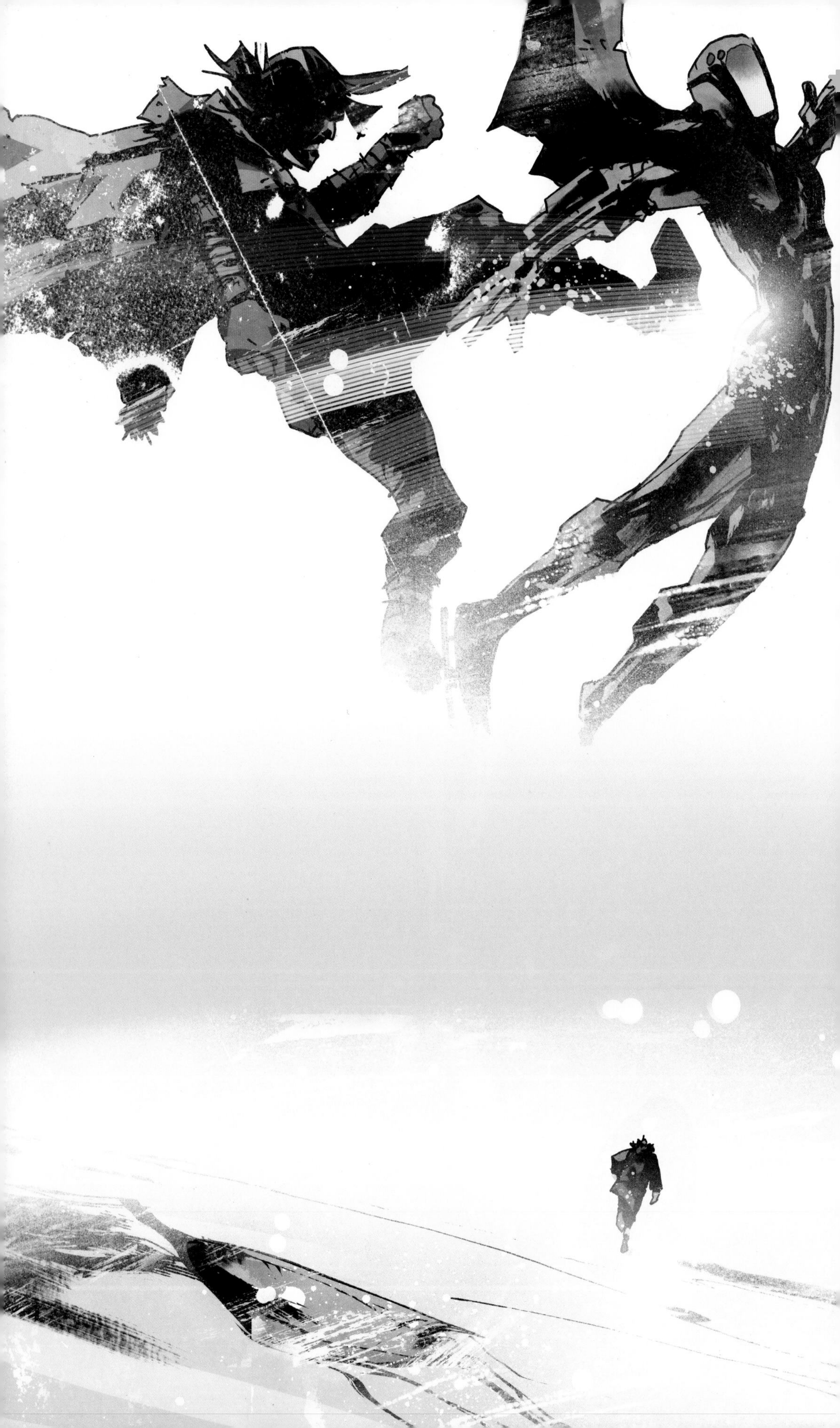

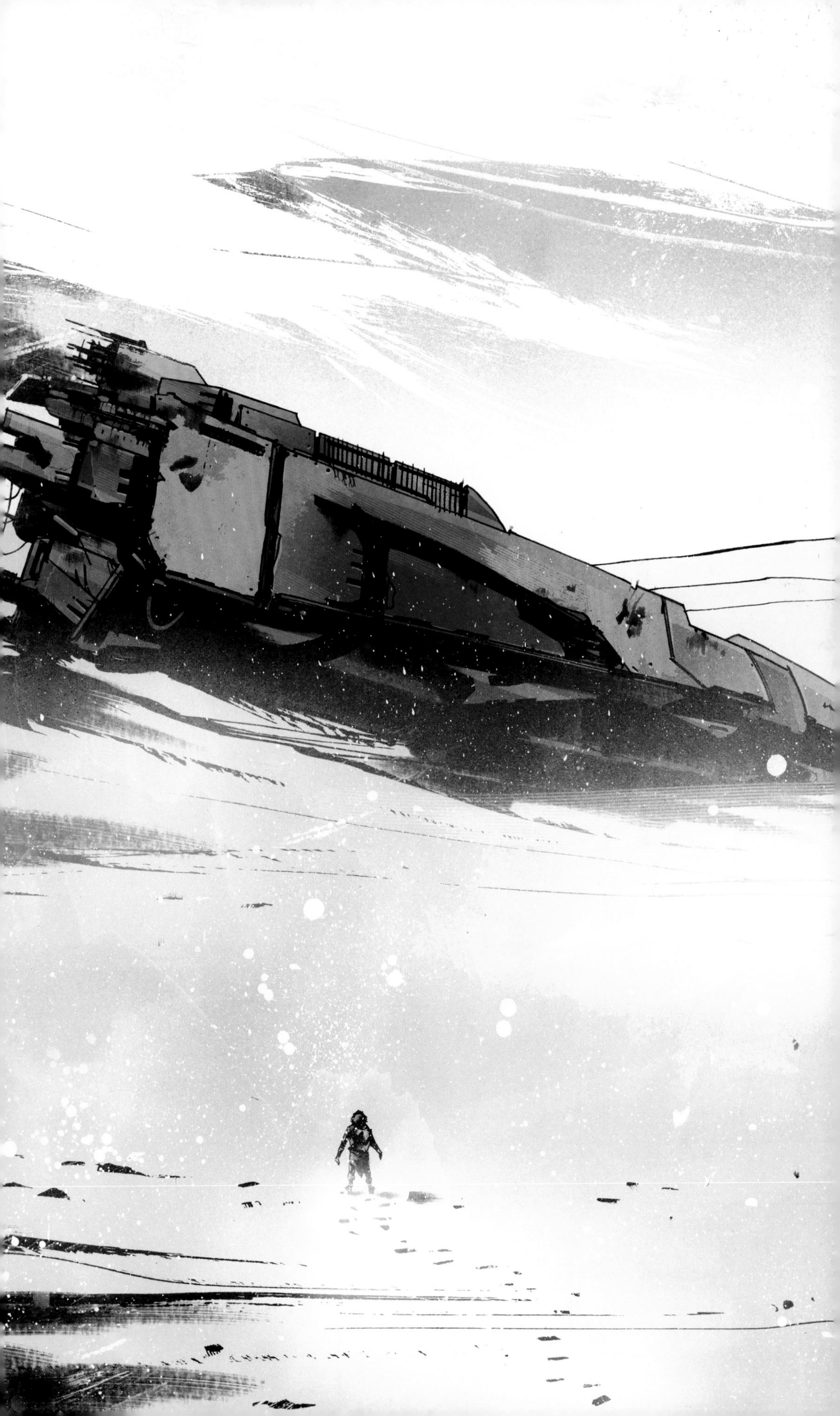

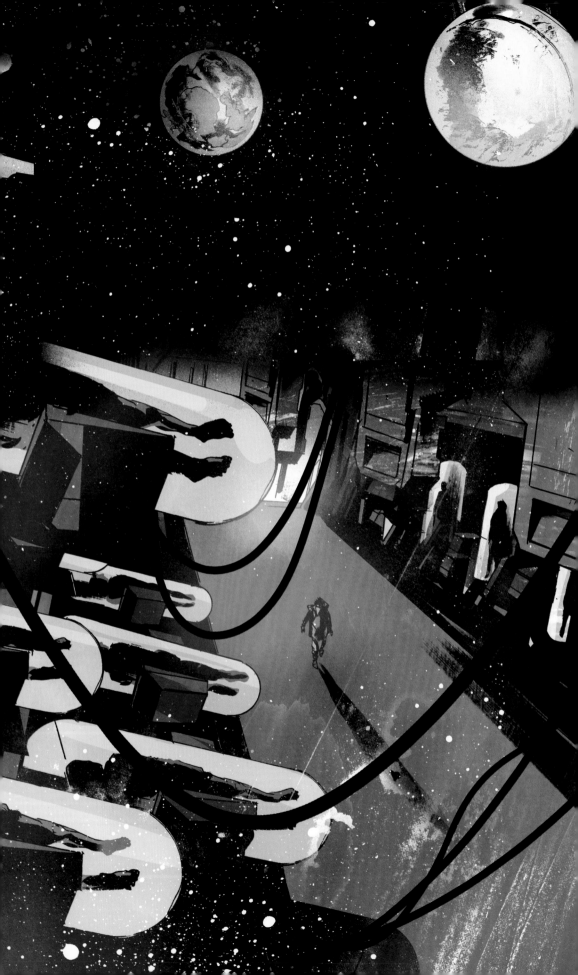

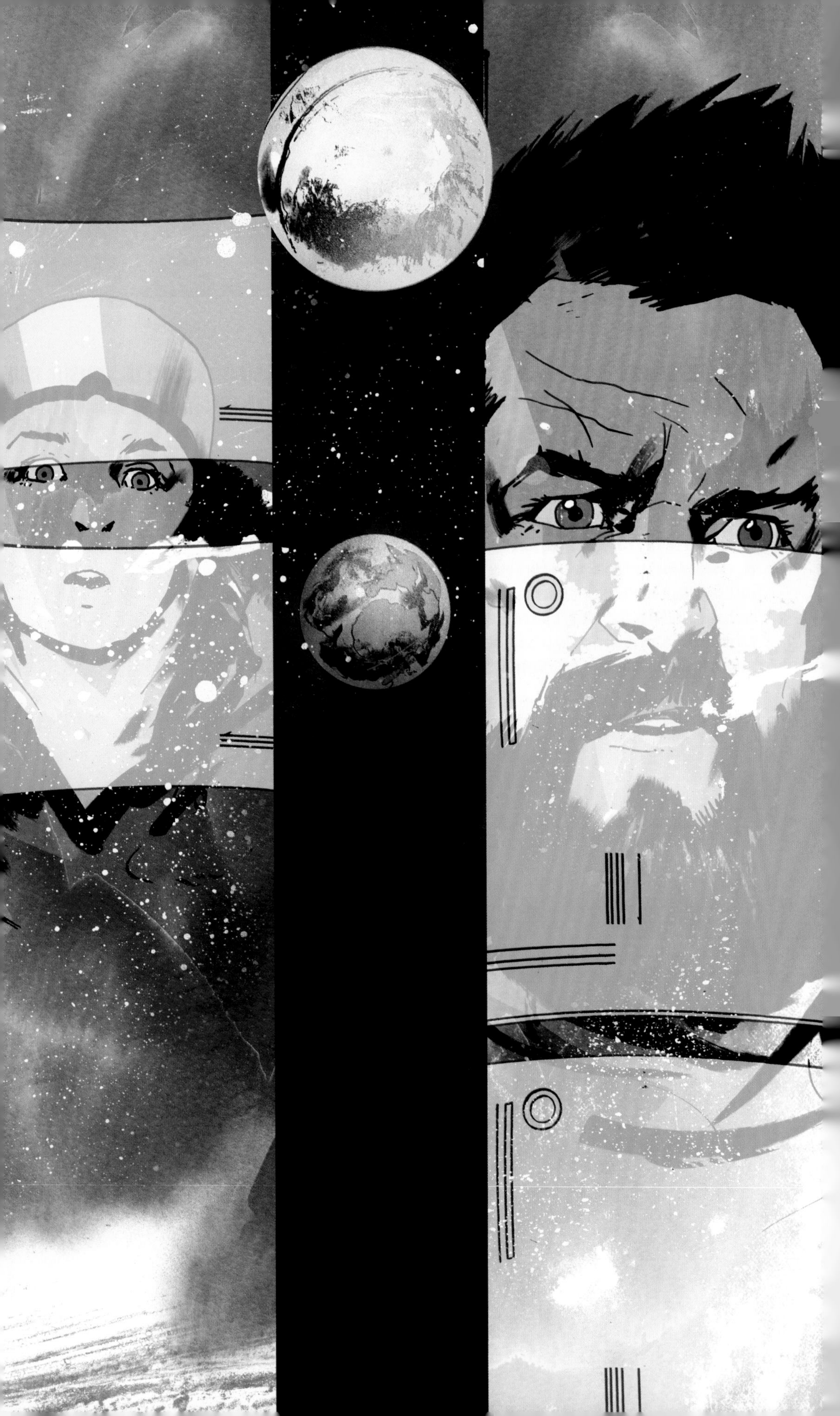

FROM THE VAULT BONUS EDITION:

SNOW ANGELS™

LIKE *BLACK HAMMER* AND *GIDEON FALLS*, *SNOW ANGELS* HAS A LONG ORIGIN STORY. AND SINCE THE COLLECTED PRINT EDITION OF THE SERIES BY JOCK AND ME IS OUT NOW FROM DARK HORSE, I THOUGHT I WOULD DO A BONUS EDITION OF FROM THE VAULT TO REVEAL THAT ORIGIN STORY . . .

I usually don't remember exactly where most ideas come from or start, but I do know where *Snow Angels* started. I used to put myself to sleep by visualizing skating on an endless river. I know this sounds cheesy, and just a little too Canadian, but it's true. It was a weird, calming visualization thing I did for a while that helped me calm down and stop thinking. And it was from this idea of an endless iced-over river that *Snow Angels* was born back in 2008 or 2009. Initially it was called *Trench Skater*, and it was about a man skating this endless river and hunting or being hunted by a dark figure called The Snowman. Very inspired by *The Gunslinger* by Stephen King.

TRENCH
-SKATER

MAN.

STORY...

SKATES.

RIVER.

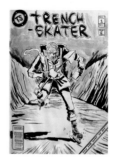

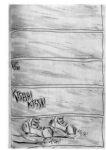

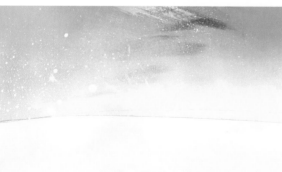

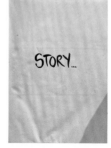

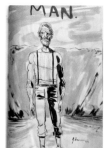

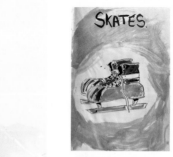

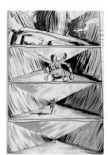

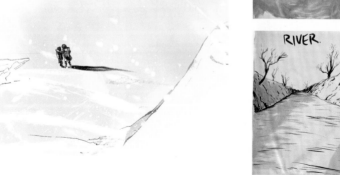

I spent a while playing with this idea in my sketchbook in 2010, before putting it aside to work on other projects like *Underwater Welder* and *Sweet Tooth*.

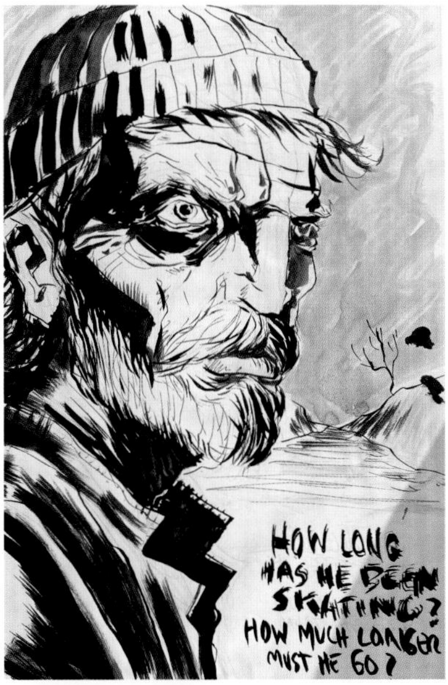
HOW LONG HAS HE BEEN SKATING? HOW MUCH LONGER MUST HE GO?

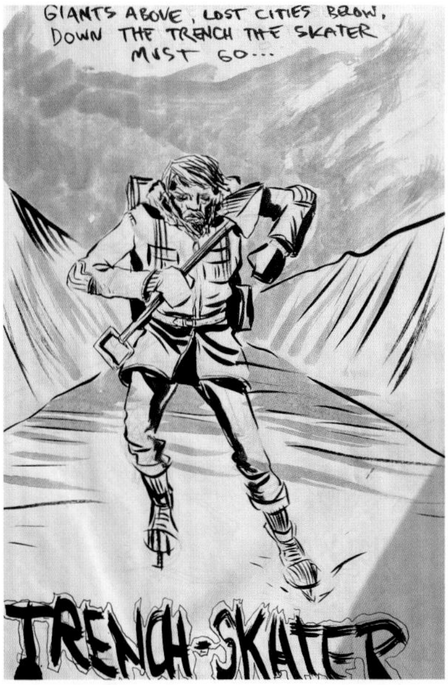
GIANTS ABOVE, LOST CITIES BELOW, DOWN THE TRENCH THE SKATER MUST GO...
TRENCH-SKATER

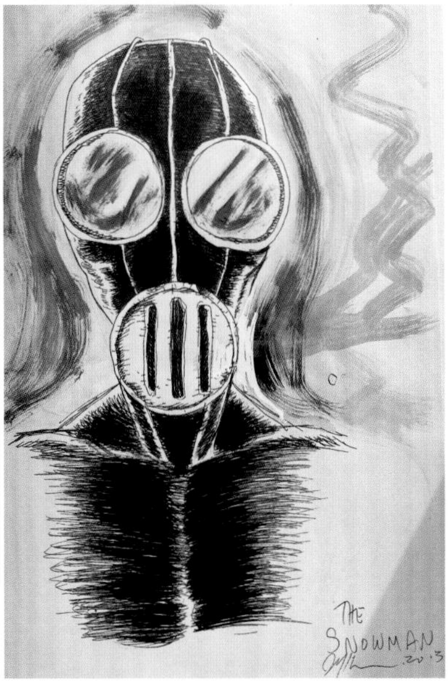
THE SNOWMAN
2013

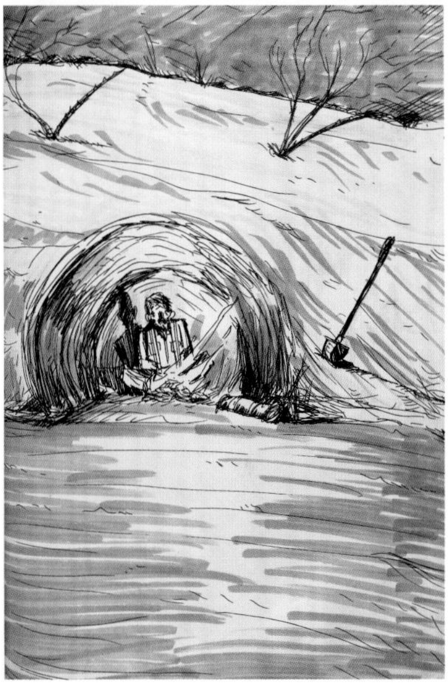

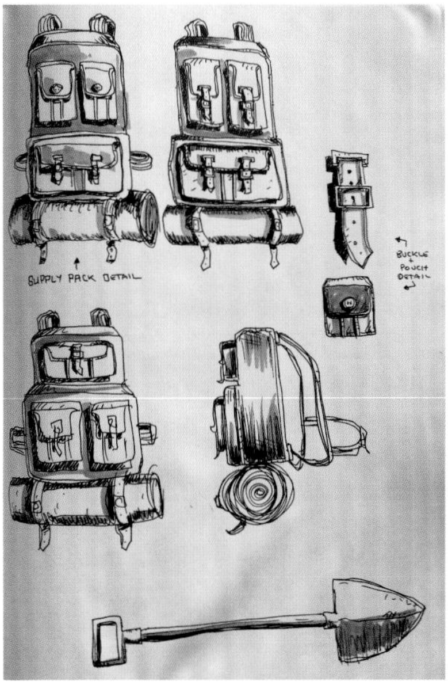
SUPPLY PACK DETAIL
BUCKLE + POUCH DETAIL

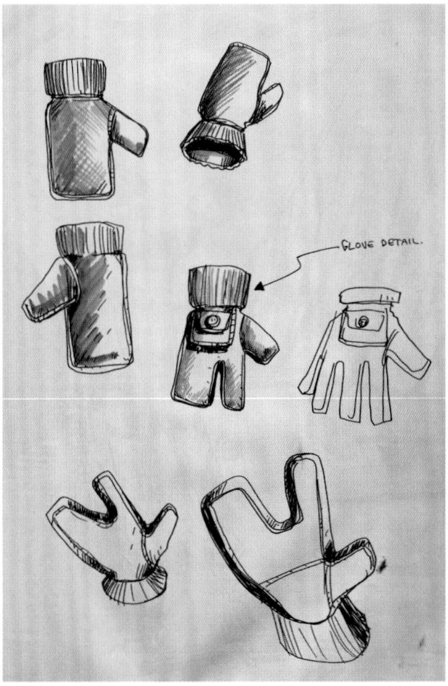
GLOVE DETAIL.

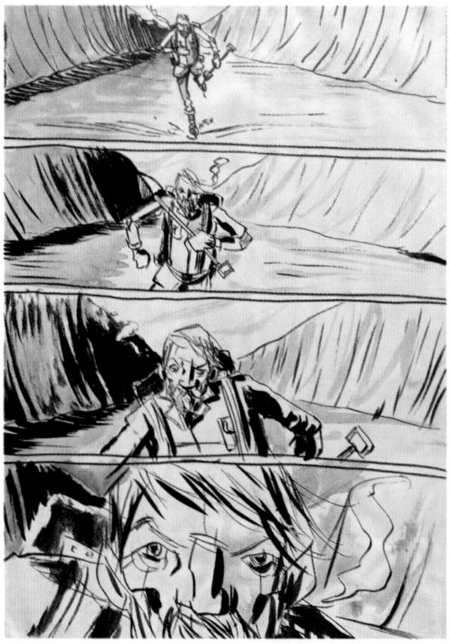

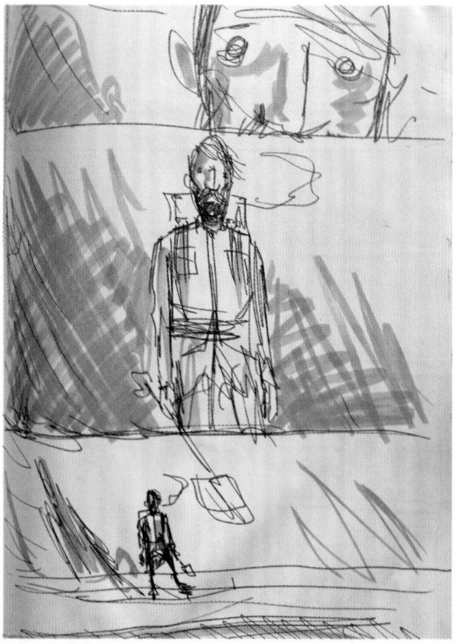

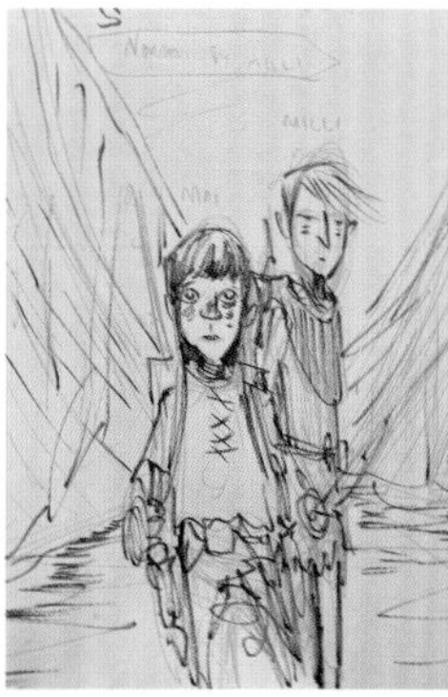

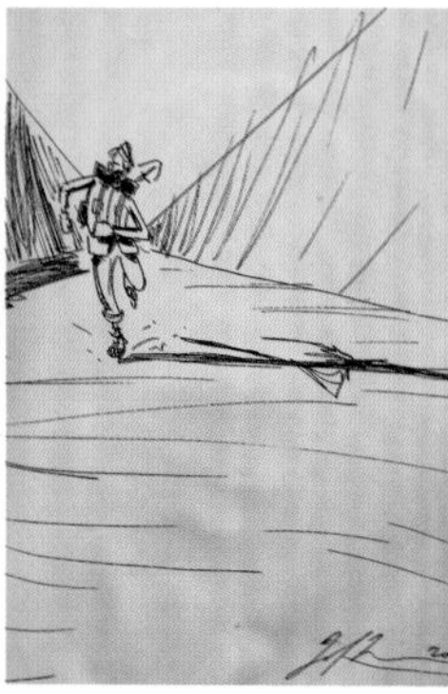

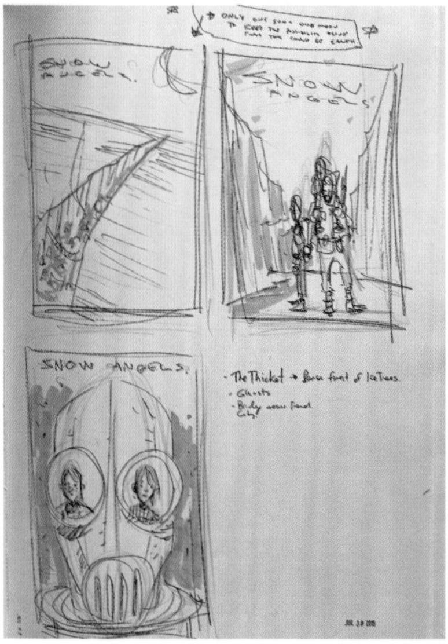
SNOW ANGELS
SNOW ANGELS
SNOW ANGELS

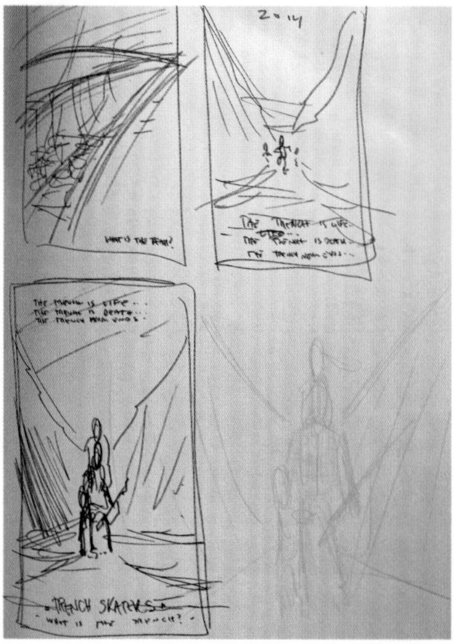
2014
What is the Trench?
TRENCH SKATERS
What is the Trench?

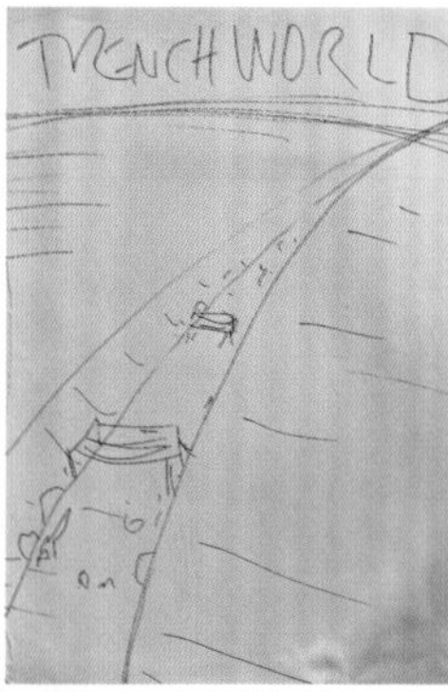
TRENCH WORLD

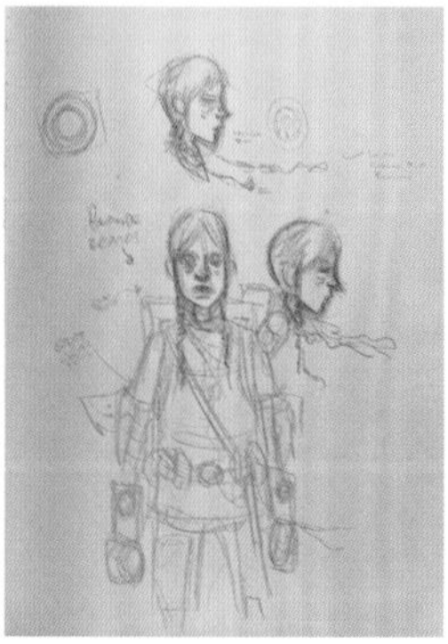

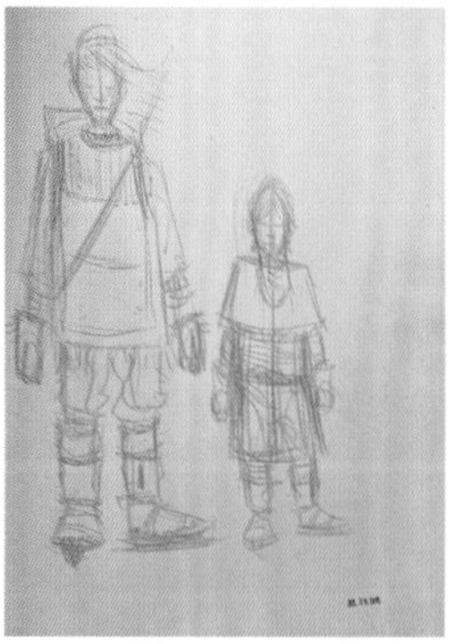

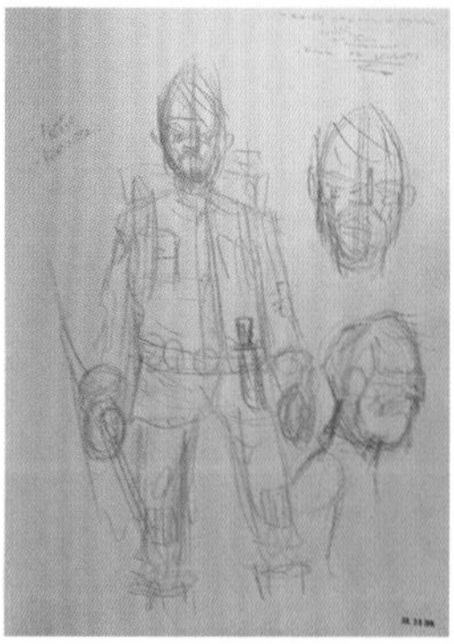

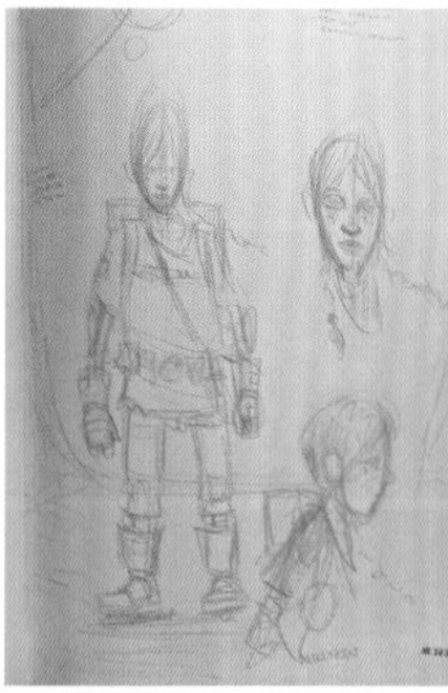

The initial version never really got past these early sketchbook drawings, but I would later resurrect the idea and pitch it to Karen Berger at Vertigo in 2014 as my follow-up to *Sweet Tooth*, with the two girls—the man's daughters—now as the focus.

The Vertigo pitch didn't really go anywhere, and I ended up pitching and doing *Trillium* after *Sweet Tooth* instead. But, of course, the idea kept sticking around, and I approached Jock about drawing it in 2015 or so. We were set up to do it as a team at Vertigo right before the imprint was shut down by DC and Warner Bros. And obviously, we ended up taking it to comiXology and doing it there as a ten-issue series last year.

I loved working with Jock and our editor, Will Dennis, on *Snow Angels*. Some ideas just don't let you give up on them. In the case of *Snow Angels*, it would take ten years and a great collaborator like Jock to see it through, but I'm glad we did it.

—JEFF LEMIRE

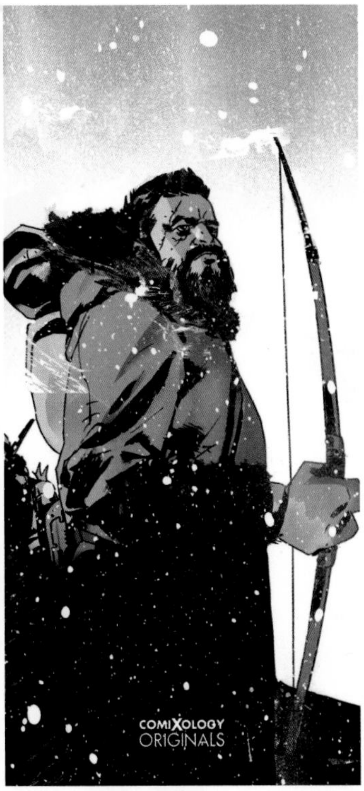
comiXology
ORIGINALS

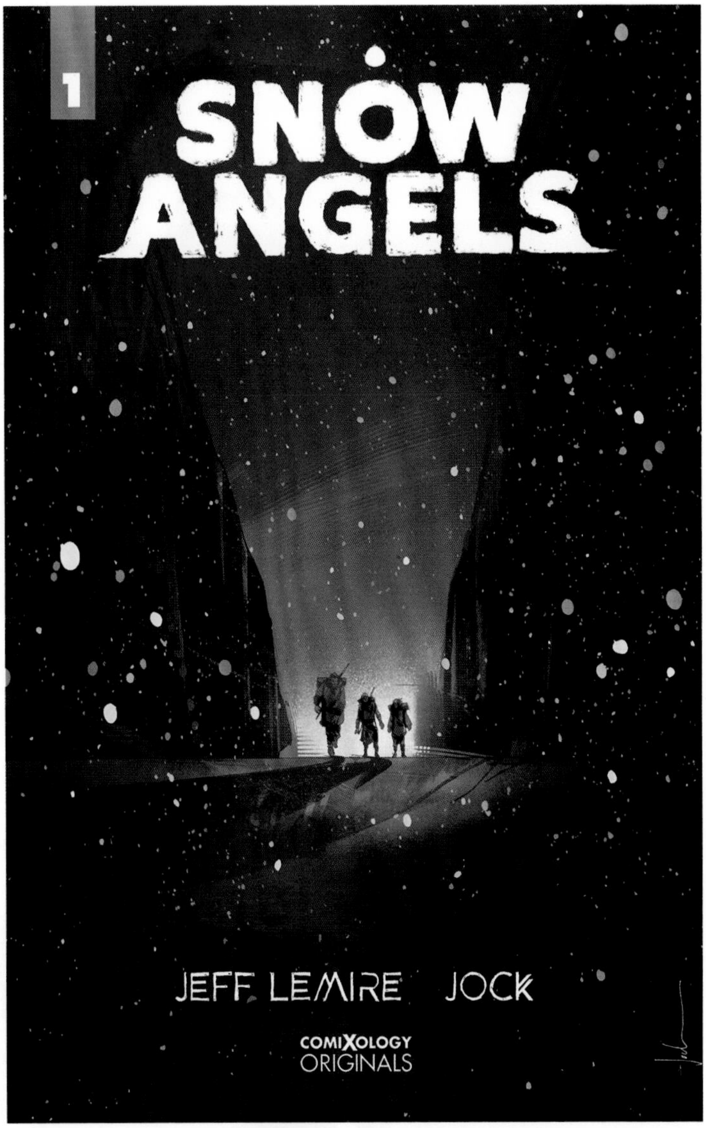
1
SNOW
ANGELS
JEFF LEMIRE JOCK
comiXology
ORIGINALS

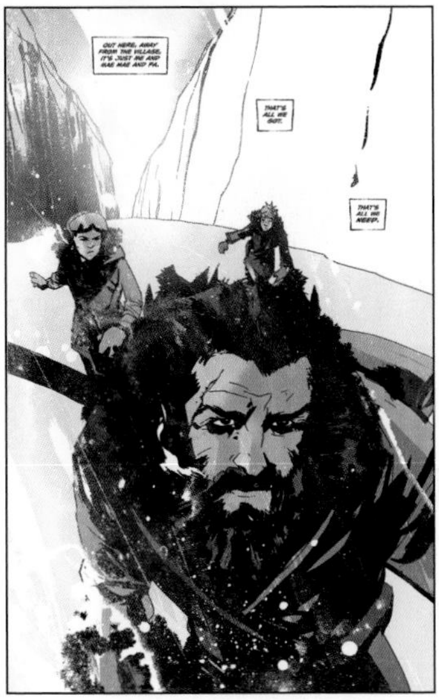
THAT'S ALL WE GOT.
THAT'S ALL WE NEED.

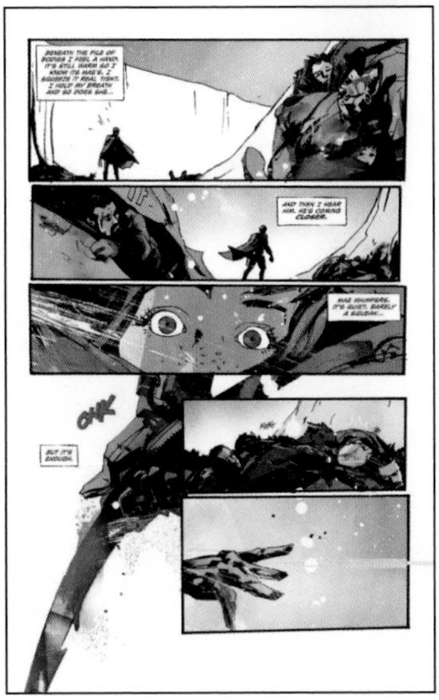
AND THEN I HEAR HIM. HE'S COMING CLOSER.
BUT IT'S ENOUGH.

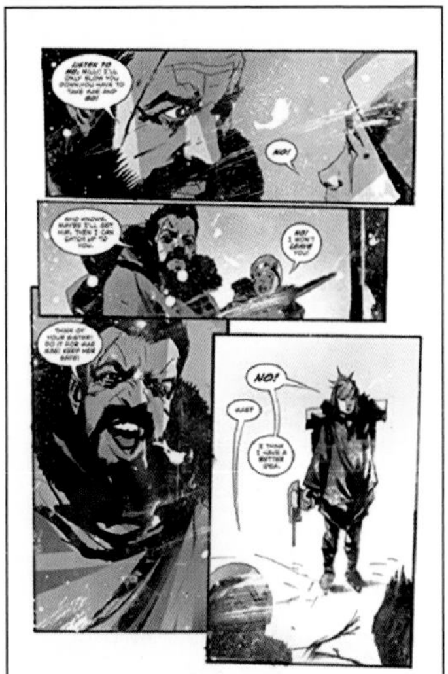
NO!
NO!

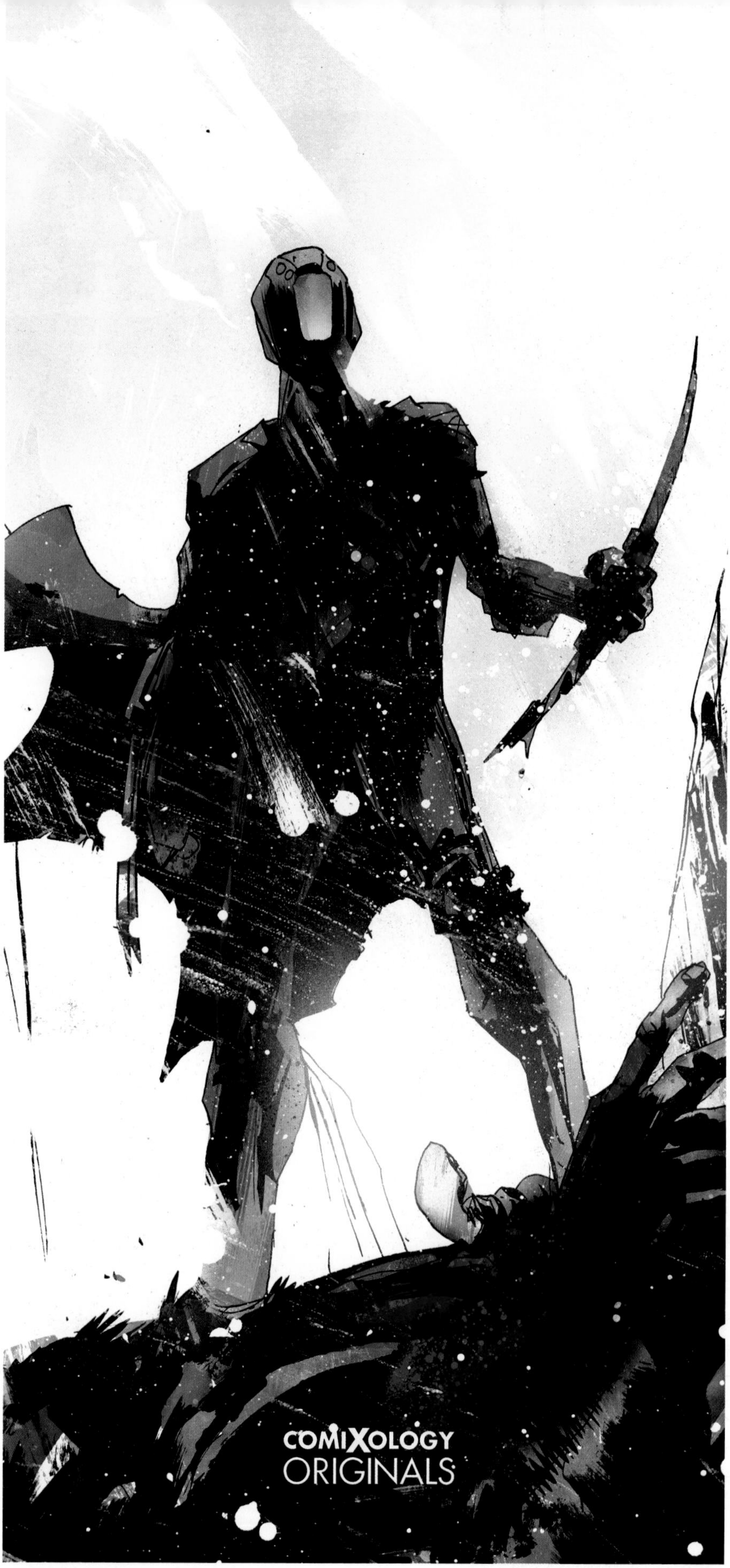
comiXology
ORIGINALS